You and the State

You and the State

A Fairly Brief Introduction to Political Philosophy

Jan Narveson

ROWMAN & LITTLEFIELD PUBLISHERS, INC.
Lanham • Boulder • New York • Toronto • Plymouth, UK

ROWMAN & LITTLEFIELD PUBLISHERS, INC.

Published in the United States of America
by Rowman & Littlefield Publishers, Inc.
A wholly owned subsidiary of The Rowman & Littlefield Publishing Group, Inc.
4501 Forbes Boulevard, Suite 200, Lanham, Maryland 20706
www.rowmanlittlefield.com

Estover Road
Plymouth PL6 7PY
United Kingdom

British Library Cataloguing in Publication Information Available

Library of Congress Cataloging-in-Publication Data:

Narveson, Jan, 1936–
  You and the state : a fairly brief introduction to political philosophy /
Jan Narveson.
     p. cm.
  Includes bibliographical references and index.
  ISBN-13: 978-0-7425-4843-5 (cloth : alk. paper)
  ISBN-10: 0-7425-4843-0 (cloth : alk. paper)
  ISBN-13: 978-0-7425-4844-2 (pbk. : alk. paper)
  ISBN-10: 0-7425-4844-9 (pbk. : alk. paper)
  1. Political science—Philosophy. 2. State, The. I. Title.
  JA66.N37 2008
  320.01—dc22   2007047146

Printed in the United States of America

∞™ The paper used in this publication meets the minimum requirements of
American National Standard for Information Sciences—Permanence of Paper for
Printed Library Materials, ANSI/NISO Z39.48-1992.

Contents

Preface

This is a somewhat different introduction from the many available to present-day readers. I try to assemble the subject from the ground up. What is special about political philosophy? Moral philosophy focuses on individual people and what they should do, how they should live. Political philosophy focuses on *government*, which has the distinctive feature that it claims, and is generally regarded as having, the authority to *compel* people to do what it lays down. Compulsion isn't very nice. We all have our own lives to lead, after all. We can all benefit from advice, no doubt. But compulsion? Someone else proposing to insist that we do something we didn't want to do and then threatening us with imprisonment or worse if we don't do it is a chilling prospect. It needs justifying. Private persons or the members of groups in society threatening to behave that way toward us are regarded as criminal (if we're fortunate enough to live in our general sort of society, anyway); yet if the government does it, that's supposed to be OK, and our duty is to put up with it rather than resist. Political philosophy for the most part has been concerned with just that question: the justification of imposing their will, forcibly, by a few people who have extensive populations under their control. The people with those sorts of powers are what we call the government.

That has been the question, and there have been various answers. One is that we don't need to discuss it because the government is just *there*, a fact of life, and there's nothing to do but knuckle under. Thoughtful people generally and instinctively reject that. They look instead for reasons why such an agency might actually help to make life better for us. I agree with that stance, and I suppose the reader does, too. But of course, that leads to the questions of what constitutes a "better life" and why it should be thought that an authoritative and powerful agency *might* be able to help achieve it. Further reflection leads us to the distinction fundamental to politics today: *Whose view* of what is good for us is to have the upper hand? Can someone else really say, authoritatively, what we should be doing with our lives? The contemporary answer is in the negative. It is we as individual people who should have that "ultimate authority over ourselves." That is the central thesis of *liberalism*, the reigning philosophy of the present, and the one I think to be correct for this purpose. That it is right is not self-evident and will be discussed and argued for rather than simply assumed.

If liberalism is right, then our resources for trying to justify the State are much narrowed. There is a classic view: The State keeps people from interfering with other people in their various pursuits of what they see to be the good life. It enshrines that idea in the form of a general right to that pursuit—the right to liberty, in fact. The State exists to protect our freedom—*period*. It exists, in principle, to do that and *only* that. But States all around us, including certainly the one you, the typical reader, live in, do a great deal more than that. Or at least, they spend a lot of their citizens' money in the process of making it look as though they do. Certainly they *say* they do, at the very least. Is that all right? Perhaps astonishingly, almost all present-day writers on political philosophy think it is. We should have our doubts about that. It is very difficult to see how government could do all these things compatibly with the basic idea of liberalism. That so many people think so is surely due to the dominance of the political system known as *democracy*, to which we will pay a good deal of much-needed attention.

This book proceeds on the lines indicated by this general picture. In chapter 1, we have a general look at the project of political philosophizing, with a methodological suggestion. We ask whether the subject is possible, really, and certainly whether there is any point in it, considering how the world goes. The first can be answered, I think; the second is very much a matter between you and your soul.

In chapter 2 we look at *force*, which is in a sense the very essence of the State; we consider the general idea that it is self-justifying, needing no further thought. "Might makes right!" The idea has been and remains far more popular than it should be, but we need to see why it is so tempting, at least.

Rejecting that, we then turn (chapter 3) to what I somewhat awkwardly call "political conservatism"—a term that has had a wide variety of uses not too easily related to mine. Nevertheless, I think the generic idea that the State can act on the basis of some view of what is good for us that it thinks right to impose on the citizens can be reasonably so termed. For good historical reasons, we can call it Platonism as well. More surprising to many readers, I'm sure, will be my classification of socialism and communism as instances of that idea—along with even less savory ideologies, among which what is nowadays called religious fundamentalism and is only too

prominent an example. Along with the more familiarly branded ultracon-
servatisms such as Nazism, I argue that political Platonism is a very grave
mistake, though one to which it is easy to see why so many have suc-
cumbed. (In earlier days and in many other introductory books even now,
socialism is paid much more attention than in this one. But my brief discussion, especially of Marx, strikes, in my view, at its roots.) The point of
this is that there is no end of differing views of what is supposedly "Good
for You" that can be and have been pressed by this, that, and the other State
(and, certainly, by the State you live under right now . . .). That is something
that should help make one think whether Platonism really makes any sense
whatever in the political sphere.

Then we turn (chapter 4) to the classic theory of liberalism, due to Locke
and others, which is the theory of the *minimal state*, the one that attempts
to do *nothing* beyond the securing of preexisting rights to nonviolence and
the keeping of agreements. In the process, we will notice that there is some
question, given these premises, as to whether the State can be justified *at all*.
That view—*anarchism*—will get more sympathetic attention in this book
than, probably, any you would normally read in a university course or on
your own. I devote the final chapter (chapter 8) to it.

After classic liberalism, we make a sort of side excursion to *democracy*
(chapter 5), which is by far the most popular theory of government in the
present era. Democracy is so completely associated with the general stance
I call liberalism that many simply identify the two. But wrongly, for the theory of *democracy* does not sit comfortably with *liberalism*, as I point out. We
may be stuck with democracy, but we are right to worry. Here, happily, serious scholars are aware of democracy's general tendencies. They are somewhat in agreement about partial solutions to those problems. I think the solutions are extremely tenuous. Democracy has caused and will cause no end
of woes. The question what to do about those is, perhaps, the most serious
one in the field—serious at the level of real-world political practice, not just
in the minds of theorists.

The next topic (chapter 6) is naturally the modern welfare state, in which
we are all immersed so thoroughly. There is a great deal about this octopus
of an institution to call into severe question—so much, that what the apos-
tle of the welfare state requires is a special story and that is indeed what he
thinks he has supplied. I have grave doubts about this, as will be seen. Democracy has led, certainly, to the hegemony of the busy modern welfare
state, which imposes more extensively on our lives than ever before. Is all
this really necessary? Does it make sense? How much does it really differ
from the hated regimes we all thought we were done with (fascism, communism, socialism . . .)?

The next chapter (7) is another excursion into international matters. Some
consideration of that general subject is a necessity in any general introduction

to politics; they also enable us to think about them in the light of previous deliberations about domestic politics. The major issues concern war and peace and global trade, with immigration a close third. Here we contemplate the situation of a multiplicity of States, many with widely varying background cultures, in a busy and populous world. Very briefly: Why we do not have peace, considering its overwhelming advantages, is something of a mystery, perhaps comparable to the mystery of why we do not have global free trade. And of course, there are the modish current issues typified by global warming. Discussing those matters will bring our attention to some very persistent and potentially disruptive tendencies in human nature. They may be the very ones that make politics happen.

In the final chapter (8), we briefly survey the possibility that society could do better without government *at all*, in the usual sense of that term. Many strange and curious ideas have been associated with "anarchism," especially in the past century and a quarter or so, but we discuss it under the aegis of liberalism, which provides considerable impetus toward asking why we do not, instead of relying on government, form our society entirely on *voluntary associations*. This possibility is not summarily dismissed as it is in almost all introductory books on this subject. It is intended to stimulate thought on the issue—as indeed is the entire book. Everything you have been told about government all your lives militates against even thinking seriously about anarchy; the anarchist notes this point with cynical disdain. Have you been brainwashed? We'll take the possibility seriously. I hope that a fresh perspective emerges.

Acknowledgments

This book emerges from over forty years of university teaching. My debt to the classic philosophers of the subject—to Plato, Aristotle, Aquinas, Hobbes, Locke, Marx (in a sort of inverse way), and Mill—will be obvious. My debt to any number of colleagues will be evident to some of them and is insufficiently acknowledged in footnotes and the like, but is real. So is my debt to enormous numbers of students, whose papers and exams and discussions have provided much food for thought. Unnecessary to state is my debt to my family and friends, who do so much to make life worth living, and while at it, make the production of books like this possible. Quite necessary to state, though, is my debt to my friend and literary helper James Leger, whose assistance over many years has contributed greatly to this and other of my writings.

This is not your typical treatise on this subject. My sympathies are not concealed, and impatience with many major ideas is evident at many points. This is an introduction to the subject in the sense that it does not presume previous acquaintance with the philosophical literature on these matters, but it is not an evenhanded tour through the area. By all means, it should be read in tandem with some more, shall we say, politically correct accounting. I suppose that if you read carefully, you'll agree with my outlook—but that, of course, is your call.

1

What Is Political Philosophy About? Why Do It?

In today's world, it is all but impossible to ignore the presence of government—local, state/provincial, and national governments impinge on us almost constantly. The newspapers spend more pages on government actions than anything else, and television news is mostly about what this or that government is or isn't doing about this or that. At the same time, most contacts with governments by citizens who aren't actually employees of governments tend to be uncomfortable: the policeman giving you a speeding ticket, the tax people to whom, likely, a lot of what you thought was *your* money goes, and so on. Probably the main thing that makes such encounters uncomfortable is that the agents of government have a relation to you that nobody else normally has. They can, as we say, "do bad things to you," and they can make it stick. Encounters with government for many people in many parts of the world can be fatal. The law, literally, is on their side: They claim, indeed, to *be* "the law." If you disagree—well, too bad for you!

Experiences of this kind may get us to thinking about this peculiar institution, government. This introduction to the ancient subject of political philosophy is intended to aid the process of reflection. Philosophers raise basic questions about it, of which the most general, certainly, is whether, and if so, how government is *justified*. That strikes some, but not others, as a reasonable and important question. But it is not an entirely clear one, and clarifying it will be one of the tasks of this chapter. We will then discuss some ideas about this. There have been several historically influential views, and we will pay them close attention, even though brief. Further basic questions concern, very generally, what governments should be doing—if, indeed, anything—and how they should do it. Are there significant principles we can identify to guide and restrict their actions?

1

The list of things it does or tries to do has grown prodigiously over the years, but we can usefully group them under several familiar headings. We could draw up a list of levels of State action, ranging from *none*, which is the anarchist view, up to *totalitarianism*, which we all, I trust, join in rejecting. But no matter how disreputable or absurd we may think a certain type or level of government may be, we can learn from thinking about it. Just what is so awful about the awful ones? And if we look at our own governments today and it turns out to be not so easy to see all that much difference between the outrageous ones and ours, that could be pretty discomfiting. In the process, we might end up with a new view. In any case, there will be a new appreciation of our old view, even if we stick with it.

A NOTE ON THE HISTORY OF THE SUBJECT

One really good way to get introduced to political philosophy is by reading the classic works in the field, such as Plato's *Republic* and Hobbes's *Leviathan*. This book is not historical in intention, but topical, aiming to analyze the subject fairly systematically. Those writers deserve a lot of attention as well as our respect and admiration, but a few things have happened in the intervening centuries, and so I will only occasionally mention, mostly quite briefly, some of these classic writers. But I hope that many readers will be stimulated to peruse some of these famous writings, which have greatly influenced my own and almost everybody else's thinking on the subject. Most of those classic writers are not only insightful and interesting but also readable, too. However, close summary and discussion of ancient writers are not the point here. What I attribute to famous philosophers is usually uncontroversial; where not, it is what I have been stimulated to think by them, and scholarly justification is not in point.

My contemporaries also influence the ideas expressed in these pages to a degree. Readers not acquainted with contemporary philosophy will find most of that material difficult or even incomprehensible. This book may help you to read other contemporary writers—with due caution. As you will see, I am not in much sympathy with most current philosophical writings on politics. But that does not mean that I think them not worth reading. A very few will be found in the bibliography at the end of this book. Those few can easily lead you to many more.

POLITICAL ARGUMENTATION

This last discussion brings up one more topic, a methodological one: How do we get anywhere in this undertaking? That, of course, is a very broad topic, but I mean here to address a rather narrow aspect of it, though an extremely important one. Political and moral arguments are *arguments*: sets of propositions, or statements, of which some, called the "premises," are intended to supply reasons for the others, known as "conclusions." In the case of morals and politics, our conclusions are *practical*: That is, they are statements to the effect that something is right or wrong, good or bad, just or unjust, or that something ought to be done or avoided. They have the force of recommendations, or perhaps "commands," issued by the reasoner to himself, at least. But not just to himself, for in a clear and important sense they are issued to *everybody* everywhere, or sometimes to fellow citizens of the issuer's country, or other specified groups.

But what about our premises, then? And can we actually get conclusions that follow, usefully, from helpful premises? At this point, we encounter a tradition in moral philosophy. According to this tradition, in effect, the answer to these last few questions is a resounding *No*. That is: It is denied that we can start with any sort of truths, at least ones that we can prove or have good evidence for, and move from them, without fallacy, to conclusions of the kind we are interested in. The name for this is the "naturalistic fallacy." According to the theory that there is such a thing, facts simply don't and can't imply values—so, forget it! People who take this seriously tend to proceed in morals and politics by simply laying down moral claims without argument, as if they could just be plucked out of the air. Or perhaps their idea is that one person's moral ideas are as good as the next, and we're all in this just for a good chat.

But the subject is too important to accept a status like that. For one thing, we can surely criticize any argument that either has false premises, or true premises but a conclusion that doesn't follow. Perhaps above all, we can object to *question-begging* arguments. These are "arguments" only in quotation marks, for their conclusions are really just their premises all over again. Anyone who wasn't inclined to agree with the conclusion will simply reject the so-called premise, and that's that. Since that really would be pretty useless, any argument guilty of that sin is condemned forthwith.

Any argument generates a conclusion that is no better—no "truer"—than the set of its premises taken together. A good argument, though, takes two or more premises and extracts from the set of them a conclusion that is not so obvious and may even come as a complete surprise. Or alternatively, the fact that that conclusion, with which we already agree, can be gotten from *those* premises might be really interesting. But it remains that the reader always has a choice: Even if it's a perfectly valid argument, you can either accept the conclusion or reject one or more of the premises. Which you should do will require a judgment about plausibility. Sometimes some of the premises will assert factual claims that can be in some degree tested at the hands of the "data" available, or perhaps of common-sense observation.

Sometimes it will be claimed that a premise is "self-evident," and occasionally that claim will look very plausible. But, you always have to be careful: What seems self-evident to Jones can seem quite nonevident to Smith— and then what? This book is not a treatise on logic, and when arguments are presented, they will be so in the hope that their premises will look so good that you will be inclined to accept the conclusion even if it's not one you supposed you would accept before you started.

RESPONDING TO THE "NATURALISTIC FALLACY"

The preceding discussions do not yet answer the challenge of the naturalistic fallacy. Can it be answered? Yes. Indeed, there is a mistake in the claim that there must be such a fallacy in all arguments in moral and political philosophy—a subtle but serious error, but one whose uncovering also points the way to a serious restriction on what kind of arguments in this subject can pass muster.

People getting into practical inquiries and arguments carry around with them many desires, interests, wants, loves and hates, ideals, and so on. Those are ideas with practical connotations already. Now, the statement that "I want a loaf of whole wheat!" implies or is, while it's at it, a *fact* about myself: It is (presumably) true of me that I have this desire. From my own internal point of view, however, this fact about me asserts what is actually, so far as I am concerned, a *value*, not an inert fact with no practical output. My wants animate me; they (often) stimulate me to action. To see that something is what I want is to have a reason to act, or more precisely, the beginnings of a reason. As Aristotle observed, "Intellect itself moves nothing." But that doesn't mean that nothing in the mind moves anything or anybody—very much the contrary. We all have, as Aristotle famously noted, "passions" (less dramatically, wants) that get us going.

Now suppose that I reason about *your* action. How do I go about it? In many cases, I do so by starting with *your own* known desires and interests and working from there, just as I would if they were *my* desires and interests. Why will I do this? I could be your doctor or your coach or your mom. But more typically, I do this because what you do affects my own interests in one way or another, and so I have a practical interest in your practical behavior, whatever I may think of you.

In political reasoning, we are concerned especially about points of practice by various people that have spin-offs, implications for many people and perhaps everyone. Notionally, they are about everyone's behavior. The lawmakers say, "Do this, or we'll fine you $100!" They say it to everybody in that jurisdiction. Some of those people may never even be tempted to do what the lawmakers want to forbid, of course. But many others will be so tempted, else the lawmaker's concern would be pointless. Virtually everyone *would be able* to do, and many do actually desire to do, that thing; and what they do may impact on ourselves in one way or another.

Consequently, the reply to the naturalistic fallacy challenge is simply that good arguments in moral and political matters must always be based on values that the people they're concerned with *do actually have*, somewhere in their souls. These premises are not *moral* or *political* values; they are simply our own values. But when we take other people into account, interesting things happen. That is because these other people can do things that matter to us, and vice versa. How best to cope with this is the problem that specifically moral and political theorizing addresses. Thus, plenty of perfectly straightforward facts can be practically, and sometimes politically, relevant, and the actions of other people and ourselves can be so. The naturalistic fallacy idea, in other words, can only be thought to have a devastating impact on moral and political reasoning by confusion. The confusion consists in not distinguishing between sheer interests or values, for this or that or anything, with *moral* or *political* values. It may be true that "de gustibus non est disputandum." And to be sure, people's views in morals and politics all too often seem like a matter of *taste*. The impact of this distinction, by the way, is explored at length in chapters 2 and 3—in case you think it's a fussy academic distinction. It's not. Moral and political theses require justifications; our taste in ice cream does not.

What isn't confused, however, is that if there is no shred of practical interest anywhere in the premises, then no practical conclusions can follow. Right. And that's important too, after all. I once heard a learned scholar lecture on the factors presumably affecting the ozone layer, the thesis being that there are "holes" in it. All of a sudden, though, the lecturer was advocating major political initiative to do something about this. Hello? He needed, of course, a premise to the effect that those holes would be a bad thing for people. Politically, indeed, that was the only question of any interest. But he acted as though no further premises were needed! Wrong, of course. We must *always* have premises of the relevant, value-laden, interested-asserting type before an argument has any relevance at all to politics and morals.

But that leaves a great deal—in fact, it leaves the *entirety* of the subjects known as moral and political philosophy intact.

THE ISSUES

Political philosophy is concerned with certain main issues, others not quite so fundamental, and many that are spin-offs or variants of relevant but more specific issues. Here, as I see it, are the top-of-agenda questions.

1. **Is government justified at all?** To ask this seriously is to inquire into the philosophical merits of an idea known as *anarchism*—the view that government is not justified and that we should not have one at all. If anarchists are to be taken seriously, of course, they will have to have answers to some plausible and familiar questions. However, the defender of government also needs good answers to those same questions. Or, perhaps, he needs a good reason why we may ignore the issue (as it generally is in Introductions to Political Philosophy). Since it is so obviously fundamental, I propose not to ignore it in this book.

2. **If we are to have government, who should govern?** How are the people who end up "in charge" going to end up there?

   The classic options here were known by the ancients as government by "the one, the few, and the many." "The one" would be monarchy, or perhaps dictatorship, and possibly what we would think of as tyranny. It was seriously thought, and for a long time, that monarchy was the best option. That is hard to believe nowadays, but we will review the situation anyway, and see why. "The few" might be, for example, the supposedly "best" people (*aristocracy*) or the wealthy (*oligarchy*) or the militarily strong (*timocracy*), or perhaps the extraordinarily intelligent. Finally, "the many" is, of course, democracy, that nowadays is universally held up as the ultimate in government. We will examine its claims very carefully, of course (chapter 5). To this list we need to add, at least in theory, the option that *nobody* is "in charge"—the anarchist challenge. Chapter 8 addresses it, a bit.

3. **What, and how much, should (legitimate) governments do?** This issue is logically independent of the preceding one but is sure to be connected with it rather closely in several ways. Here, the options are
   (a) Anarchy: Nothing.
   (b) Minarchy, or the Minimal State: protect persons and their property (including national defense where needed) and nothing else (chapter 4).
   (c) The Functional State (a name I invent for this purpose): the preceding, plus things like roads and gas lines—"infrastructure" as it's now called—and also, or including, operation of the monetary system and regulation needed for the smooth functioning of those things (also chapter 4).
   (d) The Welfare State: the preceding, plus social services including health, education, and welfare (in the narrow sense of that term), and many other services as well (chapter 6).
   (e) Socialism: operation of the society's productive industries by public, politically selected agencies (chapter 3).

(f) Totalitarianism: unlimited government, in which all aspects of people's lives are, or at least are eligible to be, controlled by the rulers (chapter 3).

These half-dozen categories are, of course, susceptible to indefinite further ramification, but these will do for bringing out major issues.

4. **What general political values may be pursued by the State?** Certain very general, normative questions will pervade all treatments of political philosophy. By far the most prominent concern these four: virtue, freedom, welfare, and equality. The questions to ask about these things, however, are easily and generally misconceived. Our questions are political *only* if they are specifications of *this general question:* What, if anything, should the State do in the way of *compelling* the conduct of its citizens? Thus: May it *compel* people to be virtuous? May it *compel* them to be free? Or even—a quite different thing—to respect other people's freedoms? May it *compel* people to contribute to each other's welfare? Should it *compel* people to equalize themselves relatively to others in various respects?

In order to answer those questions, we have to delve into individuals' value schemes and decision-making systems and ask how it is rational for people to deal with others in those respects. That sets our agenda.

GROUPS THAT MATTER TO POLITICAL PHILOSOPHY

Governments rule over people, and governments themselves consist of people. So, some people rule, or at any rate have authority and power of a political kind, over others. People tend to come in groups, of many kinds. Some distinctions among these various kinds will help to set the stage for discussing political philosophy.

Individuals

Writers often invoke a contrast between "the individual" and "society" or some other group. But groups, after all, consist of individuals—what else? The widest and most comprehensive of all human groupings is, simply, everybody—all the individuals there are.

There are two main points about individuals. First, they are *particulars*. Imagine two truly identical twins, as identical as we can imagine. Still, they are two, and not one. Particulars are countable, no matter how similar or different they might be. Second, and crucial to the subject: People are individuals in a further sense: the sense that each is *different in kind* from each other. Every person has a history that "reads" differently from every other: different interests, different aspirations, different abilities, different ways of looking at things—we are awash in differences. Still, we are all, to a degree not easy to determine, influenced by other people: parents, peers, associates, lovers, and so on. Obviously, no one is an island. Just what that implies is not obvious. Aristotle said that man is a "political animal." Maybe, but some are a lot more political than others. We all know people who are simply apolitical and others who are intensely political. We grow up among people, our political environment is evident everywhere, yet we might try hard to avoid discussions of politics or direct contact with government. Is it wrong to be like that? Many contemporary political writers think so. Most ordinary people think not.

The point is that people are indefinitely diverse and distinctive even while immersed in social life. Somehow they unite, in the ways in which political institutions imply unity, despite their differences. Whether, why, and in just what way this uniting might be a good idea is, in effect, what social philosophy is about. Political philosophy especially concerns the narrower question of which kinds of unity may properly be *imposed* on people.

Yet along with all these differences, there are commonalities. We all need to eat, sleep, breathe, and maintain our body temperatures at around 37°C and keep our various bodily bits in working order. In a way, differences are what we have in common: Everyone has a distinctive set of interests (desires, tastes, ambitions) and a distinctive set of powers (including skills and abilities), though both change over time, sometimes enormously. Are there common interests in some sense important to our subject? Is there a "common humanity" to which we can all appeal? That cannot just be assumed. Perhaps, though, it can be *argued for*. We'll get to that, much later.

Among human powers, one sort is especially important here: their ability to think about what they are doing and to make decisions in the light of that thinking. People are sometimes said to be uniquely "rational animals." That is far from obvious; other animals do reason, at some level or other. What is distinctive of humans, however, is their ability to articulate their ideas in language that is communicable to others and to plan and carry out actions more or less in accordance with those ideas. This difference from the "lower" animals may be a matter of degree, but the difference of degree is really striking. We'll see why that matters, *hugely*.

Families and Tribes

We are mammals; we reproduce sexually, and especially in our early years we require extensive care from parents or parental figures. Members of the same family have a lot more in common than they do with other people, and they characteristically have emotional attitudes toward fellow family members that they don't have toward anyone else. Beyond the level of a particular family, there are more distant relatives, who in many societies form *tribes*. Tribes have been a potent force in human history, and politically they have been, and in some places still are, very significant. Should they be? Whatever, it is implausible to think of the State as a great big "family." It's not, and the State that presumes to be everyone's parent is likely to be a nightmare State.

Communities

Next is the group of those who live in fairly close proximity to each other and have a lot to do with each other: working and playing together, sharing religions and many other practices, speaking a common language, and having bonds of affection and senses of togetherness and "identity." A recent trend in political philosophy, called "communitarianism," attaches major political significance to communities, proposing to model the State on the fact of community. It's not surprising that there should be such theories—community is a major fact in most of our lives. But States comprehend many communities, each different, invoking different loyalties and interests. The claim that the State simply *is* a community is false. It imposes on state-level society what just isn't there, again with serious consequences. We can think, with a shudder, of the Nazis and their "ideology of the Volkgemeinschaft" ("national community"). 'Nuff said?

Associations

The term *association*, like so much of the vocabulary of the social studies, is ambiguous, but there is a fairly specific sense of it that is hugely important to our subject. In this normal sense, an association is a group of people who *intentionally associate*, and do so in order to pursue fairly definite purposes. A church, a bowling club, a university, a picnic—in all of these, a number of people come together with a number of other people to engage in various activities. Sometimes the point of the association has to do with the particular other people who are members, but often not. What matters is that associations have one striking difference from all the rest: They are *voluntary*. Those who joined did so for certain known purposes; they weren't compelled to join and may leave if they wish. The problem about the State would be no problem if the same were true of it. But, of course, it isn't—quite the opposite. Alas, too many philosophers have simply assumed that the State is an association. Don't be sucked in!

Society and Societies

"Society" and "social" are of the same general ilk. Most people like to "socialize" with some others; someone might enjoy the "society" of

women, or men, or freemasons, or artists. And there are "capital S" societies such as the Society for Psychical Research. Still, the word *society* has
a fairly specific connotation. A "society" in this sense is a lot larger than,
say, a club or an association. Also, there's the case where we want to say
"*a* society" and the case where we just say "society." The latter is the
broadest sense: It's the group consisting of everyone there is but looked
at as *a* group, not just a set. The former, however, is not quite so easy to
identify. But the general idea is, first, that it's a very large group of people who have something to do with each other and a whole lot less to do
with people in other groups of the kind. Polynesians and Inuit exemplify
this idea. What's important about it is, first, that members have something to do with each other, although it's not each with every other;
rather, they are chain-connected, so that A associates with B and C associates with D and E, and so on. Secondly, you needn't, and typically
don't, become a member of a society by *joining*. Rather, members become
members by being born into that group. Because this is so, we must be
careful about imputing commonness of purpose to fellow members of a
society, and especially of society at large.

Societies, in the sense in which they are many, get some unity from culture,
especially. That is a difficult-to-define notion but familiar to everyone, and it
is enormously powerful in human affairs. Some theorists go so far as to say
that we derive *all* our values from our social involvements. Others go to the
opposite extreme and attribute all values to *ab initio* decisions. This too seems
not credible. We assume no particular theory here, and especially no extreme
one: We take people as common sense tells us they are, with a mix of biolog-
ical, socially formed, and sometimes idiosyncratic, motivations.

Nations

The category of "the nation" is not so easily defined, but we'll do best to
think of it this way: A nation is a group that *aspires to be a State*, where the
emphasis is on the word *a*. Members of the national group, if they are not
already in fact members of the same State (and we often use the term "nation" as a synonym for "State" rather than as something different), think
that they and their fellows should be wielding political power separately
from other States, rather than as parts of a current one.

The State

The subject of political studies becomes distinctive when we get to the
State. We might say that a State is *a society with a government*—government
being *a smallish group empowered with the making and administering of laws
and the creation of "institutions" under their aegis.*

This definition uses the term *society* in a way that isn't quite accurate in terms of our previous discussion, for a given society might have more than one State, or perhaps none, and social and cultural diversity within one State is familiar nowadays. More accurately, then, a State is simply a great many people, in some bounded geographical area, with the *same* government over them all. States and societies have this in common: Their members typically didn't *join* but were *born* into the group in question. That matters a lot for political philosophy. For the government of a State has a very special and distinctive status relative to anything else: Governments have the ability to lay down the law; they tell people what to do, and they can make it stick. They have "clout." If we don't do what they tell us to, things can get nasty. They can send us to jail or even to the gallows. And they can deprive us of quite a lot, or perhaps all, of our worldly possessions, our incomes, especially. But unlike a band of thieves, they claim to do this legitimately: Governments think it's perfectly OK to do this, and most of their subjects agree with them. It rarely occurs to ordinary citizens to question government's right to act as it does.

It's that special feature—the capability of telling us what to do and having the power to compel us to do it if we are inclined not to, yet claiming that's *rightful* and having most people accept that claim—that makes a government a government. They sometimes act noncompulsively, to be sure. But insofar as they do, they're just another organization. Governments as such *rule*.

POLITICAL PHILOSOPHY

Political philosophy is nowadays sometimes distinguished from another study, *political theory*. The intended distinction is this: Political philosophy is what we now call a "normative" inquiry, asking what makes government just or legitimate or good, while political theory is supposed to aim at understanding politics—to explain it, but not necessarily to judge it. How tenable such a distinction can be is a matter of much debate, but at least on the surface, these sound different. How they relate is a large and important issue.

We all discuss the actions of governments, making free to pronounce them good or bad, right or wrong, just or unjust, stupid or praiseworthy, and so on, just as we do regarding the actions of individuals. Political *philosophy* concerns the question, What are the right basic ideas and principles for controlling these discussions (if any)?

But when we examine the actions of governments and politicians, we frequently make claims about the *effects* of this or that initiative or policy. We want to know what *caused* this or that government to do such and such. Is there perhaps a bottom-level, ultimate *theory* of people that explains politics? Maybe. If there is, political philosophy would be irrational if it ignored it. But if a theory told us that people cannot in fact appraise politics at all, it would be flying in the face of the facts. We simply need both, and if they're hard to keep apart, that's not surprising.

MORAL VERSUS POLITICAL

Morals concern *rules for the group*: how people ought to act, by virtue of being members of the group in question (which may be simply the "group" of everybody). Governments themselves consist of individuals, of course; what else? This perhaps provides some reason for supposing that moral and political philosophy are presumptively similar. It also suggests that perhaps the underlying principles of appraisal are similar: not only that governments are susceptible to moral criticism but also that we can use very much the same general principles, rules, and standards in appraising them as we do concerning individuals. We must not be too hasty in making such an assumption, but as a provisional point of departure, it seems right.

If that assumption is reasonable, then in addition to the ideas listed above, we will need the appropriate vocabulary of criticism. And this in turn raises a very important question about the relation between politics and morals. The fact that some State does something is one thing; whether it ought to have done so is another. Both are discussable. It looks, then, as though political philosophy is a branch of moral philosophy—moral philosophy as applied to the special case of political action. If so, a book on political philosophy is inevitably a book on moral philosophy while it's at it. We can hardly discuss politics if we have no idea what makes an action right or wrong, good or bad.

The most prominent of the moral concepts that we apply to political matters is *justice*. It's not the only one. Was a policy wise? Was it helpful? Was it practicable? Did it do more good than harm? Was it reasonable, or even rational? These are all things we ask, and rightly, about governmental actions as well as those of individuals and lesser groups. But there is one clear sense in which *only* individuals can act, deliberate, or decide what to do, and address themselves to the rights and wrongs, or any kind of merits, of anything at all. Yet political questions are *social*. This brings up two important points.

First: Individuals have views about various other people and even views about society. We make moral appraisals of other people, and we evaluate whole societies and governments. In doing so, we are not doing the same thing that we do when we evaluate, say, the taste of coffee, or the merits of a certain piece of music, or for that matter of a lawnmower. What difference is made by the fact that our subject is the actions or qualities of *other people*?

Second: Obviously you or I are not the only persons thinking about what to do. We all do this. And when we appraise societies or governments, we may be sure that our own view about what to do will differ from some or even all other people's. Does this matter? When we differ, are some of us right and some wrong? If someone else has an opinion that we think is in error, does that very fact—that someone else has a different view—matter to my own reckoning of what is to be done? That question, as we will see, looms very large in political philosophy.

Political questions are very close to moral questions. We may well describe the project of political philosophy as that of developing the best *political morality* we can manage. What, then, is that? Well, that is the general subject of this book.

LAW

Politics is also closely related to law. Governments govern under the aegis of laws, and if they don't, we worry. If they completely ignore considerations of law, as they have sometimes done, we will doubt that the "government" in question deserves the name at all—it's more like a gang of thieves and cutthroats. Indeed, at one end of the spectrum is a view that that's how it is bound to be anyway—a thesis we will consider in the next chapter. We will emerge, of course, with the view that law is important and that we need to find out what *good* laws are.

There's a difference between the idea that the rulers cannot do without law altogether and that they are the *source* of law, even though they also govern under the idea of law. This brings up the question of what law is, and as it happens, one of the great figures in political philosophy, St. Thomas Aquinas (1225?–1274), has come up with a nice, succinct, and, I think, essentially correct answer to that question. Law, he notes, is imposed, enforced, on a community. The citizens don't have their choice about it—it isn't a piece of advice, it's an order! Nevertheless, that imposition is to be *rational*. Law, he proposes, is "an ordinance of reason for the common good, promulgated and enforced by the one who is in charge of the community."[1] This analysis has these essential features.

First, the imposed ordering is supposed to be *rational*, whatever that means.

Second, it's for the *common good*, an idea that has caused a great deal of scholarly ink to flow in discussion over the centuries.

Third, it talks about this "ordinance" being *promulgated*; and fourth, it refers to someone being *in charge of* the community, or words to that effect. In the case of the State, of course, it is the government.

Aquinas's idea is brilliant but requires thought. First, why "rational"? Rationality is one of the pervasive ideas in philosophy, and for good reason. The very idea of writing a treatise about the justification of government, or anything else, surely implies that rationality is at work. But it is one thing for a treatise to be rational; our challenge here, though, is to explain just how an "imposition on a community" can be so. Second, the formula says that this imposition is to be for the "common" good. We will need, then, to have some idea (a) of what is to count as "good" for political purposes, and then (b) how such a thing can, in view of the enormous differences among people, be *common*. Third, why "promulgated"? The fourth clause says that someone does the imposing and promulgating. Who? And where do they get the power to do that?

A question: Did Aquinas only mean to be analyzing the idea of law as ordinarily understood, that is, as what emerges from legislatures and is adjudicated in court decisions? No, actually. He thinks that there are several kinds of law: "divine," "eternal," "natural," and "human." Only the last of them corresponds to the idea of "legal" law in the narrow sense just noted. The third of them, "natural," was meant to apply to what we would call *morality*. Aquinas would have had the Ten Commandments in mind, for example. He even tried to apply this same notion of law to things like the law of gravity, the sort of "laws" that "govern" the universe.

Aquinas, of course, was a Roman Catholic priest and had a strong commitment to his religion. He supposed that the whole universe was the work of the Divine Being, who accordingly is, one might say, the "person in charge" of the universe at large. But the suggestion that the law of gravity is an ordinance for the common good is a bit bizarre to the nontheistic mind, and we will ignore it for our purposes. What we will not ignore, however, is his interesting idea that *morality* is "natural law," in the specific sense that it is somehow "founded on" the nature of things. The idea is that what's right or wrong is so because it reflects or is founded on *the way things are*. Many people, and many philosophers, have supposed that moral law is somehow a *human creation* instead. I'll suggest that the *instead* is out of place. It's both. But certainly law in the more usual legal sense is so—Aquinas calls it "human" law.

If moral law lives up to this billing, though, legal law does not. Legislatures pass laws, but they can't pass moral laws—the very idea is absurd. We can ask whether legislatures, in passing a certain law, are being just, fair, and in general right in doing so. They can't simply decree that they are and that's that. So if we are to say that morality is somehow humanly created, it must be in some other sense than that of legislation. That's another challenge, which we take up below.

Why, now, would law have to be "promulgated"? There's an obvious answer. Law is supposed to *tell us what to do*—it "imposes an order" on the community, and the community consists of us "rational beings." We are agents, organisms that think about what to do; we decide to do this or that on the basis of various considerations. If someone is going to claim to "direct" us, a minimum requirement is that that someone *convey* to us what we're supposed to do. There is no point in "laying down" or "imposing" a law that we would just be following anyway, so if this new one is to make any difference to our behavior, and especially if it's going to make that difference by being *followed*, then we have to know what it is. Thus, it has to be communicated, that is, "promulgated."

Aquinas thinks that the moral law itself is also promulgated, but by being "written on all hearts"—an intriguing but dark idea. It could mean that moral law is natural in the sense that we all just know it from the word Go. The trouble is, we apparently don't. Further, it looks as though there's considerable variation, even disagreement, about what's right and wrong. Children, at the very least, need quite a bit of teaching on that subject, and even adults don't always know. On the other hand, morality is *public*: The "rules" are spread around, taught to children and others, and so on. There can't be any moral secrets, since the idea is to guide everyone.

Finally, there is the urgent question of the "people in charge." Aquinas talks rather as though the "powers that be" are just *there*, perhaps appointed by God in the end. That's a pretty unsatisfactory view, of course. Moreover, as just noted, moral "law" cannot be *imposed* by some one or some few. No matter who proposes to "impose" something like that, we can question their pronouncements. Morality just is like that. It can't "belong" uniquely to anybody.

The main point here is that human law is subject to moral law that is nonarbitrary and nonlegislated. We have our work cut out for us in explaining how morals apply to politics. Can we sensibly, rationally, criticize politics in light of morals? Is the idea of morals solid enough to provide a basis for such criticism? We will see.

LEGAL POSITIVISM

In modern times, there has been much support for an apparently quite different idea about law, called "legal positivism." According to it, law can be identified without any normative assumptions. Positivists deny that law *must* be for the common good, or in any other way be a "directive of reason"; rather, law simply is the output of legislatures or other entities with similar powers.

But what is this output? It is no good saying that it is "law," of course, since that is what we are trying to analyze. Certainly law is a general directive to all in the relevant polity, and enforceable. *Which* general directives, and how we tell that the right people have put it out, is tougher for the positivist to specify. Somehow the body is appointed or intended or otherwise endowed with the task of doing this, but for what are they thus appointed? We don't, after all, have people printing up sentences like "it is henceforth illegal to deposit garbage in the streets between the hours of x and y" just for the fun of it. And no matter how much intending you or I might expend on the production of such a sentence, it won't be law when *we* try it. It takes a legislature or the equivalent.

It has been proposed that law comes with a capacity of being recognized—a "rule of recognition" as it is called—by which the citizen can tell whether some precept was a law or not. But it's unhelpful to appeal to a capacity to recognize a law if we don't know what it is that is being recognized. We must agree that the citizen usually knows that something is being claimed by his government to be a law. We might just say, "Of course, that's the law. It says so right here!" by way of defining the term. This turns *law* into a label with no content. But in fact, as we know, the thing is put out with the intention that *we* have to *obey* it. What we really wanted to know about law is *why do we need to obey it?* No amount of talk of rules of recognition, etc., will tell us that.

Law makes a claim on us. Why should we respond? Aquinas's answer is Because it's for the common good, and you, Mr. Citizen, are one of those "commoners." That makes sense. If indeed a law is for my good, then I can see why I should obey it. If it's for everyone's good, then evidently it's for mine, too. But now, suppose I confront what is claimed to be "a law," and I ask: *Is* this particular sentence on paper, issued by variously costumed officials, and saying I am to do this or that, one that I should take seriously? *Would* it be for my good? How? If it's because it is aimed at the *common* good, does that mean that I'm included, or does it mean that I might be left out and asked to sacrifice my own good for that of a bunch of people I don't know and perhaps don't care about very much? The answer had better be, for starters, that I'm included, for if I'm not, then there's no obvious reason why I should go along with it. This confirms Aquinas's point: To be an effective law, it has to be for the common good, so that it provides each and every one of us with a good reason to do what it says.

OK. Are there any such laws, in fact? We can agree that it makes sense for a legislature to *try* to make laws with those properties. Whether they can actually succeed is quite another matter. We'll be back to that kind of problem in the ensuing pages.

THE RULE OF LAW

The idea of law is central to political philosophy, but which idea is it? Here we must make some distinctions—three, to be precise.

(1) Laws must be distinguished from *decrees*. Suppose the dictator, one fine morning, says, "Hey, let's roast Phil Jones on a skewer today!"—no reason given. He has minions around who will jump to his command, so Jones is duly rounded up. Jones asks, "Why are you doing this?" and the dictator replies that he, Jones, has no business asking him, the Big Cheese, why he does what he does, and off Jones goes to the roasting pit. (In the discussions, contemporary as this was written, of what to do about Mexicans "illegally" in the United States, a frequent claim is that the reason—the *only* reason, it seems—for sending them back to the destitution of their native land is that in getting to America they *broke the law*.) Insofar as the community's rulers behave like that, I suggest, we do not have the rule of law—though we certainly have *rule*.

Even rule by decree is possibly a step up from the worst condition, in that the powerful simply act, without any effort to impart their wishes to anyone. But if the decrees can be completely irrational or arbitrary, it's scarcely better.

(2) A major reason for having laws is precisely to avoid the previous condition, which is, after all, tyranny. How serious a tyranny depends, of course, on what sort of whims the particular dictator of the day happens to have—but then, that's part of the point. One political view is that "benevolent despotism" would be the best of all. But as soon as we try to put together a political system that ensures that your dictator *will* be benevolent, we see that this is just wishful thinking. Instead, we insist that our government proceed, especially when it proceeds *against* some citizen or citizens, *only* on the basis of general rules, applicable in principle to all, knowable in advance, published in accessible places, and applied to individuals on the basis of fair procedures such as a jury trial, with good standards of evidence. The generality of law is especially what provides this considerable protection to the individual citizen. At least the citizen can then know in advance what's required and thus what he must do to keep out of trouble, and he has some recourse if the government tries to get him into that trouble.

How much recourse? That will depend further on the procedural safeguards recognized and perhaps provided by the State. Is he entitled to trial by jury? Are there rules of evidence? Is he entitled to legal representation? All these things will matter, but details are not obvious.

The idea is to rig them with the general goal of protecting the innocent and yet making sure that the guilty are plausibly *found* to be so and duly dealt with. That is often not easy.

An important subissue concerns the administration of whatever laws there are. Are they enforced in every possible case? Or is there room to recognize some cases as ones where "the law is an ass"? Every driver on modern highways is familiar with the custom of police allowing a certain excess over the posted speed limits. Rules never fit all cases. Should administrators act accordingly? Plausibly, yes they should: We are better protected when the law is applied according to the "spirit" rather than the "letter." The rule of law does not call for all laws being applied at all times. How far this point reaches is an interesting question that we can't pursue further at present.

(3) The idea of the rule of law sketched in (2) is undoubtedly a huge improvement over the situation of despotism envisaged in (1). Still, though, there is a very large question: Why do we have the particular laws we have? What are they supposed to be like, in order to pass muster? A government must have a lawmaking institution of some sort—a Parliament, Congress, Assembly, or at least a Council of Ministers—whose job is to formulate and certify these general orders to the populace. But does just *anything* go? One hopes not. After all, general rules known to all, and uniformly applied, could nevertheless be downright silly. "All citizens will wear brown slacks only!" is clear enough. But will it do? Should such "laws" even be allowed in a decent country? Or worse. Suppose the laws forbid marrying people of differing race from one's own, or compelling us to poison our neighbors? Is there a way to prevent that? If so, is *it* to be reckoned a part of the "rule of law"?

It helps a bit to say that laws should be "reasonable"—there's Aquinas, holding that laws must be "ordinances of Reason" rather than just any old sort of command, however general. But what *is* reasonable? Again, Aquinas helps when he says that law must be for the common good. How much that helps now depends on what is allowed to count as an element in that "good." It is easy to imagine the dictator making some awful pronouncements on the subject. "Death is the only thing good enough for persons of Jewish ancestry!" is, alas, not even a fanciful example, in view of over twenty centuries of history.

So our highest-level idea of the rule of law is this: We are indeed morally obliged to obey a given legislated law if and only if this law meets the specifications laid down by the True Theory—the right theory about the "essence" of law, the gimmick, so to speak, that really makes a given law "swing." This would be the theory that says exactly which proposed laws pass muster as the right thing, and which do not. We could then object to a given output of our legislatures on the ground that it failed this test. (Some famous ideas will be considered later.) The term "natural law" could be brought in to designate this superstandard, knowable prior to any actual legislating. The main question, of course, is whether there can even be such a thing—some formula or principle such that to be an acceptable law is to live up to its specifications. This is a third understanding of rule of law, because it imposes a filter on the set of items that would qualify something as a law under (2) above. In the present book, much later, such a very strong filter will be proposed.

Meanwhile, we can now make a useful terminological distinction for our third level as compared with our first: It would be the rule of *law*, as opposed to the rule of *laws*. In a polity where the rule of law holds sway, the officers of the law are told to look beyond the "letter of the law," as the popular phrase has it, and instead act according to the "spirit" of the laws (as in the famous book by Montesquieu[2]). They do in fact do this now to some extent. On a normal day on an American highway, the police will not arrest you for exceeding the posted limit by less than a certain amount. In numerous ways, the letter of the law will be ignored, and mostly, that will be a very good thing. What the officers do in those cases, however, is not contrary to the idea of law. Just the opposite: They will be doing better what the very idea of law sets as the right sort of agenda for a good community.

THREE THEORIES OF GOVERNMENT

I conclude with a note about where we're headed. The next four chapters of the book are organized in terms of a division of political theories. Our question is how to be rational about political matters. One way of putting that is, How does a rational person deal with political issues? Especially, what would the person in the position of exercising political power do with that power?

The answer to this question takes us along three very different paths, one of which, I think, and I think we nowadays all think, is the best one, but all of which make sense and are extremely important. Each is more or less formulated or illustrated by a character in Plato's famous book *The Republic*—the first, and, quite a few would say, still the greatest book on political philosophy. The three are these, with my brief explanations.

(1) *Realism* (or "Realpolitik" or "power politics"): The tough-guy character in *Republic*, a brash young man named Thrasymachus, bursts into the conversation proposing that justice is *"the interest of the stronger party."* Thrasymachus goes on to propose that the rational possessor

of political power would use it to promote *his own* wealth, power, and glory, and that to act otherwise is to be a fool. He would, in short, be a tyrant. Thrasymachus's ruler regards his subjects as just so many sources of potential gain for himself. His view of the citizen is that there's a sucker born every day! Much later, the Italian Renaissance writer Niccolo Machiavelli wrote what is widely taken to be the classic treatise in this vein, *The Prince*, and the sort of politics meant by the term is typically referred to as "Machiavellian" (perhaps unfairly, as it turns out[3]).

(2) *Conservatism* (or "Platonism" or "Guardianship"): Next we have Plato himself, via his mouthpiece Socrates, who exemplifies the Philosopher. The ruler or "guardian" devotes his life to figuring out what's good for people, and he then *treats people accordingly*. He absolutely disagrees with Thrasymachus: The ruler rules not for his own good but for that of his subjects. But what the people themselves think about it is more or less beside the point—they're not very bright, and they are short on virtue, especially the intellectual type. So the good ruler becomes a sort of supergoverness ("guardian"), and the State is to be run by the "Guardian" class, composed of (supposedly) very wise people selected especially for the purpose of seeing The Good, then getting it realized.

(3) *Liberalism*: Finally, Plato's character Glaucon, who seems to represent ordinary people, proposes that morality is something we might prefer to avoid, but, given the way things are, avoiding it is a bad idea. In Glaucon's view, what the citizens *want* is what counts. What the rational individual, mindful of his or her own interests, wants is such that his indicated solution is to make an *agreement* with his fellow citizens—the "social contract" as it later became famously known. The terms of this agreement consist, especially, in staying out of each other's way; keeping off each other's back, as we might say. Glaucon's idea was taken up much later in a more thorough and allegedly "scientific" way nearly two millennia later by the Englishman Thomas Hobbes, to whom we will be paying rather more attention later on.

My three titles—"realism," "conservatism," and "liberalism"—fit only very approximately with current usage, which is not at all stable anyway; but they are the nearest thing among labels in common use to the requirements of political theorizing, so we'll use them. The important thing is the basis for the categories.

1. The political *realist*—the "Machiavellian"—holds that rulers should get what they can *however* they can and forget about niceties like

morality. The ruler on this view will be what has lately been called a "kleptokrat"—a superthief.

2. The *conservative* wants to promote the public good, as long as the "true" view—which of course will be his own favored view, inevitably—of what's good for people is what is used for this purpose. The view of the people themselves is beside the point.

3. And finally, the *liberal* takes the view that each person should be regarded as the final authority on his or her own good; the public good is simply your and my and everyone else's good, *as seen by each person for himself or herself*. The practical question for liberals, then, is Which political arrangements conduce to this end? A very serious theoretical question along the way is What do we do when one person's good is not compatible with another's? How do we resolve the conflict in a way maximally true to the idea of individual self-rule?

Three Theories of Government, with a Dialogue . . . (and apologies to Plato)

We'll introduce the three fundamental views of government, as I think they are, with this little dialogue.

MacThrash ["M"]: a sort of Thrasymachus/Machiavelli [as in *The Prince*] hybrid

Platocrates ["P"]: the Socrates of Plato's *Republic*, who is thought to be mostly Plato by scholars

Alfred E. Glaucon ["A"]: roughly the common-sense character in the *Republic*, plus a measure of "What, Me Worry?"

****

M: Look, you guys, there's really no point in prattling on about the essence of justice—you've all got the wrong idea. Actually, it's just a tool of the strong. Justice, we may as well say, is the interest of the stronger party.

P: You mean to claim that whatever any "strong man" tells us to do is *ipso facto* just? That sounds like a perfectly crazy theory of "justice" to me.

A: Well, to be fair (if that's the right thing to try to be with a bull in the china shop like MacThrash!), he must mean not that what we *mean* by "just" is "in accord with the will of the strong," but rather that the voice of reason and common sense tells us to recognize facts when we see them. We simply have to obey the guy with the most strength and might as well try to do so with good grace.

M: OK, I accept Alfred's adjustment. What I'm saying is this: Everyone thinks that obeying the laws is just. Well, the laws are made by the strong, and of course it is their interests that impel them to make the ones they do. Therefore, people who believe they are acting justly are in fact promoting the interests of those strong people who make the laws.

P: You realize, of course, that some of us (present company a case in point!) do *not* think that the laws are just no matter what they are like and no matter who made them or why. When we act justly, we are not conforming to the will of the strong, *unless* the strong happen to have made just laws in the first place. But if they did, it wasn't just because they did make them that they are just, nor because they happen to promote the leaders' interests (if they do). It could hardly be more obvious that we need a deeper theory about what makes things just.

A: Yes, indeed we do. Now, you, Platocrates, are famed for having such a theory: Justice, you say, is the Harmony of the Soul. But this seems to me a puzzling and implausible idea. It's not, of course, entirely clear what this "harmony" consists in, but I want to hold up as cases for study various dictators whose souls seem to be in pretty good shape. They know what they're doing, they have their act together, and unfortunately their very possession of a pretty high level of personal virtue of that kind enables them to pursue their unjust projects all the more effectively.

P: Well, I claim that a man cannot *truly* have his soul in harmony if he goes around murdering people, say.

A: That would be nice, indeed: But how do you prove this? How can it not be a fatal problem for your theory that people who, in any nonquestion-begging sense, have "harmonious souls" might nevertheless do horrendous injustices to lots of people?

M: You'll admit, I think, that one of those strong men who does, as Alfred so neatly puts it, have his act together, will ignore fancy theories about "justice" if those theories call for anything other than doing what serves his own interests best.

P: But his *true* interest . . .

A: What on earth is a "true" interest? If I have an interest, say, in having the fine house of that person over there, who on earth are you to say that it isn't "true"?

P: Speaking both as your professor (ahem!) and as a normal citizen, I say that it isn't true because it'll make you miserable if you act on it—in the longer run anyway. And that'll be because what you would have done is unjust.

M: Sounds pretty speculatively chancy to me to say that. In the process of taking over the house, I'll just have my henchmen throw the current owner out—no problem!

A: Anyway, there's a much better theory about what justice is than either of you guys seem to be plumping for. Who on earth would want to live under Mac-Thrash's rule, if he had any choice in the matter? And who wouldn't be worried about a government trying to "improve his soul"? But on my theory—which I think is the common sense one—justice is simply a sort of agreement among us rational people, in particular an agreement to refrain from damaging each other at will. You don't hit me, I don't hit you. Fair deal! Once we are all pretty much at peace with each other, the rest is, simply, to each his own. Can either of you offer anything more appealing than that?

M: Well, that assumes you have some choice in the matter. But if you don't, what am I supposed to do about it? Given the power I'll have, I reiterate that what I will do is what I damn well please!

P: It looks as though we're in for a very long slog before my Republic is realized!

A: Yes, no doubt. But it's not so hard to set up something else that will effectively prevent people like MacThrash from ever getting all that power he is so ready to misuse. A constitution that sets up pretty good procedures that keep the power hungry in check and enable the wheels of government to turn pretty much in the public interest—surely that's what sensible people will aim for.

* *

My three characters represent the three basic ideas in my division of political theories. Our question is how to be rational about political matters. One way of putting that is to ask: How does a rational person deal with political issues? Especially, what would the person in the position of exercising political power do with that power?

WHERE WE ARE AND WHERE WE'RE GOING

The twentieth century was dominated by two political systems or ideologies that are widely rejected today: communism and fascism, each of which turned into versions of totalitarianism. We are right to reject them, but we need to know our enemies. They are most nearly associated with the conservative among my three types, though it is unfair to stick conservatism with any of them automatically. There are plenty of conservatives who denounce these extreme systems. No doubt Plato would have hated Mussolini, Hitler, Stalin, Mao, Castro, and the many others who play the role of dictatorial arbiter of the fates of their subjects. But, still, there is a connection, as we will see.

Liberalism is in the ascendancy among philosophical writers today, though that is not always easy to tell. At any rate, a project of this book will be to explain why it should be so and to explain the support for it. But just where liberalism takes us is a much-disputed issue. We will see that it comes in two sharply divergent general strains and explore why this should be so and what there is to be said on behalf of each. The transition from the one to the other has arguably been due mainly to the political system known as *democracy*, and accordingly we will take a close look at that. It is an important relative of liberalism but by no means the same thing.

My final chapter takes us back to the subject of *anarchism*. Would it be an improvement on all the others? Maybe so, I suggest. I hope the reader will be interested enough to follow the path from anarchism thought of as chaotic and nightmarish to anarchism regarded by its advocates as the ultimate in peace and prosperity. Political philosophy is by no means at an end!

NOTES

1. St. Thomas Aquinas, *Summa Theologica*, Treatise on Law, #90. A good source is William P. Baumgarth and Richard J. Regan, eds., *Saint Thomas Aquinas on Law, Morality, and Politics* (Indianapolis, IN: Hackett, 1988). The definition in that volume is on p. 17.

2. Charles-Louis de Secondat, Baron de La Brède et de Montesquieu (1689–1755), *De l'Esprit des Loix* (*The Spirit of Laws*). This book is one of the classics in the history of political theory and law, published in 1748 in two volumes.

3. It has been argued that *The Prince* was written tongue-in-cheek. See, for example, http://www.mala.bc.ca/~Johnstoi/introser/machiavelli.htm, which is the transcript of a lecture by Ian Johnston, Research Associate at Malaspina University-College, Nanaimo, British Columbia, Canada. He says, for example: "My take on this book is representative of a widely held (but distinctly minority) view of *The Prince*; namely, that the book is, first and foremost, a satire, so that many of the things we find in it which are contradictory, morally absurd, and specious are there quite deliberately in order to ridicule two things—first, the Medici family itself and, second, the very notion of tyrannical rule embodied in the government of the Prince (hence, the satire has a firm moral purpose—to expose tyranny and promote republican government). Such a way of reading this text, it should be clear, is distinctly at odds with any reading that assumes that Machiavelli's analysis and text are totally without ironical undercurrents that qualify, indeed contradict, his literal 'message.'" (Mr. Johnston gives permission to use without charge given recognition of the source.)

2

Right and Might

From the Jungle to Civilized Government?

"THE INTEREST OF THE STRONGER PARTY"

Governments compel. They impose. They have muscle. That's what forms the background for our subject. If government were just another club down the street, nobody would be writing scholarly treatises about it. Given that it can and does use force, and given that force, or more precisely *coercion*, has a way of working, the thought certainly suggests itself that force is, as the kids say, "where it's at." And it is central, indeed. But how? The interesting thesis was famously asserted in Plato's *Republic* by the character Thrasymachus that justice is "the interest of the stronger party." The justification of using force is that it works, and that's the end of the matter—anyone who questions it is whistling in the wind. A twentieth-century update was provided by Mao Tse-Dong: "power comes from the barrel of a gun."

Socrates pointed out that rulers as we know them sometimes make mistakes. When they do, there'll be a problem: Is the ruler to do X, which is in his interest, or Y, which he thinks to be in his interest, but wrongly? Socrates is certainly on to something there. Indeed, he brings up a problem for which there is no solution: ignorance. In one sense, of course, the solution to the problem is simple: Learn the truth. But that sweeps the problem under the carpet. What if the dictator *does* know what's in his interest?

A different and more useful thing can be said. Insofar as someone is ignorant in a way that is relevant to what he or she is trying to accomplish, that person *is* weak. There is considerable truth in the saying that "knowledge is power." Some knowledge is virtually useless ("What is the diameter, in light years, of the galaxy Monstro?"), and a lot of power is not a matter of knowledge at all, but of physics. Niagara Falls is extremely powerful, but

25

it rules no one. The sort of power we are speaking of, however, is *political* power. This is interpersonal power and is wielded by people with goals, ambitions, interests to be realized. For them, knowing what works and what doesn't is of vital importance. Thrasymachus responded to Socrates by insisting that the *true* ruler makes no mistakes: Insofar as he rules, he gets it right. If we adopt this usage, there is no logically open question of the form, "will the ruler do what works?" But then, there is another open question: "Is Jones, who is generally considered the ruler, *really* the ruler?" As soon as he makes a mistake, the answer will be negative, and nothing about his current status on the throne will assure that he doesn't make those mistakes. The device of redefining the term *ruler* in Thrasymachus's way is unhelpful.

POLITICAL POWER

Not all power comes from knowledge, by any means. Another widely quoted slogan, noted above, from recent history was attributed to the Chinese dictator Mao Tse-Dong: "Power comes out of the barrel of a gun." Mao was right in two different ways, but it's very important to distinguish those two ways. One way is crudely physical: If you shoot someone dead, then that person is now out of the way. His body might be in the way, but that's quite a different kind of obstacle from the case in which it's his actions you were concerned about. This latter way is not at all irrelevant; it is the very stuff of politics.

If you shoot someone, he's dead. But if you instead *threaten* to shoot him *unless* he does x, there's a very good chance that he'll do x, almost no matter what x may be. There are two important points about this: First, the "do": what threatening does is to induce *action*, not just physical motion. The actions you might induce someone to do by threatening him with death might be very sophisticated; he might be a highly trained scientist who can do things almost nobody else can do and that you yourself don't know much about. And those actions are, in a sense, voluntary: That person *could* choose not to succumb. If you do shoot him, he isn't going to do what you wanted him to do, of course. You might nevertheless shoot him, but that is very different from the case in which he cooperates. Indeed, there is paradox here. Insofar as you actually use the force you threaten, you fail to get what you wanted, which was for the other person to do your bidding. If you don't use it but merely threaten it, you might succeed in that. But if the other person thinks through it, he could alternatively just refuse, and then where are you? That is the classic game theorist's situation known as "chicken": What's worse for your victim is also worse for you. But clever and courageous players, knowing this, may induce you to back down. Most people are neither that clever nor that courageous, and they do back down. The art of politics, says the Thrasymachean, is getting the maximum out of your subjects before they refuse to put up with any more. (Think of current income tax levels, for example!)

Trying to get things done by this method—*coercion* as we call it—has its limits. When A coerces B, what A essentially does is to narrow B's range of options, *for the worse*. B was working in her lab, meaning to finish her experiment and then go home to dinner with her family. A's interruption makes this impossible. What's more, it's the one she prefers; A deprives B of an alternative that B prefers to all the alternatives A leaves her with. She now needs to choose between being dead and revealing some serious secret or concocting some dangerous substance, or whatever it is that A wants her to do, knowing that what A will do with it will be pretty awful for many people. But B will decide on this matter by deciding which is on the whole the greater cost: being dead or doing those things.

Some subjects of coercion will not do what the coercer wants. History is full of resisters who refuse to go along even at the cost of death. Think of the famous Zealots at Masada, who committed mass suicide rather than submit to the Romans. Should you be one of them? It would be nice if that question never had to be raised, but if it ever does, it's very important to be aware that the answer just might be Yes. With this thought in mind, let's return to our subject. Thrasymachus claims that justice is "the interest of the stronger party." What could he have meant?

One thing he might have meant is what he literally said[1]: that the word *just* means "fulfilling the interest of the strong." But if that's what he really meant, then the suggestion is obviously wrong. As we normally use this word, the weak can be in the right and the strong in the wrong, or vice versa. Thrasymachus must have had something else in mind. He might have meant something more like this: "You guys think that justice is something else, but you're deluded. If you look carefully, you'll find that at the end of the day, it's all a matter of brute force." That too is a puzzling and implausible claim, but at least it's not the implausible claim that we don't even know what we mean when we use the word *just*. But what, then, might Thrasymachus mean that is at all plausible?

There is a good answer to that, actually. Thrasymachus is talking about political power, not just any old use of force. Political power enables people to make laws. Now, most people do think that to obey the laws is just. But then, if the laws express the will of the politically strong, it will turn out that justice is in the interest of the strong. QED?

Well, sort of. There is an implicit assumption in the argument that "the strong" do make the laws in *their own* interest. If that's true, and if their interests are opposed to those of the people they are governing, then you and I are likely to think that what they do is unjust in the usual sense of the term (rather than Thrasymachus's, if he has a special one). But it might not be.

Perhaps the rulers, strong though they are, are nevertheless public-minded people who are trying to promote the public good. In that case, it might be just to obey the laws they make, but not merely *because* they express the will of the strong. Rather, it might be because those laws are just. Or it might be because it is just to obey the law. Our broaching of the subject of law in the previous chapter leaves ample room to deny this, in that usual sense of the term *law* in which laws can be and are made by legislators and other rulers. Such laws can certainly be unjust. The claim that we should obey them anyway doesn't look promising—even though some very smart people have professed to think so.

GENGHIS KHAN, AND PEOPLE LIKE THAT

History is replete with famous conquerors, such as Alexander the Great, who is sometimes said to have conquered "the world"—an overstatement, though he did conquer a lot of countries in the Middle East. The British had a huge empire, though much of it was not exactly "conquered," and Adolph Hitler and his Nazis managed to conquer virtually all of Europe in the early stages of World War II. The people who had the misfortune to be in the paths of these conquerors sometimes had the choice to surrender or fight. A good many did surrender, and many in each group chose to fight and paid with their lives. The question is whether their conquerors acted justly. You and I surely think not. Part of the motivation behind this book is the hope that we can show that we are right about this. Might does *not* make right.

An urgent question is whether those of their victims who chose to surrender rather than fight were acting justly. Does justice require that we resist injustice, even unto death? Almost all of us, I suspect, think otherwise. Certainly almost all of us do otherwise. We think that the victims of robbery or political conquest, faced with the unhappy alternatives of fighting (and probably losing) or surrendering, do *have* the latter option. Justice permits us to surrender, though it doesn't usually require us to do so. Why? That crucial question will occupy us at some length in the ensuing pages.

Those who might be attracted to the idea of justice as power in the sense of "force"—superior strength of body, skill at arms, and other military attributes—will do well to study the histories of these famous conquerors. Take, for example, Genghis Khan (1162–1227), whose exploits are instructive and, for our purposes, typical. Of greatest importance is that what the one Great Conquerer does is to lead a great many others and to use political devices that enable the job to be done by securing the more or less voluntary assistance of those others, including the people conquered. Thus we are told, ". . . [T]otal destruction of cities in Central Asia by the Mongols

. . . was more of an exception than a rule. If a city capitulated, Genghis Khan was usually content to let them be, once their defenses had been pulled down. Only those who resisted faced the sword. This not only wiped out resistance, but more importantly, word quickly spread of the wrath of Genghis Khan, and many peoples found it easier to submit than to resist." This and many other things about his methods and his background make the example of this fierce warrior a fascinating one. "While normally thought of as a despot Genghis Khan was also generous and loyal. A highly charismatic man, he nonetheless also expected loyalty from everyone, including those who served his opponents." Genghis Khan, then, did have moral principles. He enforced the idea of loyalty to one's leader, not only to Khan himself. "He is reputed to have put to death people who, thinking they would gain his good graces, betrayed their lords to him."[2]

Conquest is never a matter of sheer brute force. Consider the striking case of Masada, a fortress rock at the edge of the desert in Israel. A group of Jews not happy with the Roman occupation took refuge there for several years. When the Roman emperor decided to deal with them, his legion surrounded the rock, making escape impossible, then built an enormous ramp up to the top using slave labor by conquered Jews, smashed the entrance, and planned to invade the next morning. But the Zealots chose to frustrate the conquest by committing universal suicide (including some being chosen by lot to kill the others, then themselves). In the morning, the Romans were greeted by dead bodies. They did find a handful of women and children who survived to tell the story.

If the object of the Romans was to *subjugate* the Zealots, they *failed*. The Romans wanted obedience. All they got was a lot of dead bodies and a major mess to clean up. If what you want to do with the people you conquer is anything that requires any kind of human activity on *their* part, then you simply won't be able to get it from people who are so determined not to give it to you that they'll choose death in preference—and that's an end of the matter. That end, however, is so far from most people's ideas of how to live that force usually works, sort of. But at what price, and to what end? And what are we to infer from all this?

Parts of the answers to both questions are provided by a bit of thought about the nature of human beings and interpersonal conflict. Genghis Khan did not win all of his battles, and plenty of his soldiers died in the process of winning the ones he did. His tireless horsemen went to battle with their own food "which usually consisted of powdered yak milk . . . and when food was scarce the soldiers would open up a vein of their horse to drink its blood." Hmmm! One might just wonder whether a life of frequent bloodthirsty battle, sustained by reconstituted milk and the odd glass of horse blood, with a fairly short life expectancy, isn't a considerable price to pay for the supposed glories of conquest and occasional celebrations of victory. This would be especially so in the cases where your army slaughtered all of the inhabitants of the places they conquered, thus leaving themselves with no human services at all from their victims and another awful mess to do something about.

But what about the many cases in which they enslave the victims in question? The case of slavery is a fascinating one. The slave owners have to devote a great deal of time and effort to compel their slaves to work and of course to keep them from running away. (Jeffrey Rogers Hummel has plausibly argued that if it weren't for the Fugitive Slave Act, which required the bordering American states to return runaway slaves to the slave states, the institution of slavery simply couldn't have been sustained.[3]) In a free society, no such effort is necessary: You simply offer a payment, and the potential worker either takes it and does your work, or declines, in which case you have to go elsewhere or raise your offer. Both parties benefit, nobody suffers injuries or is even threatened with any such, and no one is left with a lingering sense of having been forced to do something he or she really didn't want to do. (Some workers and many philosophers who purport to speak for workers have claimed differently; we'll discuss their ideas later on.) The contrast with slavery is stark and dramatic.

How shall we decide about this? There are two things, actually, to be "decided." One is whether the life of the soldier or the slave owner—not to mention the slave—is the life for you. The fact that essentially nobody would volunteer for the life of the slave, given a real choice, is significant, but let's table that point for the moment. Meanwhile, the point about the soldier, even if he's on the "winning" side, is that he leads a dangerous life and one that is heavily dependent on the support of others. The soldier does no useful work, except insofar as defending people from other soldiers is useful. But of course, the same points apply to the soldiers on the other side: They too are devoted to subduing other soldiers of whom precisely the same thing is true. If we consider two nations, or two tribes, or even just two individuals, at war, the spectacle presents itself of all concerned doing no useful work insofar as they are busy making and preparing for war and so producing nothing of value to the folks back home. The two societies, on the face of it, will make themselves worse off by their warfare. You don't need to look too long at photographs of Germany in April 1945, or of most of the war-torn cities in Europe of the time, to see what the costs of war can be. Even America, which is often claimed to have prospered due to World War II, suffered 400,000 dead and emerged with a civilian economy no wealthier at the end than at the beginning (unless you count possession of war weaponry as "wealth"—a tendency unfortunately widespread[4]). The point is clear: The victors in war can expect to pay severe costs for their supposed gains, and it is unclear what the gains are anyway, unless you count the sheer sense of conquest as a "gain." Which some have, to be sure. Are you one of them? Seriously?

Meanwhile, however, the gains to a small set of people at the top might indeed be considerable. Generals are paid more highly than foot soldiers, and members of governments who send men to war do pretty well. The question for the folks back home, though, is why they would find it a great benefit that the leaders are enriched at the home folks' expense while the sons (and now daughters) of those folks are put in mortal danger as well as kept off the farm or the shop for the duration.

This, actually, is one of the intriguing phenomena of political philosophy—as we might call it, the Nationalist Rah-Rah factor, or perhaps the Gung Ho factor. What's in it for *you* if Your Country is the Top Country, militarily, while you sacrifice a large share of your income and expose some of your family to wounds, dismemberment, and death to make that possible? We are given the impression by Greek playwrights that lots of people, women included, would have no problem with that question. We may be forgiven for thinking that they *should* have a problem.

This brings us to the other question, and the relevant one for our purposes: What about the issue for political morality? But of course, to answer that we need some idea what this consists of. So that's next.

DOES MIGHT MAKE RIGHT? SHOULD IT?

It is familiar stuff that might doesn't make right. Thrasymachus seems to be challenging that. Plato paints Thrasymachus into a tight corner when he points out that even a gang of thieves is going to have to practice justice. Suppose that each thief is fully as much a danger to the other thieves as he is to the bankers and corner-store operators he victimizes. Will they even succeed as a gang? Of course not—as Thrasymachus agrees.

Another question is whether a well-organized gang of thieves operating against the rest of society will, or should, be hailed as heroes. We can be sure that the banker and the corner-store owner don't think so. Nor do their customers who, after all, share in the losses. And what about ordinary people trying to go about their lives without molestation? Does it make any sense for them to approve of people using force to get their way and taking the view that all that matters is who comes out on top? To ask such a question is virtually to answer it. If you have any choice in the matter, such approval would be absurd. Still, an obvious reply is that if you *can* get away with it, why *shouldn't* you? That was, after all, pretty much Thrasymachus's thesis. Few of us, of course, *can* "get away with it."[5] Does that matter?

HOBBES ON GOVERNMENT

For the most relevant and interesting discussion of this, we turn to the work of Thomas Hobbes (1588–1676), whose argument about the rationale of the State is worth our most careful attention. Hobbes imagines a "state of nature"—the condition in which people who are in touch with each other, and so are a society, are without government. What would happen in such a condition?

Hobbes identifies the main features of people that enable us, he supposes, to predict this.

1. They are, he says, equal. Equal how? Interestingly, he specifies a roughly equal capacity *to do violence to each other*, equality of "vulnerability" to each other, as we may call it: "for as to strength of bodee, the weakest hath enough to kill the strongest." Death is the great leveler, and (virtually) anyone can inflict it on anyone.
2. They live in a condition of general, but relievable, scarcity. The "relievable" specification is important: If we can cooperate, we can improve on nature, producing what unaltered nature does not. But can we? That's where the next three features become crucial.
3. They don't generally love each other. Each acts with a view to seeing to his or her *own* interests, whatever might happen to others. Yes, they love their families, but that doesn't get us to love of our fellows generally. If anything, it may make that less likely, as people defend their own families against the dangers presented by others. So far as those others are concerned, if it comes down to a choice between *me* and *them, mine* and *theirs,* Hobbes assumes that it'll be *me* and *mine.*
4. Hobbes takes it that we are *not moral by nature.* We have no innate scruples about damaging, even killing, each other.
5. Pervading all, they are *rational:* Humans can put two and two together. One of the ways they put them together is by noting that other people also have the preceding characteristics, and so, if we come into competition with them, we'd better watch out.

Now, natural scarcity assures that we often will come into such competition; nonaltruism and amorality mean that we won't hesitate to take what we want by force if we can't get it otherwise. People determine the best means to their ends and follow it up in action.

Conclusion: We are in for a very rough time! For if you can be pretty sure that the other guy will get you if you don't get him first, you will be motivated to do just that—and he knows you will. So the whole thing degenerates into a fracas, the "war of all against all," where everybody is everybody's enemy. Given the undoubted physical capability of the normal individual, this condition would be truly intolerable. There would be

> no place for Industry; because the fruit thereof is uncertain; and consequently no Culture of the Earth, no Navigation, nor use of the commodities that may be imported by Sea; no commodious Building; no Instruments of moving, and removing such things as require much force; no Knowledge of the face of the Earth; no account of Time; no Arts; no Letters; no Society; and which is worst of all, continual fear, and danger of violent death; And the life of man, solitary, poor, nasty, brutish, and short.[6]

What to do? A thought would be to mutually agree to be peaceable instead of using our powers to "invade and despoil." But the perennial question arises: Will this work? The trouble is that agreements, says Hobbes, are "mere words" and "of no strength to protect a man," not to mention that it is hard to see how, in such a condition, people ever would or could negotiate such a thing anyway. And so he concludes that it isn't going to work. Morality isn't enough. Hobbes proposes government as a solution: Let's hand all our powers over to some one person or small group of persons, who will then see to it that miscreants who try to make their way by violence will get punished for their efforts. Given that sort of an agency, we will at last be able to rely on each other to keep their agreements, and in general, civilization can then get off the ground.

MORALS, POWER, AND "NATURAL LAW"

Hobbes's argument for government is elegant and captivating, and has in fact captivated virtually everybody, in one version or another. Few writers from that day to this don't virtually concede Hobbes's argument: We need government to keep us from cheating, stealing, murdering, and just generally making life awful for everyone.

Is he right? There are two huge problems. In the first place, there is a logical problem about getting government off the ground on Hobbes's stated terms (or anybody's). Hobbes says that there are just two ways to acquire government. One way is by universal agreement: We all "confer our power" on this one person or small group, and then Presto!—they have it! But *can* we do this? After all, this too appears to be a verbal agreement and therefore, if the previous argument is right, not worth anything more than the words that convey it. So how can it do what is claimed for it? Or if it would work, then why wouldn't other agreements be worth something too? A large part of the point of erecting a sovereign, after all, was to enforce agreements. If we need one to have this kind of superenforcer, Hobbes's argument is in trouble. But if we don't, then it's also in trouble. Maybe anarchy is a viable option after all.

The other problem is a familiar one since Plato. Plato was of the view that government required trained, wise people who would devote their lives to the public good. Critics over the millennia have asked, "Who guards the guardians?" With Hobbes the same problem arises, perhaps even more virulently. For Hobbes doesn't have us choosing the wisest and best to do the job—just somebody, anybody: King Joe Schmoe! But once this person gets his finger on the trigger, why would he do the job Hobbes assumes and hopes he will do? Why will he use his power to protect us, instead of turning into Thrasymachus and using it to rob and despoil?

Indeed, many critics of government are of the view that governments will do just that. (More of that later. . . .) But that isn't the main point, exactly. Rather, the real problem is that Hobbes has no way to block that. Hobbes makes a distinction between *just* government and *good* government and holds that the former expression is pleonastic—*all* governments are just, because to *be* a government is automatically to be just. But Hobbes, to his credit, is clear that government is not automatically *good*, and he has a brilliant agenda for appraising governments, on which I'll be drawing later. But the former? It's surely bending way too far over backward to insist, against all common sense, that the pronouncements of hoodlums and maniacs on the throne are necessarily *just*. Stalin, Mao, Nero, Hitler, and the other famous tyrants of history were evil, and they were unjust in the extreme. If subtle philosophers argue otherwise, what can they be thinking? Maybe they need to look again.

As things stand, Hobbes can't have the particular cake he wants and eat it too. Something has to give, and what has to give is the claim that familiar moral ideas don't apply in the "state of nature" in his sense, namely, that they don't apply in the absence of government. Of course they do.

In a sense Hobbes agrees with that. Hobbes himself is the source of a first-rate theory of morals his rules known as the "Laws of Nature." They tell us that we are not to proceed by invading and despoiling; that is, by aggressing upon others—in short, by making war. His reasonable First Law for us all is to "seek peace and follow it"; only when attacked do we get to use the "helps and advantages of war." Justifiable attack can only be counterattack; just war can only be *defensive*. From this Hobbes deduces many interesting theorems: We should allow each other the most liberty compatible with all having it; we should keep our agreements; we should confine punishments to those useful for preserving peace rather than just to get back at the bad guys; and much else.[7] The question is, though, in the absence of government, would these excellent precepts have any "clout"? Hobbes says not, but the right answer to this, as we will see, is yes, at least *some*.

Hobbes overlooked two factors of enormous importance in human social life. One is our ability to influence each other's behavior. Interaction along the lines of Hobbes's battlers is, frankly, stupid. Since it is enormously contrary to my interest to have you going around clubbing people to get what you want, and vice versa, and since we can often keep an eye on each other, and better still, get our friends to do so, the prospects for nongovernmental control of interpersonal behavior are actually pretty good. And the fact that we'd all be dead if Hobbes were right should also be allowed to count. No human community could long survive with everyone regarding everyone else as his mortal enemy. Natural selection weeds out the war-of-all-against-all types, leaving lots of human communities that have survived and do survive, for indefinitely long periods, without government, strictly speaking. Small bands of native peoples everywhere have "ruled" by consensus, not by coercion from a centralized source. (Whether "bands" with millions of members could do so is, of course, another question.)

The other thing he overlooked is that interaction with our fellows is rarely a "one-shot" affair. We encounter each other again and again. You kill this man now, and in the future you are forever deprived of whatever he could have done for you, and vice versa—not to mention what you can expect at the hands of his family and friends. When we deal with people over and over, day after day, the superiority of peace becomes apparent. The basis for expecting considerable compliance with the rule of peace is therefore much better than Hobbes thought.

Morality is not a perfect form of behavior control, but it is pretty good, surely good enough to raise the question whether sovereignty is really superior. The laws of nature, he says, are "eternal and immutable." To be reliable, honest, and nonviolent is always a virtue—*if* others are reliable, honest, and nonviolent too. But even if we both know that, how can we be sure? Perhaps we should agree that we can't: It is just barely possible that my friend will slay me tomorrow while my back is turned. Maybe, but it's immensely unlikely, and especially unlikely that he only refrains from slaying me *now* because he thinks the police will get him if he tries.

And then, there is that problem about Who Guards the Guardians—of constraining the "Sovereign." John Locke, writing not so long after Hobbes,[8] asks whether a king with unlimited powers couldn't be worse than the state of nature. It couldn't easily be worse than the *worst* conceivable Hobbesian scenario, true; but it could easily be worse than the relatively peaceable condition that Locke depicts as the plausible state of nature.

If, of course, people had not only no government but also no morality either, that would be another matter. But that is not about to happen, under remotely normal circumstances. Truly awful circumstances do happen, and when they do, many if not quite all bets tend to be off. But Hobbes, if he's to be effective, must argue for the typical, normal case—not wildly improbable scenarios. In normal cases, it's not every man for himself and devil take the hindmost. Instead, it's every man being tolerably helpful and unit-ing against really bad people. When there's a crime in a small medieval vil-lage, the "hue and cry" goes up, and the robber, or whatever, is assailed by an angry crowd. Who is the "stronger" party, a 240-pound thief or a crowd of 150-pound neighbors who are really mad at him? In numbers there is strength, and the numbers will go for protecting the innocent, not heaping praise and honor on murderers and robbers. (But let's not forget the down-side, such as the stoning of allegedly unvirtuous maidens.)

Things get complicated, however, when we consider sizable groups united in interest against isolated individuals or against other groups. They indeed present problems. But for the present, let's just point out that we can turn Thrasymachus on his head. Might gathers on the side of right, not be-cause might *makes* right but because it is hugely advantageous to almost all of us to have people behaving at least half-decently to each other. It may be nearer the truth, then, to say that right makes might! Thrasymachus's "strong men" are not strong because they are individually supermen but be-cause those subject to their rule by and large find his reign peaceable enough to enable citizens to get on with their lives.

THE LOCKEAN ARGUMENT FOR GOVERNMENT

John Locke (1632–1704) was as convinced as Thomas Hobbes of the ne-cessity of government, despite his insight that morality is more effective than Hobbes allows. People have, Locke says, a "natural law" to guide them, and in fact that natural law is the same as Hobbes's, if put a bit dif-ferently: "No one ought to harm another in his life, health, liberty, or property."[9] Harming others amounts to aggressing or "making war" against them and is thus what Hobbes's First Law of Nature likewise for-bids. Even though Locke thinks this will get us somewhere, he doesn't think it will get us nearly far enough. We may all agree that we ought not to steal from each other, but what if you think that this cow is yours, while I claim it's mine? We may all agree that certain acts are wrong, and punishable—but you may think he should get nine months in prison while I think he should get life. So the state of nature has severe "incon-veniences": All agree on the law of nature, yet if everyone administers that law as he thinks best, we could have big trouble. What we need, he argues, are three things:

(1) a common police force, instead of the ill-assorted bevy of ragtag pri-vateers that we would have in the state of nature,

(2) a common set of more detailed rules that apply the law of nature in all kinds of cases where it isn't so obvious what it says, and

(3) "learned and impartial" judges to decide disputes in an authoritative and fair way.

These three functions—administration, legislation, and adjudication—are general functions of government. Without them, things will go badly, if not as badly as Hobbes claims. With them, we have a functioning, effective community in which we can get all those desirable things done that are, as Locke agrees, the point of it all. And he assumes that we could only have them with government. On the former point—that things will go badly without such functions being seen to—he is right. On the latter, however—that we must have government to perform them and that it will for sure perform them well—the case is far less clear. Read on!

THRASYMACHUS REVISITED

Previously, we have understood the question for political consideration in these terms: If we didn't have a government, should we create one? Its co-ordinate question: If we do have a government, should we get rid of it? The argument to be addressed now is that we waste our time considering either of these questions, since government is going to happen, no matter what we want.

It is not entirely clear that this is so. Indeed, since governments are social devices made by people, it cannot be so at what we might call the abstract level. So argument is needed. What would the argument be? In short, it is this: Violence has a way of pressing the issue upon us. When determined, armed men are at the door, proposing to impose their will on us, we must either give in to those wishes or resist. Resistance may consist in suicide, but that is hardly the kind of answer that helps out our side. What we want is to live, but to live in a manner of our own choosing, that we are comfortable with. Resistance more typically will consist in armed resistance, which can be effective if we are well-armed, militarily astute, and courageous. It is also expensive, both in terms of the amount of time and energy we must invest in military training and production and in terms of life and limb lost in battle. The trouble with armed resistance is that it is almost certainly incompatible with that "life we want to live." So, violence, the use of force against others, is *compulsive*. It eliminates choices, and especially it eliminates our *most preferred* choice, which is to keep right on doing what we were doing before. We'd rather do that than fight *or* change—but those who live by the sword do not allow us that option.

Government consists in a "monopoly of force": That is to say, a government, or at any rate an institution that can plausibly claim to be a government, commands sufficient force that no one else in the community is able to prevent it by force from carrying out its will. And what is its will? Governments have had innumerable "wills" in regard to the sort of social, economic, and political programs they have proposed to carry out. But they do have one thing in common: They want to maintain and, almost always, to expand their power over people. They will do a great deal to achieve those ends. What, then, are our options, realistically? Indeed, how is it that "we" have any options?

The answer to the last question is that we do actually have those choices, and we always have them. There are the guys with the guns, or the pieces of paper that assert that they, despite having left their guns back at the station, can use them if needed. Here are we, faced with the choice to comply with what they demand or to resist in some way. The kind of resistance that consists in armed confrontation by one or a few people is, in the case of typical large contemporary States, certain to be futile. Hardly any of us will even consider it an option, though of course it is one, as shown by the fact that on occasion someone does take it. Subtler variants exist that may be more rewarding. We can tell the people at the door that we are in the process of complying with their demands, and if they'll come back tomorrow, we'll have what they want for them. When they leave, however, we will too, and in such a way that they'll have a very difficult time locating us. Possibly we'll end up safe and sound in Antigua, or in the vast Canadian wilderness. But again, this is chancy and it rarely gets us what we'd have preferred, which is for the government agents to just stay away, thanks, while we continue to live as before. The power of government consists in its ability to eliminate that most preferred option. That is the same as the power of armed robbers.

The armed robbers, however, arouse the ire of governments as well as of most of the population. Why? In the case of governments, it is because gangs of robbers are *competitors* for the kind of power that governments have and want to maintain. Government is a monopoly, and it does not like rivals. Eliminating competitors has been a prime concern of governments since they first appeared. The winners of power leave a trail of corpses, and the losers fill a sizable establishment of jails and graves. In the foreground are taxes, taxes, and more taxes, supporting bureaus, bureaus, and more bureaus of civil servants carrying out the will of the power holders. These latter are claimed by those civil servants not to be robbery, even though the process of separating us from our money does have many of the earmarks of that unlauded profession.

We may well ask, where in all this is the good of the people? The general answer lies in the fact that social power cannot be wielded in a vacuum. Those who hold power wield it over the populace, yes, but it also comes from and is supported by the populace. The question is What keeps the people from revolting against the regime? One answer is that they can't succeed because of the superior power of those they would revolt against. Another, however, is that the regime does enough for people to make them decide that *acquiescence* is preferable to revolution. And what's more, we must agree, it often gets not just acquiescence, but enthusiastic support.

So, what do governments (claim to) do for our involuntarily contributed support?

1. First and foremost is protection. Government claims, first, that it will protect people from foreign invasion.
2. It protects citizens from other citizens, or at least punishes those who attack them. It does not, of course, claim that it won't assault the citizens itself: The government's mandate is to protect everyone from everyone *except itself*. Hopefully, there are constitutional documents presuming to limit this tendency. Stay tuned!
3. It supplies provision of basic "infrastructural" services. High on the list are roads, bridges, canals, airports—things that we need, but defenders of the State claim to be not providable by the market, even though that market provides a great deal else. In recent times, on similar grounds, the State has gotten into the gas, electricity, water, and telephone business as well.
4. It supplies more sophisticated services: In the late nineteenth century, the State got into education in a big way as well. Present-day theorists of almost all persuasions agree that education should be the responsibility of the State. And while we're at it, there's health care too, and finally, "welfare." Oh, yes—and protecting the environment and promoting the arts. In all of these, relations between government and the various individuals and institutions who would provide them are complex to the point of being Byzantine. (See chapter 6.) The government, typically, converts all these things into *rights*, or more precisely, *entitlements*. The citizen comes to think that government *owes* her all these things.
5. Another expansion of the State into hitherto private territory is found in the history of socialism, where committees of the State undertake to guide no less than the entire productive system of the nation.

How much of this the State should actually be doing, or even has any legitimate business doing, and of course why, are questions that will be getting close attention in the rest of this book. Here the point is only that these many undertakings by government are *not surprising*. For in each case, we have an expansion of the power of the State, with attendant increases in the number of its employees working at the command of those in power, and a corresponding decrease in the areas for enterprise by the citizens themselves. (Often nowadays, the expansion of government goes together with an expansion of private businesses—usually very large ones—whom the

State contracts to build or operate the service. But the taxpayer pays nevertheless. The authors of a major study on such things[10] point out, for example, that "Compared to forecasts for opening year traffic, actual passenger volumes ranged from just five percent of predictions (Calcutta metro) to 18% for the UK-France 'chunnel' to 25% for the Paris Nord TGV [ultrahighspeed train] line." When you spend other people's money, it's easy to be optimistic. Thrasymachus doesn't pay the bills—*we* do!)

The challenge of Thrasymachus, then, is this: Is the government, despite its honeyed assurances to the contrary, just a very much larger and more powerful gang of thieves? When governments govern, are they really just trying to maximize the share of wealth that *they* can grab from the whole product of society? Or is this false, or if true, true only in an innocuous way, since whatever the effect on government of its exercise of power, it does actually benefit us after all? In that question lies the point of political philosophy.

THE PEOPLE UNITED—SORT OF

At the same time, there has been an interesting change in the typical structure or form of government. Nowadays, we may say, democracy is all the rage. It will get attention in chapter 5, but some notes here will be useful for starters.

Very generally, to have a State is to have a social arrangement in which some smallish number of people administer a measure of compulsory control over everyone in a certain area. Democracy may be thought to be rather different, and indeed it is, in a way. At the least, we will need to distinguish between the fairly small set of people who administer the laws, a typically different set who legislate those laws, a still different set who interpret them when there is question about them, and finally, the set of people who have the power to determine membership in the above sets. In the case of democracy, this last set is, notionally, *everybody*, or at least every adult, and the distribution of this ultimate power is *equal: Democracy is the equal distribution of fundamental political power.* One person, one vote, and everything is done, in the end, by voting, or more especially by persons who have been elected—that's the democratic idea.

But, of course, these people are never of one voice. In a democracy, "the people" are allegedly "united," but what unites them, insofar as they are "united" at all, is the decision to abide by the will of the majority; or rather, more precisely, the will of whoever can get elected by a procedure in which numbers of votes are what count. A welter of laws is quite likely to emerge from this procedure. If each citizen were asked, individually, in regard to each law passed, "If you had your choice, would you want *this* law?" it is extremely likely that we would get a negative answer regarding a lot of them, probably most of them. The sense in which democracy expresses the "will of the people" is therefore a subject in need of some considerable thought and discussion.

Democracy concentrates political power behind the winners of elections. It gives an effective reply to "the strong" by bringing out the fact that nothing is stronger than a whole lot of people who are fairly well united. Machiavelli observes, ". . . it is now more necessary to all princes . . . to satisfy the people rather than the soldiers, because the people are the more powerful."[11] Maybe the majority makes a *better* Thrasymachus than warlords or hereditary monarchs or the denizens of some aristocracy—but Thrasymachus it is, for better or worse.

CONSTITUTIONS AND CONSTITUTIONALITY

One of the basic ideas in politics is that of a "constitution," a term used in two related senses. In the first sense, a constitution is simply the basic system or organization of the political entity in question. In the second, however, a constitution is a *document* that sets forth, in words, how the political entity in question is to be arranged. Absolutely all political entities have a constitution in the first sense, but by no means all do in the second. Great Britain is generally classified as having a (mostly) "unwritten constitution"— an understanding of how it is constituted, and an understanding so precise that courts can rule on its basis. Americans and others with written documents puzzle at this, but we will not press the issue here. What we are interested in is, first, the variety of possible constitutions, and second, how we might rationally choose among them, if possible.

Even anarchy, in the sense of the system prescribed by *anarchism*, the view that there should be no State, is in the first sense a "constitution," even though, by definition, what it is the constitution of is not what we call a State, since it would have no government. But then, nongovernment *is* its constitution, and a problem for any anarchist is why or how an anarchy would remain such, rather than sliding over into statehood. A further interesting question about anarchy is whether it makes sense for it to have a written constitution. Clearly it could not be authoritative in the way that a written constitution such as the famous American one is, for there can be no general authority of that kind in an anarchy. Still, we can imagine that some people write up a document declaring that governments are not allowed in this area, proposing that everyone in the area "sign" the document, either literally or at any rate by some kind of implicit understanding, and that practically everyone does so sign. The document might also summarize or literally state the basic "natural law" that all understand to be the fundamental moral law for all. But having slightly opened the lid of this particular Pandora's Box, we close it again, for the present. In the rest of this book, until the last chapter, the State's existence will be provisionally but generally assumed. Our question then is this: What should it look like, and what should it do?

States come in florid variety. One fairly useful organization of this variety, for openers, lies in the ancient division of States into government by The One, The Few, and The Many.

(1) The One: monarch, czar, or dictator or whatever the one ruler is called; in principle, all political decisions are fundamentally the decisions of this one person, the sole supreme ruler.
(2) The Few: this might variously be the military, the rich, a hereditary ruling class, or an "elite" as in Plato's *Republic* or the Communist Party of the former Soviet Union.
(3) The Many: democracy, as already described briefly above.

These are constitutions: The understanding, in a written document, to the effect that the specified ruler is the monarch, etc., or that members of the Select Few are the supreme source of political decision or that everyone is entitled to one vote, with all significant decision makers to be elected or at least selected by people who have been elected.

In the frequent cases in which there are designated legislative bodies— assemblies, parliaments, congresses, etc.—the constitution will have to specify how their members come to be members, and what they can and cannot do. We may call this aspect of constitutions the "formal" aspect, specifying how the general machinery of government is put together.

BILLS OF RIGHTS

Some constitutions also deal with "matter" in addition to "form." Bills and charters of rights are of special interest in that they lay down a list of *rights of citizens*. We could, with a bit of stretching, impute such a list to any and all constitutions, but it is not, I think, worth the effort. Very definitely worth the effort, however, is the job of trying to identify, in some fairly general way, what should be on such a list, and what its effect is to be.

Specifically, the point of a bill of rights is to *limit the operation of the legislature* and thus the administration of the State in question, and thus to provide *some* protection of the citizen *against the government itself*. The American Bill of Rights, rightly regarded as one of the great classic entries of this type, begins with the pronouncement, "Congress shall make no law respecting an establishment of religion." What that constitutional provision says, bluntly, is that Congress doesn't have any business telling people what or whom or whether to worship. Cool! But, what if Congress goes ahead and does this anyway? Then what? It is to be hoped—but is perhaps realistically too much to ask!—that the administration of the time would refuse to carry out such a law even if passed. However, in the American case (and many others), what will happen next is that somebody will challenge the constitutionality of the law, and the case will come to a court, and ultimately to a Supreme Court that, at least in theory, will have the last word on the matter. The Court, presumably, would find that the law in question did indeed transgress the First Amendment, and it would be declared null and void. And that would be that. Hopefully.

What is the basis of that hope? Here we arrive at an interesting and puzzling, and perhaps wonderful, thing. The how and why, in the end, is that a whole lot of the right people would sustain, uphold, adhere to, act in accordance with, that document. The document intends and somehow reflects this very widespread understanding of how things go and are to go in this polity, and that understanding is, in the end, the *real* constitution—the final end of the line in politics.

Which is why there is room for political philosophy and political thinking. Can a constitution, given that it is the sort of thing just described, ever be *wrong*? My, and I'm sure your answer is You bet! But suppose that one lone thinker, such as Kant or this author or yourself, believes he or she has found a defect in it, then what? In the American case, there is a prescribed procedure for amendment. It is a fascinating procedure, and can itself, of course, be discussed and criticized. But, once again, if the would-be reformer is to have any hope of carrying through his or her proposed reform, there is, literally, no realistic option of doing it in any other way.

Well, except for one important thing: revolution—probably violent—or military conquest by some outsider. Using force successfully would reduce the citizens' options to a few, and probably the top option would include knuckling under and accepting the new regime, like it or not. In this way most of the world's most nightmarish social regimes came into being as well, we hasten to add, as some of the good ones. And we present-day citizens of the world, looking into our history books, hopefully learn from all this and take care that the constitution we have will at least not be seriously worsened or eliminated altogether by such means; we will all, or so many of us as makes no mind, uphold that constitutional arrangement insofar as we can do so. And it works—here. But in many other faltering or politically immature places, it does not work and life can be very difficult, as in contemporary Iraq, Zimbabwe, North Korea. . . .

Recently, an article, followed by a book of the same title, made quite an impression by proclaiming that the End of History was at hand, sort of. The author, Francis Fukuyama, suggested that all States either already were or were on their way to becoming Market Democratic Welfare States. We will see why he is, probably, mostly right. Having previously mentioned the classical division of governments into the One, the Few, or the Many, we can see why "the many" is the hands-down winner. Or rather, this more limited thesis: That, *if* we must have government at all, then democratic government, warts and all, is the constitution of choice. Still more precisely, the choice is for *constitutionally limited* democratic government. This leaves two very big question marks: First, what sort of constitutional restrictions should there be? Which list of Rights of Citizens will be selected to control the Leviathan that democratic government inevitably consists in? Second, and more fundamentally: Is government really necessary? At the end of this book, we will revert to that interesting question, briefly. But not so briefly as most, who dismiss it with a wave of the hand. This is a real question, not rhetoric. But before that, the rest of this book intervenes.

MONARCHY AND THE LIKE

Contemporary young people have a way of learning virtually no history to speak of. They might well be astonished to learn that, historically speaking, monarchy or some other version of one-person rule has been, overwhelmingly, the major form of government. The history of England, until quite recently, is a history of monarchs. So too France and Germany, and on and on. America is a spectacular exception, maybe—if we ignore its first seventeen decades of monarchical rule by the British monarchy. But then, America is a bunch of English citizens sailing across an ocean, taking along a huge stock of political lore and using it to create the world's first, and still functioning, near-democracy. The founders of America, as it were, cheated: They looked up the answers in the back of the book and didn't need, and certainly didn't want, to relive history.

Why was there ever monarchy? A superb answer is provided by Jared Diamond.[12] Monarchies in smallish, fairly technologically primitive settings work as nothing else to enable the group *as a group* to act. For monarchs to work, society needs roughly the following, a structure that almost all societies have more or less had up until recently. First, if it is sizable, it contains a number of subgroups with a certain amount of internal cohesion and potential loyalty—usually tribes, which in turn break down into sizable families. Second, these subgroups come to have leaders, more or less. Third, these leaders all acknowledge (more or less) the one superleader, the king as the general authority across the land, instead of fighting among themselves. With a small number of fairly powerful and not greatly unequal people in charge, a single decision maker at the top is a great way to avoid highly suboptimal developments (which happen often enough) *provided* the ideas of the king about what to do aren't too greatly at odds with those of the powerful chieftains functioning under his alleged leadership. Which is to say, if it isn't already obvious, that no monarch has ever, or could ever, function as a "strong man" ruling entirely by his own will. Why don't the underlings murder the chief? Well, for one thing, every so often, they do just that. By definition, the ones who survive as kings do not meet that fate, and that can only be because they succeed in exercising the sort of direction that is fairly agreeable to those being directed. They in turn exercise the sort of direction that is fairly agreeable, despite all, to the people they lead, which is why they in their turn are able to lead.

Now let's try to think our way back to the technology and society of, say, the ninth century, and we ask, what about democracy? The answers come flooding in. Hardly anyone is literate, so having our kind of electoral campaign is out of the question. Maximum travel speed is the speed of a trotting horse, and if the kingdom is 300 miles wide?—forget it! Of course, there possibly could be a gathering of a few "representatives" of "the people," but again, they aren't going to be represented in the sense of elected, for the same reason. And the gatherings in question aren't so easy to bring about. Chieftain A may be back home fighting off some invaders from Chieftain B's or somebody else's territory, and so on. What economists call *transaction costs* are just too high for democracy to function in biggish countries until quite recently.

An interesting question is why most kings most of the time were busy either fighting wars, planning them, or trying to prevent them. For an answer, see especially Thrasymachus: You put people on a throne, and what do you expect? Even if they are not themselves superambitious (and a lot are), they have neighbors who are and who don't leave much choice. Moreover, most kings will spend a fair bit of time making sure that the competition doesn't have a chance. Rivals to the throne will be assassinated, or bought off, or beaten in a fight, fair or unfair. Between that and concerns with "foreign" warfare, the king will also be busy collecting the funds needed to support this expensive habit.

Down at ground level, so to speak, what is to be expected? The short answer is that kings collected taxes, or rather their underlings did, and once they did that, they pretty much left you alone. If we suppose that the various foreign rivals to a throne would do at least as badly or likely worse, and if the effect of all this government is to provide at least modest deterrence to robbers and murderers, and when we bear in mind the enormous military superiority of professional soldiers to ordinary people, the result is that general acquiescence to monarchy made sense.

If we ignore those realities for a moment, however, and ask what *we* think of rule by "One," *now*, we will quickly get what appears to be quite a different result. What's wrong with monarchs, in short, is that they aren't *us*. That isn't necessarily a problem; after all, there are about 6 billion more people out there nowadays, none of whom are "us." The trouble is, monarchs would have all this power, and their own ideas of what to do with their power, and that needn't include much attention to yours truly. And we, of course, don't like that. Prima facie, kings can't be trusted. If I am the king, of course, that's just fine, but the chances that I am are $1/N$, where N is all the people in the kingdom. Actually, it may be much less than that, for once you are born to the wrong people—as almost all of us are—our chances of becoming king are, pretty much, nonexistent. So, forget monarchy!

That is the short of it. The long of it is quite different, as we saw above. We aren't much concerned about the full story today, not only because, after a couple of hundred years of democracy (in the case of Americans), or at least a half-century or so of it (for most other readers), we just aren't "into" that anymore. Anyway, the times have changed, especially technologically, to the point where monarchy no longer makes much sense.

This needs considerable qualification. Typical democratic presidents arguably have more real power than most monarchs ever did—apart from things like arbitrary power of life and death over any citizens at any time. However, those presidents emerge from a recurrent electoral process. They aren't even *allowed* to retain all that power for terribly long, for they must submit to reelection, often with just one further try. And they are hamstrung by legislators, courts, and such. Presidential power solves some problems and presents still others, but for the most part it's not surprising that it should exist and be quite substantial. The claim, then, is we have the best of both worlds: an efficient near-monarch and a procedure for keeping him from getting out of hand, especially for very long. It's pretty hard to deny the relative merits of the new type of government, in this respect. But reasons for more extensive optimism about democracy will not be quite so plentiful as ordinarily supposed, as we will see (in chapters 5 and 6).

THE ROLE OF THE FEW

What about government by "the few"? Contemplating even the idea of this brings up many problems. Suppose that there is a hereditary class, and all rulers come from or are somehow selected by this class. Does the idea of "rule by a few" mean that the country is run by a sort of supercommittee? Large committees, practically speaking, turn into small committees, that turn into monarchies, though the monarchs are limited in turn by their support bases.

Which "few" will it be? Whatever rule will be military (*timocracy*), since all rule, inherently, is by force. In the end, those who aren't inclined to go along will be manhandled by those in power—that's what being in power consists of, after all. But then, who controls that military, and how? The rich are a plausible candidate. Soldiers cost money. They don't produce anything, and they consume a lot, not only in food but also especially in such things as horses and their maintenance, armor and arms, and later, of course, very expensive means of destruction. The money must come from somewhere. Ultimately, of course, it might be thought that all wealth is created by a "proletariat," an idea not the exclusive property of Marxists, and with a grain of truth to it, no doubt. Nevertheless, the wealthy who got that way by directing large concerns are likely to be effectual controllers of large sums, which is what is needed. So *oligarchy*—rule by the wealthy —is a likely option.

What about intellectual elites? Historically, intellectuals have been a sideshow, depending on how we define our terms. If we allow the priestly set to count as "intellectuals," then it must be admitted that the success of that subset has been substantial. Even so, however, some distinctions reduce the spectacle. First, in the West, there has been separation of church and state; that is to say, that the power of the priesthood has been indirect. Priests dispose ordinary people to accept the rule of nonpriests, but the nonpriests have usually been susceptible to manipulation by those claiming to be in touch with Higher Powers. In the Muslim world, where separation of church and state is roundly denied, things are different. But how much so? The Muslim religion has nothing in the way of official church hierarchy, for one thing. And dictators dictating in the name of Allah look and act awfully similar to dictators elsewhere, including exercising the power to do what ordinary people take to be forbidden to themselves—have any woman they want, for example.

We owe to Marx the dictum that religion is "the laudanum of the poor." But in fact, the churchly opiate has been effective far beyond the realm of the poor. It galvanized, for example, the Moorish armies that swept across the Middle East and North Africa in the seventh and eighth centuries, with more forays all the way to the seventeenth when the Ottomans were at last repelled in military confrontation at the walls of Vienna, putting a final stop to the expansion of their empire.

When we contemplate this last option, we immediately run into the sort of problem that terminates in the adoption of a strong civil right of freedom of religion. All who adhere to the Ruling Creed will be more or less happy with rule by the priests, and all who do not will be extremely unhappy with it. And here too is where we see the problem in accounting the priesthood an "intellectual elite." For despite huge investments of mental horsepower by assorted prophets and such, it remains that religion is simply not rational in the way that science is. Disputes between religion X and religion Y will not be won on the playing fields of reason. They will instead be largely political: The tail will soon be wagging the dog. And so we are back to where we started, with rival contenders for power trying to settle their differences by force, except that now the participants will fight with the fury that comes from belief that the gods are on our side, and moreover offer remarkable rewards for our efforts even if, as is all too likely, we end up dead on the field of battle. Given all this, sober persons of all faiths must eventually come to the only possible conclusion: Let's keep religion out of politics, guarantee to all the secure practice of the faith of their choice, and accept an overwhelming restriction against trying to impose it by force.

The conclusion is as with monarchy: Rule by the few may be OK, if you are one of the few. But what if you are not—as by definition you probably aren't. Will we entrust our lives and fortunes to someone else, even if the "someone" is a fairly large class of people, and perhaps one that claims to have our best interests at stake? But if they do, why don't they *ask us* what we want? Come to that, why don't they let us in on the action?

In short, we are again driven to democracy, where everyone counts for one, none for more than one, and the victor will at any rate have the greater numbers on his side. What further we are getting ourselves into with democracy will be explored at length below. But it should be noticed that what gets democracy so prominently into the picture is that the greater number wins. And isn't the greater number the "stronger party," just as Thrasymachus says?

Meanwhile, the remainder of this book will be concerned, not with niceties of democratic organization, but with substance. For democracy does not determine substance, or at least not directly. We will have what people vote for, but what *will* they vote for? More to the point, what *should* they vote for? Are there reasons available for directing the citizen's vote? Those who vote do so for *some* reason or other, and that is to invite the question whether it's a good one, and whether something else might not be better. Generally speaking, then, the rest of our inquiry will concern this question of what we should be doing, rather than precisely who does it and how.

HOW MUCH GOVERNMENT?

This can also be put in terms of *how much* governments should be doing. The options, as we saw earlier, run roughly like this:

(a) Nothing: Anarchy
(b) Very, very little: the Minimal State
(c) A modest amount: the Functional State
(d) Quite a bit: the Welfare State
(e) A whole lot: Socialism
(f) As much as possible: Totalitarianism

Of course, answers to this question will be a function of *why* government should or should not do whatever it does. On this, not surprisingly, there has been much discussion.

WHY LIBERALISM?

What is the State for? That is the crucial question. There have been various views. But there is a rather new, very good, fairly familiar, and in a way perhaps disconcerting, answer: The State is not *for* anything. It is, rather, the *servant* of its public. People have interests, values, ends. Government is there to help them achieve *their* ends—if and as it can. This is the *liberal* view. The question of what the State is for does not allow a general answer, unless we say that government is to help promote public happiness as an "answer." But if what constitutes happiness for person A is quite different from what does so for B, and C, and so on for the rest of the 6 billion, then that answer is not very helpful to the aspiring ruler(s).

Why should we accept liberalism? The brief answer is that we are people, not machines or even animals. People think for themselves. They make up their minds what to do, in light of ends adopted or at least adhered to by them. If someone else thinks that he can provide a better answer than Jones regarding what to do with Jones's life, there is an easy formula: Suggest it to Jones and see what she thinks. But suppose Jones doesn't accept the formula; Now what? How can it possibly be rational for Jones nevertheless to accept this other person's idea? Liberalism, it seems, is based on a deep understanding of human nature—namely, our own, of ourselves.

The problem, however, is that with all these people, each with his or her own values that their bearer hopes to promote, we obviously have a potential for conflict. This was anticipated by Hobbes, who responded, as we have seen, by proposing that we all hand over the reigns of power to a central agency, government. This runs into the same problem: How do we know that this agency will do what we want? Hobbes's response is that it will keep the peace, and that's what we need. But our answer is that a government that makes war on its own people is not obviously much of an improvement over their making war on each other, and what is to keep Mr. Leviathan from doing just that? Surely we can do better? We will want to tame Leviathan. But how?

Interestingly enough, the general principle for such correction was admirably formulated by Hobbes himself. The trouble with the state of nature, he saw, was, in a word, violence. People wanting something and seeing that it could be got by simply taking it from others without asking, were, he reasoned, the basic problem in that condition. What's needed is respect for others. Instead of simply taking by force, we *ask*, and we proceed by agreement. Thus are we able to cooperate, pooling our resources and talents with the people we choose to do so with, yielding a result that is better for all participants. Cooperation leads to all the good things in life: plenty to eat, clothing both warm and attractive, comfortable housing, education, art, sports, and so on. The clue is to stop people from just batting along on their own, without thought of others, or with negative thought of others.

The threat of violence can only be countered in two ways: reason and force. Reason could easily not work, so force is going to have to be available for defense when required. But really, reason should usually do the job. Anyone short of a complete idiot can see that the general allowing of violence is going to be completely counterproductive. Anyone can also see, with a bit of effort, that violence begets counterviolence from those attacked. Hobbes's proposal is *general* peace—peace for all, except those who initiate war.

Given the State, he supposes, peace is preserved by force when necessary, against those who aggress against others. Was Hobbes right? In part, for sure. The police will attempt to punish malefactors, and presumably that makes us safer. In fact, though, the modern State does much more; and while it's at it, it continually intervenes in the lives of citizens, which itself looks to be a sort of aggression. But at this point, we will adjourn the discussion of liberalism until we have looked at its main rival—conservatism (in, I hasten to add, my somewhat special sense of the term.)

NOTES

1. That is, what the translators have him saying. I am at their mercy, of course.

2. See also http://www.greenkiwi.co.nz/footprints/mongolia/ghengishistory.html and http://www.fsmitha.com/h3/h11mon.html All accounts agree on essentials.

3. Jeffrey Rogers Hummel, *Emancipating Slaves, Enslaving Free Men: A History of the American Civil War* (Chicago: Open Court, 1996).

4. Robert Higgs has argued the point well in *Crisis and Leviathan: Critical Episodes in the Growth of American Government* (New York: Oxford University Press, 1987), chapter 9.

5. Or can we? Our later chapter on democracy will raise some questions about that.

6. Thomas Hobbes, *Leviathan*, chapter XIII. Hobbes's *Leviathan* was first published in 1660. There are dozens of editions. All of my summaries and extracts are readily found in chapters XII–XVII.

7. See *Leviathan*, chapters XIV–XV.

8. John Locke, *Second Treatise of Civil Government*, published in 1690. (Again, there are innumerable editions.) See especially sections 90–93.

9. Locke, *Second Treatise.*

10. Bent Flyvbjerg, Nils Bruzelius, and Werner Rothengatter, *Megaprojects and Risk: An Anatomy of Ambition* (Cambridge: Cambridge University Press, 2003).

11. Niccolo Machiavelli, *The Prince*, XIX, numerous editions.

12. Jared Diamond, *Guns, Germs, and Steel: The Fates of Human Societies* (New York: Norton, 1996).

3

Pushing the Good

Conservatism and the Guardian State

CONSERVATISM AND POLITICAL CHANGE

In this chapter we are concerned with a set of political outlooks that I label, with some hesitation, "conservative." The hesitation is due to the fact that my choice of analysis does not correlate very well with a familiar employment of this term, in which conservatism is said to be resistance to change while liberalism is characterized as readiness to change. Consider this nicely typical statement that everyone will recognize as being in the conservative mode: ". . . a nation is defined not by institutions or borders but by language, religion and high culture; in times of turmoil and conquest it is these spiritual things that must be protected and reaffirmed."[1]

There is a major problem with this use. Someone being against change must think that the status quo is somehow good, or at least all right—good enough to be worth preserving. A wag has said that "a conservative is a man who thinks that things are going downhill, and wants to keep it that way." The quip brings out the problem. A conservative in the Soviet Union in 1965 would presumably be a staunch Communist, and meanwhile over in the United States, a Communist was regarded as a radical extremist. In short, conservatism could be advocacy of any political system so long as it was actually in place, liberalism advocacy of any political system so long as it was not in place. What is the use of such designations? Surely there is a prior question: whether a given system is any good in the first place, and why. If it isn't, we should surely want to change it if we can, and if it is, we should not want to change it.

To be sure, political change is likely to be hard on some people, and that's bad. But suppose it is also good for some people—well, that's good. Perhaps

a conservative would be someone who thinks that the cost of change is typically not likely to be worth paying, while the liberal thinks the reverse. But
that is sure to be highly variable. Neither is obviously right, and cases would
have to be gone into in some detail. Consider the adoption of the metric system in Europe during the Napoleonic era and its adoption in Canada in
1970. The change in Europe was probably good, as the weights and measures varied greatly all over the place, making trade and travel confusing for
all. The change in Canada, on the other hand, imposed a system that had no
real advantages for ordinary people to replace one that was useful, well understood, and workable. The costs of change in Europe were not very great,
but the costs in Canada were enormous—to this day, pounds, feet, inches,
and even degrees Fahrenheit continue to be widely used—not surprisingly,
given that 85 percent of Canada's trade and a great deal of its travel is to and
from the United States, which continues to use Anglo-Saxon measures with
no end in sight. You need not be a conservative to think the first was a good
idea, the second a bad one.

A further useful case concerns "rule of the road." In the UK, Japan, and
several other countries, the rule is to keep to the left. In the rest, including
the United States and continental Europe, it is to keep right—a nuisance for
car manufacturers and tourists. But the costs of general change are enormous. Sticking with what they have makes sense, and you needn't be a political conservative to think so.

These examples illustrate the point that whether to change something or
not is a quite discussable matter and that everything depends on the real
merits of the existing system compared with the proposed new one, plus the
costs of making the change. The taking of a general, systematic stance of either opposition to or support of change as such looks irrational, and so the
familiar identification of two supposedly general political outlooks with
those attitudes is either a device for identifying opponents as "straw men"
or is philosophically useless.

A MORE FRUITFUL ANALYSIS: CONSERVATISM AS IMPOSED VALUES

It is much more plausible to look to their values to determine whether a
theorist is conservative—something about their view of the proper fundamental bases of political action.

In the analysis here adopted, conservatism is the imposition, by compulsion (if necessary, which it is presumed often to be) of values against the desires of those upon whom they are politically imposed, and on the ground
that the imposed values are the right ones, those recalcitrants who resist
the imposition being held to be wrong or perverse. We may also call this

"Platonism"—again with some apologies to Plato and Platonists. This usage, while hardly perfectly aligned with standard usage (if there is one) does capture an element present, I think, in all of the "conservatisms" normally so called. For conservatives don't just wish to avoid change, they wish to prevent people who do want to change and who would do so if only the laws permitted it from doing so, on the grounds that their values are wrong. Conservatives on sexual behavior want to prevent, by law, various practices such as homosexuality (and currently, homosexual marriage); conservatives typically uphold legal restrictions on the use and sale of "recreational" drugs; conservatives about abortion wish to prevent people, by force of law, from having abortions, and so on. In all these cases, those "in favor of change" favor the removal of obstacles put in the place of various actions by individuals. They do not insist on everyone doing the things that would be allowed if the obstacles were removed, of course. Insistence that we all become homosexuals, for example, would be illiberal in the extreme. But insistence that we all adhere to heterosexuality is similarly illiberal.

Liberalism is the view that individuals are authorities on their own good and that their good is what politics ought to be concerned to promote. That is an intelligible and important distinction. But there is an important point about liberalism, and failure to see it can lead us astray: The liberal does not need to maintain that individuals are necessarily *right* about their own values. He is free to disagree with the values of others, thinking them to be in error or low of brow or insufficiently clued in or shallow, etc. What makes him a liberal is not that, but rather his accepting for political purposes that we are to take the individual's own evaluations insofar as they concern himself rather than others, as what we, the rest of the polis, are to accept in his case. In short, we will be disposed to have the political system respond to the wants of people, without further judging them. The conservative, on the other hand, thinks he knows what's good for people and knows it better than those people themselves. At the extreme—which we will look at later in this chapter—we get authoritarianism, government assuming the right to direct us through and through. This is a striking difference, and it greatly affects practice. For example, the conservative will support the illegalization of drugs, despite evident demand for them and comparative absence of negative effects on others. In the remainder of this chapter, we will survey some important varieties and sources of conservatism.

PLATONISM

It may be unfair to Plato and his younger colleague Aristotle to stick them with the label "conservative." Plato might argue that the things he claims are good for the soul are such that, if any individual thinks about it, he or she would come to agree that they are indeed as good as he says they are. Yet he is not ready to say that people should get what they want just because they want it. Aristotle makes clear that the State's main business should be to inculcate virtue, as expounded in the previous books of his *Nicomachean Ethics*. Moreover, he believed that many people were naturally fitted to be slaves[2]—a status they were not accorded by asking them whether they'd like the job.

The logic of what I am calling Platonism is clear. Most of us have values that we think are valid beyond our own cases. We think we have insight into the human condition—and perhaps some of us actually do. We suppose that certain things make for a good life, and others don't, and if people out there don't see it that way, it's because they are ignorant or corrupt. Why, then, shouldn't we be ready to impose our views on the rest, seeing that we are so obviously correct and that our motives are so high-minded?—We seek the people's good, after all!

But then, if we look at it from the other person's point of view, things might look quite different. There seem really to be people out there who don't understand about Bach violin sonatas, for example. I don't understand these people. How can they have missed the nobility, the cogency, the magic of these amazing masterpieces? I don't know—but it seems that they have. And it doesn't seem that there's very much to be done about it, either. A conservative might insist on teaching the classics to all, like it or not. Liberals do not. Instead, we of highish brow and enlightened lifestyle will just have to go our way, and they go theirs. That's the liberal idea. The conservative, however, sticks to his guns. Literally, by the way: Not a few wars have been fought with the intention of compelling others to live in the way that the invader claims to be right. Nazism is only the most spectacular of many cases in point.

ARISTOCRACIES

Throughout much of history, there have been designated smallish subsets of the populace who command either a monopoly or at least a substantial proportion of political power. Sometimes their claim to this measure of power is simply based on force, as with military dictatorships. But sometimes their power is also claimed to be merited: The way of life, the values they uphold, are alleged to be better than those of the lower orders. Keeping those lower orders "in their place" is thus a main preoccupation of this sort of ruling class (some would say, of *all* ruling classes!). That is the aristocratic principle.

Our question here is simply whether conservatism as so understood could ever be true, in a sense that would make it relevant to politics; that is, a sense that would make it rational to support such a ruling elite in the important cases where one is not oneself a member of the elite class in question. When we put it that way, however, we will have to make a distinction between the question taken in a general, theoretical, and philosophical way and the question as it may arise in specific circumstances and against a given political background. It may rightly be objected, against a high-level analysis of the sort that you will find below, that it is a mistake to try to proceed from such abstract considerations straight to political practice. Another abstract argument readily persuades one that the objection can have weight. In some circumstances, it may be that support of a certain group, whose merits in the abstract are hardly a credible ground for awarding them the power they have, is nevertheless a better alternative than support of anything else actually available. Compromise is a familiar phenomenon of practical politics. However, this book is a philosophical exploration, an exercise in theory, and the point of view being considered here is that being right in our fundamental principles is a pretty good idea both in its own right and as a guide, at least eventually, to practice. Abstractly, then, let's ask what might recommend rule of an "elite" group. There have been many, of course, but we may usefully reduce the variety. I pick five types, thinking them to be the major ones of interest: military, hereditary, economic, intellectual, and religious.

Martial Rule and Martial Values

All rule involves the capability, and to some extent the actuality, of using force to get the laws obeyed. But some societies have been dominated by their military element much more than others. You will be hard put to find a soldier in Canada today; you will be hard put to overlook them in North Korea. In ancient Sparta all youths spent most of their time in military training; mothers were happiest if their sons died in battle, and no shame was greater than that provoked by evidence of cowardice in war. A society might exalt military virtues above all. Is that rational?

The problem is that fighting seems so obviously a means to other ends that one is hard put to know what to say to the proposal to convert it into an end in itself. One idea, though, makes a certain amount of sense. We might consider war as a kind of competition, having the same kind of interest as sports. That can indeed be a lot of interest, yes—but when the competition is of the military kind, entailing early death for many and severe costs for all, the stakes look to be far out of proportion. And, of course, many people actually like eating well, getting a decent amount of sleep, engaging in leisure activities, and not living in perpetual fear. A militaristic society forces people to spend their time in ways that will understandably be perceived as counterproductive, as well as legendarily unpleasant. The peaceable among us will object to militarism as—to put it bluntly—a stupid waste of time. Military activity is not, of course, "stupid" if indeed it is necessary, as no doubt it sometimes is. But beyond that, it mainly uses up resources that could be put to much better use. All those other parts of ourselves that are diminished, extinguished, or distorted by the military way of life will clamor for putting the military in its proper place: strictly under the control of civilians, and generally in the background. We must, certainly, regard with gratitude and honor those who are genuinely needed to defend us and who do it well. But turning militarism into the very purpose of the community and entrusting government to the military class is a drastic mistake. To suppose that the good society is essentially an army, to spend its days in drilling and, worse, in fighting, is to convert this inversion into large-scale social insanity. If war is indeed too important to be left to the generals, social life is yet more so.

Besides, there's a plausible alternative: athletic and other competitions, with or without bodily contact. Football, hockey, martial arts competitions, chess, and many more—all of these give people the opportunity to hone physical or intellectual skills and to compete for glory with the immense advantage that if you lose today, you can come back next year and try again, or just go back to doing something else. As an outlet for aggression, many sports are superb. The aggression is contained and restrained by the rules, which enable boxers to pummel each other, fencers to thrust at each other, and hockey players to bang into each other with much the sort of satisfaction that soldiers had in former days but without the horrendous costs, either to themselves or to bystanders.

In all, then, the case for having a military class doing the ruling as well as the fighting looks to be abysmal. Civilian control of the military is a hallmark of good government, and a tiny to nonexistent military, in peacetime, one of the hallmarks of a prosperous and successful society.

Hereditary Aristocracy

Can there be an argument for having an "Ancien Régime"? Perhaps it would go something like this. Take the set of people of superior virtue in some long-ago time, suppose that the virtue in question is passed on to their offspring, due in part to selective breeding and in part to the natural operation of genetics, and then society is guaranteed a steady production of virtuous people to exercise political power. Cool!

But it has to be appreciated that this sort of argument logically presupposes that the traits to be passed on by breeding really are virtues—qualities for all to look on as models to try to emulate and such as to qualify their possessors for making wise public decisions. Yet if these are genuine virtues, why give power to the offspring of those who have them? Why not, instead, give it to those who have those virtues? For one thing, heredity isn't very reliable. There is regression to the mean and recessive genes; some members of the lower orders have more virtue than the hereditarily appointed ones, and many offspring of the aristocrats have a lot less. Mediocre academic, athletic, economic, and even military performance from the aristocracy is legendary. Such facts would torpedo the case for hereditary aristocracy even if there were a case for it to begin with.

So far we have not questioned which virtues are relevant but only the efficacy of the hereditary principle to sustain their incidence among the rulers. A more fundamental case is made against aristocracy if one simply denies that there are any such virtues—that ruling is not really the sort of thing that can plausibly be done by "the virtuous" as such. Not, of course, that we want rulers to be vicious. It's rather that, in one important sense, we don't want "rulers" at all. If these people are so virtuous, after all, why won't the rest of us be sufficiently impressed that we will be inclined to emulate them without their imposing it all on us by force? What's so virtuous about that?

We may need government—or something—to help defend us from assault, battery, murder, and fraud. The disposition to refrain from such things is indeed virtuous. But to have government imposing courage, loyalty, affection, wisdom, and the rest on us is another matter. An efficient government might be nice; a self-congratulatory supernanny is an embarrassment, or worse.

Oligarchy

One of the historically important political systems was rule by the rich. Indeed, it is easy to find critics who claim that that's what we have right now, in countries such as the United States. Yet the rich do not literally rule in the world's advanced countries now, whereas in ancient Greece, that's what they did: Public offices were held by the rich, and those less well-to-do were excluded from political power. Our question is whether that is a good idea. A main point in its favor is that the rich, provided they got that way by honest dealing, are indeed important contributors to the good of society. Usually those who get rich this way have organized large enterprises to bring it about and sold useful things to many people. One could do a lot worse as a qualification for political office.

Still, there is a great difference between:

(a) Laws that enable people to prosper from trade, and
(b) Laws that load the dice in favor of the currently rich, with subsidies and penalties against competition and grants of political privilege.

Oligarchy involves the latter, not the former. The presence of wealthy people who have got that way through enterprise is an indication that considerable parts of the populace, at least, are doing well. But laws of the second kind interfere with those good effects of commerce and enterprise. Having the way of businesspersons paved for them by governments who see to it that they have no competitors is not an efficient promoter of the public good.

When businesspeople are given the powers of political office, they will likely use those powers to promote business in the second way rather than the first, warping the public services to the benefit of the already rich at the expense of the rest. But we, the public, have no reason to favor artificial lining of the pockets of the already wealthy. On the contrary: We want hardworking, enterprising, and honest merchants who will make money by catering to our needs and wants, thus promoting rather than diminishing our own wealth as well.

Support for oligarchy, if anyone is actually in favor of it, confuses (a) and (b). But (a) provides the case against oligarchy, not for it. Businesspeople benefit the public only when that public is not subservient to them.

Rule by the Intellectuals

Plato's official view is that we should have government by the wise. But just what is wisdom? Part of it is intellect, by which is meant two very different things: (a) IQ and (b) having interests of the intellectual type such as in mathematics and philosophy. But there is more to wisdom than either of those. Some of modest intellect have nevertheless exemplified the virtue of wisdom, while many intellectuals commit folly. Wisdom is a matter of knowing how to deal with major practical matters, and that can't be reduced to being good at differential equations or interpreting Aristotle.

The trouble is, of course, that identifying the "wise" is no easy matter, and it is more than just doubtful that any political process can be very good at doing so. Much easier is to turn government over to people with Ph.D.s or high IQs. But should we entrust *them* with political power, either?

Here it is essential to distinguish carefully between literal rule, that is, political power, and leadership of other kinds. Bright people will produce books, inventions, and artistic productions that enrich our lives. They also shape culture in many ways—their creations typify and distinguish their societies. Society's numerous informal leadership roles are likely to be occupied by the bright. But as with businesspeople, those roles should not be political.

To see why not, we had first better make a distinction between two quite different types of reasons for employing the brilliant. Roughly, this is the distinction of means and ends. Brilliant people may know a lot of the things that we need to know if we are to make good social decisions. Science and organizational and technical know-how have their place in any decent regime. Yes—but they will also have their place in indecent regimes. Hitler's scientists used their intellects for evil ends—evil at levels not previously considered quite possible. The 9/11 pilots were not morons. This point is alone enough to explain why "rule by the smart" is a bad idea. It is bad because having the right ends, doing the right things, is not necessarily correlated with merely being smart. It is correlated with being *wise*—but then the problem is how to identify those in such a way that we could reliably get them into the positions of power. And then we have the question as to whether they would remain wise after they got there. The very bright are far from immune to the corrupting influences of political power.

Other types of intellectuals would be typified by pure scientists, mathematicians, philosophers, and artists. Such people advance human knowledge and add to the cultural riches of civilization. All fine things to do, indeed—but what justification is there for compelling people to share in these things, against their wills?

We (try to) do this now, to be sure, in public schools, in government support of the arts and of many sorts of research. The money comes from everyone, not just intellectuals—often from people who wouldn't even approve of the studies in question. Should we be imposing on people for these ends?

The ancients had a way of confusing rationality with intellect. They are not the same. There are highly rational hockey players, insurance brokers, flower gardeners—and, torturers, assassins, terrorists, and politicians. To some extent, the good politician is a smart politician. But none of this implies that intellect and intellectual attainment as such has any necessary relation to good rule.

Plato supposed that people could be trained, over many years, to moral and political leadership. Who would train them? Not the lower orders who he thought were hardly capable of such things. They train each other; previous ones train new ones. The guardians guard the guardians. Looking at such a scheme, we will want to ask, Where are the controls? Where do we, the ruled, come into the scheme? If there is an uncomfortable sense of having been left out of the picture, the point is made. The question is, of course, how bad that is. But the evidence should come from us, not from the guardians purporting to look after us.

Rule by the Priests

1. Theocracy and Civic Peace

As we saw, law, according to Aquinas, is an "imposition of reason" on a community to promote the common good. Details apart, the central issue concerns the common good: What is that? Partly, he gives the right sensible answers: peace and prosperity. But when Aquinas gets down to the nitty-gritty, it turns out to be the good as seen by Roman Catholicism. He holds this to the point of insisting that heretics who can't be brought to "reason" by priests will just have to be executed.[3] This part of the "common good" is clearly not common in the sense that everybody accepts it. Rather, it's claimed to be good for them whether they think so or not. And for those who don't? Well, as Candide has it, "It's a wonderful day for an auto da fe!"[4]

This is clearly not the way to peace in a community, unless that community happens to be populated exclusively by Roman Catholics. (Currently, the cited example might concern Islam rather than Catholicism, but the point would be exactly the same.) But that's where the difference between community and State comes to the fore. The State comprehends all those within its borders, whatever faith, color, or other variables they may exemplify. If some of those people don't share a certain spiritual belief, then St. Thomas's way makes the nonsharers into enemies, to be dealt with, if need be, by the sword. Liberalism, by contrast, says: Let them live with their alleged errors, so long as they don't harm others in the process. This has become one of the absolute truths of political philosophy. Because it is so central, we will look into it further now.

As understood here we will take religions to be concerned with god(s). (Not all beliefs and practices called "religious" are like that, and some of what is said below may not apply to some religions.) Two crucial features of religion frame our moral and political concerns. First, religion claims to provide the ultimate truth—to be "comprehensive doctrines,"[5] including, especially, the truth about how to live. Characteristically, religions include a claim that this felicitous kind of life extends beyond the grave, indeed unto eternity. The religion in question insists that in order to avail oneself of this unfathomable benefit, one must believe "in" the god alleged to exist in the sacred writings and other sources of the religion. It is characteristically claimed that god commands its subjects to have the beliefs in question and to live in the prescribed ways. In fact, it is characteristically claimed that the reason why we should do what it says are the right things is precisely that the being in question insists on it. (The absurd circularity of this procedure is not readily noted by the faithful. If I don't believe that G exists, you aren't going to help matters out by telling me that I should believe it because G will get me if I don't, or that G will reward me if I do.)

Along with that, there is the very important point that somehow adherents of religions adhere to very different religions. What makes one religion different from another is often rather obscure to outsiders, and for that matter, characteristically, to the insiders as well—but even so, these different sets of believers are often very greatly at odds with each other. They build different places of worship and those who attend one are often reluctant even to set foot in another's. All too often, there is intense enmity and rivalry among the adherents of different sects.

The next point is that despite the intensity of religious beliefs, they are not provable, nor even rationally arguable, so far as ordinary reason and science are concerned. Of course what I have just said is often denied by religious persons and theorists. But I have in mind two things. First, when philosophers examine arguments for religious beliefs, they invariably find them wanting in rigor. At some point, things are assumed that are quite incapable of any sort of proof: Either you accept them or you don't, but as for evidence and plausible rational support of any other sort—forget it. It isn't just that evidence is lacking, it's that it's unclear what is even supposed to count as evidence. And as a matter of empirical fact, practitioners of different religions do not expect to change the minds of devoted followers of other religions. Atheists and agnostics are often converted away from previously held religions by the very absence of reason for their previously held beliefs, but adherents of religion X very rarely accomplish the feat of "persuading" adherents of religion Y that X is the rationally more acceptable view.[6] They sometimes exert an emotional appeal that draws in some of those hitherto "rationalistic" nonbelievers, but the new converts never are able to explain to the satisfaction of any of their erstwhile rationalistic colleagues what happened. That is not the way of science or scholarship. Science requires canons of reason that religion inherently cannot live up to. Inevitably, religion is a matter of faith in a sense antithetical to scientific reason.

2. Religion and Tolerance

The problem for society is that the first of these two properties—the claim to be the last word about life—has the important consequence that believers do not, in principle, have much intrinsic potential for tolerating other creeds. If yours is the absolute truth, all the others must, of course, be seriously in error—error about the most important things there can possibly be, and so, the sort of error that it will be very difficult not to identify with evil, rather than honest mistake. But the other property, its nonrationality, ensures that the best the believer can manage to do is to condemn the others as victims of sin, since he won't be able to demonstrate his claim—that the others are wrong—to the satisfaction of anyone except himself and fellow believers.

How, then, can religion not eventuate in political conservatism (as understood here)? The temptation to take one's religious beliefs as the exclusively correct basis of political action is all but irresistible. But if it is not resisted, what is there to do but fight? Argument is impossible; one's view apparently justifies using absolutely any method of getting nonbelievers into line, and if they don't see it (as they likely won't) then it's out with the sword.[7] Shouts of "The sword of the Lord and of Gideon!"; "Allah Akhbar!," etc., will ring out in the land, the clash of arms will ensue—or nowadays the sound of suicide bombs exploding—and there will be an enormous amount of bloodletting—all of it utterly futile.

Why "utterly futile"? Because the one thing that matters to the religious person cannot possibly be accomplished by these methods. The other chaps will end up dead, yes—but they won't end up believing the right things; if they live, they won't have changed their minds, and if they die, they are beyond reach. The Thirty Years War (1616–1648) left a great many people dead, a great deal of property destroyed—and nobody believing anything they hadn't believed before. Europeans learned the lesson. The general Western view since then has been the liberalism advocated here.

3. Its Fundamental Circularity

It matters also that the fundamental moral theory that appears to be implied by these religions is logically unsustainable. That is because the claim that we ought to do what god tells us to makes no sense unless we assume that god will tell us the right things. But what will make those the right things? It cannot be the fact that "god" tells us this. That is not because the very existence of the god in question is unprovable—true though that certainly is. Rather, it is because the very claim that the being who tells us this is "god" rather than some impostor is the claim that it is the "perfect" being, the being beyond all praise. Very well: and what could possibly make him so perfect, if not that his properties are such as to call for our admiration, devotion, etc.? But why do those properties call for this? Obviously, because they are good and admirable properties. Which means, of course, that in order to have a picture of a "supreme being" we must have a prior understanding of what sort of properties make for the sort of moral supremacy that is claimed for him. Thus the claim that those qualities are supreme just because god has them and that we are right to do what he tells us just because he tells us to are strictly incoherent. The moral story of religion is impossible.[8]

We may darkly speculate that there are reasons of a different kind for the political role of religions. Religions exploit people's capacity for credence, garnering unthinking and unstinting loyalty, all of which plays very well into the hands of the astute seeker after power. Since the sacred mysteries are mysteries, the demagogue doesn't need to explain himself—he needs but speak sternly to the doubters. (Having his followers pull out their knives at this point will also help.) Lurking beneath the surface will be all the usual motives: lust for power and wealth, tribal loyalties and jealousies, and so on. The effect of injecting religion into these controversies, however, is inevitably to provide motivation for digging one's heels in, for utter intransigence, and in general for potentially unlimited violence in the name of the sacred.

It is of great importance to appreciate that there is no way in which religious sanctioning of what would otherwise be great evils can be correct. A god who sanctions the murder of people just for believing this or that or for not being loyal to him is not a wise and good being, but a megalomaniacal, spoiled child. There is no room in politics or morals for accepting some religion as the central determinative set of ideas in it. Politics and morals are for our mutual guidance. Reflection on our characteristics and general circumstances is what has to generate that guidance— guidance that, remember, is essentially interpersonal. The idea that this interpersonal set of rules for us all to follow could emanate from the unprovable beliefs of some people, beliefs known not to be shared by all and incapable of being demonstrated to any who don't already accept them, is subversive of morality and so of political justice. Religious tolerance is the only acceptable rule concerning religion. Beyond that, no politics can be based on religion without leading, inevitably, to war, of the most bitter and intractable kind. The effectual separation of church and state, then, is a prerequisite to rationally civilized society.

Religions need to learn, as most have done, to live with other religions in peace and cooperation. The rule of tolerance is to tolerate all who tolerate others. But it is also not to tolerate those who don't: A disposition to murder nonbelievers just because they are such is absolutely unacceptable, and it is not a sign of liberal humanity to accept religious communities sworn to undying hostility to all nonbelievers of their views.

A community that denies the separation of church and state will also be a community in the political grip of its supposed spiritual leaders— the religious establishment. An individual citizen giving his soul to god gives his body, especially in the form of his pocketbook, to the church while he's at it. Observers from the outside will have their doubts that this is a coincidence.

ETHNICITY, RACE, GENDER, AND NATIONALITY

If religion is perhaps the foremost source of the kind of politics I collect under the label "conservative," it is far from the only one. The story of politics is very considerably the story of specific groups, especially those identified by ethnic, racial, national, or for that matter sexual makeup, jostling for a greater share of political power, while others try to prevent this.

The problem for such aspirations is analytically similar to that for religions. Any such group—call it Group A—has a problem if it proposes to make A's distinctive values into ones that are to rule over others. Since those other people do not share A's values—they being, after all, distinctive—those values will not be seen by the others as providing reasons why they should accept whatever programs are founded on them. So if Group A is to have its way, it will be due to one of three things:

(a) Luck: that is, the sentiments of the others, who are, fortunately for the A group, willing to accept the impositions in question. This, of course, is not very likely. (A special case is when the A group is or claims to be needy. We will address that later. Here, though, we are concerned with ethnicity, gender, and the like).

(b) A good sales pitch: the A group proposes to extend some benefits to the others, to compensate for the imposition, and the others accept.

(c) Force: The A group compels the rest to submit.

Liberalism rules out (c). And (a), as said, is unlikely though by no means impossible. This mostly leaves us with option (b), so the question is, what does A have to offer?

A groups characteristically have some attractions for others: White people enjoy black music, black athletic prowess, and much else. The catch is that these are things anyone is welcome to offer to others on his or her own, either for free or for a price, and the others are welcome either to take them up on the offer, or not. The question is why any A group should be constitutionally enabled to do better than under the standard liberal baseline of mutual forbearance, nonviolence, and reliable adherence to freely negotiated agreements. Why should some be favored at the expense of others? There is no reason. The liberal program offers the best we can all do.

Many A groups claim to be, and some have sometimes been, the object of intolerance by others, to be sure. The most spectacular case in history is that of the Jews in relation to the Nazis in the 1930–1945 period. A less spectacular but more extensive case is black slavery in North America over a period of about 200 years. Certainly there is no lack of cases. But A groups seeking redress for past bad treatment are not our main interest here (see chapter 7). Rather, it is A groups claiming to be entitled to dominance by virtue of being themselves. The slave-owning class in the American South, the Nazis with their so-called Aryan racial characteristics (e.g., tall and blonde, like Hitler, say . . .), and no doubt assorted others, asserted their special right to hold other groups in subjection because they were the "superior" group. We have already discussed the claims of intelligence, and in broad terms the claims of "inherited virtue," and found them sorely wanting. It is no surprise that the sort of personal characteristics that go along with being of some race or ethnic group aren't going to impress us either. There's nothing much to say to this kind of racist and imperialist other than "If you're so great, why are you behaving like contemptible gangsters and psychopaths?!"

SLAVERY

When a particular subgroup in society comes into a position of political dominance, that dominance is a matter of its being able, for the time during which it dominates, to command greater coercive force than the others—enough to hold the reins of political power. Those who are thus coerced will not be very happy about this and may be expected to become troublesome, unless the dominant group does a pretty good job at option (b) above. As an interesting case in point, the lot of black slaves in America, while pretty bad, was usually not as bad as many suppose. They could keep out of trouble by working well, usually, and their supply of needed food, clothing, and shelter was steady if not exactly first class. Their lot seems, in typical cases, to have been much better than their counterparts elsewhere, as in South America. While many escaped or tried to, many more did not, deciding that putting up with it, all things considered, was better than taking the risks of escape plus the unknowns of life in Canada or wherever they might end up. At least the option of staying home was usually tolerable. Some slaves developed loyalty to their masters so intense that they did not want to be set free at the end of the Civil War.

But these modest amenities offered by their captors do not justify the institution. What could the criterion of justice be to support it? The most promising—indeed, the only one with any claim to intellectual respectability—was offered by Aristotle, who claims that there are two sorts of slaves: slaves "by nature," and others who ought to be free and are wrongly enslaved. He's unsurprisingly poor at identifying the features that supposedly fit one for slavery, but he is very good at identifying the feature that would be needed to justify it. Namely, they are better off under the direction of others.[9] Of course, this immediately raises the question: better off according to whom? Aristotle and his fellow upper-class Athenians, no doubt. But what about the slave himself? Given his choice, would the slave in question prefer to remain one? Not likely! But of course, if the intellectual makes himself the judge by claiming that slaves aren't qualified to discuss the matter, it's game over for the slave—not a very appealing procedure from the slave's point of view!

In fact, we may strongly suspect that there is a confusion here, between

(a) one person working under the direction of another, and
(b) one person working under the compulsion of another.

These are altogether different. When we go to our doctors, we typically accept their direction, for the good reason that we think they know a lot more than we do about the biophysical matters they help us with. When we work under the direction of our employers, it is because they pay us to do so and we judge that the pay (or other aspects) makes it worthwhile. The slave, however, works because otherwise he gets beaten, left in the cold, killed, and so on. The two cases differ so drastically that one must suppose that only a sort of bias could have induced so intelligent a man as Aristotle to say what he does.

Apply the same thing, now, to any group in a political society that claims the right to extract benefits from others without compensating advantages for them, and we have the same result.

MARXISM

Next we look at the theory behind history's most potent ideology—Marxism. It may seem odd to classify Marxism as a species of conservatism, but the relevance of doing so will become clear in this discussion. If Marx could be resurrected for a day or two and shown the consequences of his influence, one must wonder what he would say. Would he recognize his mistakes as such? Or did he really have a point?

Marx is famed among his followers for his so-called materialist theory of history and especially for his critique of capitalism. That critique, in turn, is comprised of three elements: his theories of value, of capitalist exploitation, and of class conflict. Of these, the first is the most purely theoretical; the second has appealed enormously to what Marxists call "the masses"; and the latter has done, probably, the most damage, as practitioners have talked themselves into believing that it is perfectly OK to murder and despoil "capitalists."

Marx was wrong about all three. The field of social theory is rife with matters about which there is genuinely reasonable difference—but not here. Marx is wrong in a perfectly demonstrable way. His general thesis belongs, in his own memorable phrase, in the "dustbin of history." The following few pages are intended to show this.

(1) The Theory of Value

Marx's critique is intended to show that capitalism suffers from internal "contradictions." The first step in the argument is a version of the "labor theory of value."[10] And what is that? To answer this, we must be careful to be aware of what this is a theory of. It is essentially a theory about market exchange, and specifically price. Marx distinguishes "value in use" from "value in exchange," price belonging in the latter category. What is the relation between these two things? People buy what they do, for the prices that they pay, because they have an eye to their utility; that is, the uses to which they will put what they get and an eye to their budgets, which are finite and which they want to use to the best advantage. How do they come to pay the prices they actually do? Marx's answer is that, ultimately, it is labor that explains price. X costs more than Y because there is more human labor "embodied" in X. Right at the start, there is the point made by some keen students of Marx that we could be talking about the "amount of labor" that it took to make the last lot of X—or we could be talking about the "amount" that it would take to make the next lot—which just might be a great deal different, since in the meantime, clever people, including many of the laborers themselves, will have thought of better ways to make X. Then the "amount of labor" embodied in a given amount of X will change, perhaps drastically. Cyrus McCormick's mechanical reaper reduced the number of people-hours needed for cutting grain by something like 80 percent; the price of wheat, of course, declined sharply. A reaper operator's work was worth several times that of a flail-thresher.

Meanwhile, however, the consumer will pay no attention to the fact that prereaper wheat has more labor in it than postreaper wheat. Since in recent times the story of economic life has been the story of increasing product per unit of labor, what is the "labor theory" supposed to say? Its primitive version, as Marx knew, is plainly hopeless. Obviously, products of a lot of labor competing with products of much less in them are not going to command the higher price that the simple theory would suggest. But which price will it command? Marx supplies a famous formulation: Value is "socially necessary labor." What is meant by the claim that a certain kind of labor is "socially necessary"? It sounds as though this is just another "kind" of labor, or perhaps an improved way to measure labor, as it were. But that is a mistake. It is nothing of the sort.

Consider an automobile factory where much of the "work" is done by robots. Highly paid technicians fix the robots when they go wrong, but as to the work that attaches the various bits of the car to each other, no humans do that. What now? "Socially necessary" labor is a matter of what the producer needs to hire, given the technological background against which his company produces what it does. But why do you need to hire the ones you do and pay them what you do? If people with the needed knowledge and skills are rare, you pay them more, and if they are abundant, you pay them less—even though the "amount" of labor put forth by those working at high wages would be exactly the same as the amount exerted by the lower paid. The trouble with the "labor theory" is that the variable "quantity of labor" in Marx's more sophisticated theory cannot be identified and measured without invoking the very phenomenon we are trying to explain; namely, the determination of price by supply and demand. The value of any sort of "unit" of labor defined independently of its relation to markets is absolutely indeterminate. In consequence, you can't use it as a basic explanatory variable for price. Marx's theory has the tail wagging the dog—how much work A is claimed to have done is measured by the price A can command for it, rather than B having to pay A only the "value" of his work as measured by its amount, measured in hours or calories.

There is an underlying reason why the theory has to fail; namely, consumer sovereignty, which is an essential component of the market. The purchaser of anything decides whether to buy on the basis of budget and perceived utility. She does not independently care how much work goes into the production of X or Y or Z. And the price asked by the merchant is a function not only of the merchant's costs of production but also of market conditions, that enable him, characteristically, to make a profit—and without profits, there would be no businesses.

(2) Exploitation

Given a labor theory of value, Marx saw, there would be a problem. He claims that in a free market, "equals are exchanged for equals." Ignoring for the moment the fact this axiom is meaningless in any sense in which it is not false, the problem would be that if the quantity of labor involved in X is the same as in Y, Y being the price of X, then how is profit possible? Marx's answer is ingenious and correct. He notes, in effect, that we must distinguish between the amount of work the worker performs—"output" labor, as we will call it, and the amount that it takes to enable the worker to work—"input" labor. The question now arises, How are they related? The answer is that output has to exceed input. The worker works, say, eight hours in a day, but the amount required to pay for his work is say, six hours. If output doesn't exceed input, profit is impossible.

Exactly what is to count as "input" labor, unless we simply stipulate that it's his wage, whatever it is? Anything else is going to be exceedingly difficult. How many hours did the worker's parents spend bringing him up? And so on, almost indefinitely. As usual, the assumption will simply be that such costs are somehow covered in the process of A's arriving at the workplace and working for an agreed-on wage. Of course, workers' wages vary enormously. Workers in a Chinese factory get 30¢ an hour for doing what those in a Mercedes-Benz plant in Germany receive $30 for. But whatever the worker's "input" is, his output must be more, else the owner would make no money.

At this point, the Marxist maintains, in several variants, that the worker is being cheated, robbed, given a raw deal, and in general "exploited." There are more things that Marx regards as a matter of relative detail, such as the money the capitalist spends on things other than labor—plant maintenance, interest costs, whatever. But the important question is whether "exploitation" is an interesting charge; that is, whether people's being "exploited," in that the worker's wages are less than the value of his product, is somehow unjust or otherwise objectionable. And there's the rub. In a free market, all labor is voluntary. Jobs are offered and they are either taken or turned down by applicants. Those applicants look at the situation from their own point of view. They take the job because it is better than their alternatives, in their view—not because some employer is cracking the whip over them.

Nor is that all. The employee might have the alternative of remaining in her cottage turning out products with enormous labor input but no "exploitation"—unless you wish to say that she is exploiting herself. But if you do, you depart from liberalism, which makes the individual the judge of such matters. The point here is simple: A's working for somebody else, B, in a way that makes B some money, is often a good idea from A's point of view, even if B makes a lot more than A does. In fact, most of us do that, most of the time—and most of us are, we think, doing all right!

Thus, the problem with the Marxian theory of "exploitation" is that what it names is, in general, a good thing rather than a bad thing. So why knock it? The grounds for doing so turn out to involve pure fallacy: inferring from the perfectly true premise that people make money for others the conclusion that they are being unjustly treated. It does not follow and is in general not true. If we allow people to be the judges of what is good for themselves, we'll have to allow them to make trades that benefit others as well as themselves, including one that benefits those others, in some commensurable way, more than themselves.

(3) Classes and Class Conflict

In Marx's view the social classes that matter are the "capitalists" and the "workers" (or "proletariat"). Why? Because, he thinks, what explains the course of history is that class controls the means of production. History is a series of revolutions in which different classes come to be in the driver's seat as a function of changing technology utilizing new "forces of production." In the case of capitalism, the supposed problem is the capitalist class, which oppresses the workers, turning means into ends and setting society at odds with itself. In the allegedly needed revolution "the proletariat seizes political power and turns the means of production into state property."[11] Whether the cure isn't a lot worse than the supposed disease is considered next, but in the meantime, is there actually a "disease"? The class conflict thesis is that there are irreconcilable antagonisms between the two classes. Are there?

Marx's economic theorizing had led him to the empirically false conclusion that the inevitable tendency of capitalism was to concentrate capital in the hands of fewer and fewer larger and larger companies and to expand the proletariat enormously—"polarization." "Along with the constantly diminishing number of the magnates of capital, who usurp and monopolize all advantages of this process of transformation, grows the mass of misery, oppression, slavery, degradation, exploitation. . . ."[12] Uh, huh—so say we now, as our highways are crowded with proletarians equipped with SUVs, haul-ing their powerboats to vacation sites, and so on. What, we must ask, went wrong (or, better, went right!)?

What went wrong is another bad argument. Each capitalist does indeed have an interest in minimizing his or her costs of production, which in-cludes of course, wage costs. They want, naturally, to hire the cheapest work-ers they can get. Those cheapest workers may cost you $35/hour, but never mind. You could say, with a bit of squinting, that there is a situation of "an-tagonism" in this respect between any particular company and its employ-ees. But does it follow that there is a situation of antagonism between the capitalist *class* and the proletarian *class*? No! If we suppose with Marx that there are but two classes and that the capitalist class is small and shrinking, the working class large and swelling, then Marx has a problem. The capital-ists make their money by selling a whole lot of stuff to a whole lot of peo-ple. Who? Given his premises, there is only one answer: to those very pro-letarians with whom they are supposed to be "antagonistic"! You aren't going to sell 10 million identical shirts to the capitalists, after all. And with-out markets, you make no money. It follows that not only do the capitalists have an interest in their own employees making as little money as they can manage to pay them but also they have an interest in the other employees in society being wealthy enough to buy lots of their own company's prod-ucts. Obviously, this does not add up to an overall "antagonism"—quite the contrary. The welfare of employees depends on the same thing that profits do: increasingly efficient production, with its corollary, increasingly high real wages—the very things that the efficient investment and direction of capital make possible.

End of story. That is to say, the Marxist argument that the "cure" for soci-ety's "troubles" lies in "expropriating the expropriators" suffers from ex-treme myopia. The "expropriators" turn out to be the worker's best friends. There will doubtless be tensions and struggles about wages, but the fact is that in the larger view, we all—capitalists and workers alike—do better as a result of free market competition. With decent economic policies from above (see chapter 6), we can have a situation in which there is full em-ployment, generally increasing wages, and good profits all around. That is hardly "antagonism." It is, instead, symbiosis and interdependency. What's so bad about that?

SOCIALISM

The essence of socialism is "social control of the means of production," where "the means" refers fundamentally to all means of production. In-stead of many owners, each doing his best to improve his own situation as much as possible, we are to have, somehow, just one supreme direction of the economy. That is the most obvious model. In more recent times, "market socialism" became popular: The various separate factories will be worker cooperatives instead of having typically independent owners for whose profit the factory is operated; these worker cooperatives, however, will behave quite a lot like separate capitalists in that they will be in competition with each other. But not—so the idea goes—with society as a whole. Or something like that. (Working out the theory of "market socialism" as it came to be called, is no easy matter.[13])

The socialist needs to tell us why this is supposed to be better. One view is that capitalists make too much money, or make it the wrong way. Since they make it only by successfully providing things that a lot of people want, the latter doesn't look too plausible. And the former? Perhaps it's egalitarianism; perhaps the socialist thinks that all people inherently have a right to an equal share in the product of "society," never mind who makes what in particular. But how will he support this claim? As usual, the answer is that he doesn't— he just asserts it. But what he's asserting is false, and obviously false. Any manager can tell you that some workers contribute much more than others; the stock market shows that some firms are much better managed than others. Some inventions have revolutionized or created entire industries. Their inventors, manufacturers, and distributors, as well as the investors who supported them obviously did a great deal more than their fellows, if we look to results rather than ideology. "Social production" is understandable as the sum of individual productions, but not vice versa. An individual's work transforms the inputs to his productive process into something else of higher value—higher in the sense that people are ready to pay more for the product than for the inputs in prealtered form. (It needn't be and never is "all" people. It's simply that there are some people ready and able to do this. The claim that these consumers' wants would be better satisfied by a committee representing "society in general" rather than by individual producers doing their best on a free market is not credible, unless you are ready to switch to nanny mode and say that consumers shouldn't be allowed to be exposed to a choice of 37 different kinds of breakfast cereal, dammit! Let them eat gruel—it's good for 'em!)

What else, then, might make a case for socialism? The social managers, so the story goes, have the interests of society as a whole at heart, whereas the individual capitalist producers have only their own interests at heart. For purposes of discussion, let's accept this otherwise implausible premise. Of course, socialist managers claim to have the interests of society at heart; otherwise, one would think, they'd be out of a job! But that's their pitch. The question is whether it's in any relevant way true. Individual capitalists may have all sorts of other people in view—or not—as they plan their investments and run their companies, but still, what they do is in fact highly beneficial to society. That looks pretty promising. Turning industry over to politics does not.

But let's assume for the sake of argument that the socialist is right here. Now what? A very large problem for the socialist manager is that without markets to set prices, he turns out to have quite a problem doing his managing. How will he know what and how much to produce? For the capitalist the solution is absurdly simple: You invest where you can make the most money, buying your production inputs for the lowest price you can find, and you produce as much as will continue to turn a profit, after which you quit. But the socialist manager has no prices to go by, his fellow revolutionaries having abolished those bourgeois niceties. Where, then, do we go from there? Socialist planners trying to use "real labor values" will be (and was) ruinous to all. The problem here was fought out in the pages of journals for most of the twentieth century under the heading of the "socialist calculation debate." According to the capitalist economists, spearheaded by Ludwig von Mises, socialist managers cannot make rational decisions. According to the defenders of socialism, they can. The best socialist writers did understand the problem and did not reply with dogmatic shibboleths. What they supposed is that the managers could do a sort of theoretical reconstruction of the market and get their price information from that. There would be "shadow prices" of various goods, and so rational decisions, based on maximization, could be made. But it was a vain hope, and this fascinating chapter in intellectual history is now closed. The supporters of free markets have won; the socialists have lost. The problem is that the kind of information needed to manage a socialist society simply can't be had without real markets, and socialism remains hopelessly inefficient by comparison with capitalism.[14] No diagnosis is more plausible than the obvious: Letting people settle things on their own terms is likely to be a lot better for them, if we take it that people are the ultimate judges of what's good for them, than trying to get some supposed expert to figure everything out for everyone else.

Socialism was and is shot through with inattention, or the wrong kind of attention, to people's interests on all levels. Inevitably, people who are allowed simply to choose among products offered by others, *provided they are free to reject those offers*, will do better than if instead remote officials try to decide what they want and how it is to be provided. According to the official view, "Communism deprives no man of the power to appropriate the products of society; all that it does is to deprive him of the power to subjugate the labor of others by means of such appropriation. . . ."[15] But this shibboleth turns out to be the reverse of the truth. Communism does deprive people, massively, of precisely the "power" in question—the power to close a deal by arranging with someone or some few others, to the benefit of both buyers and sellers, independently of what someone in Moscow or Beijing or Havana thinks that these individuals ought to be doing or having. Socialism obliterates people's freedom to act as individuals, and if the point of having a political system is to enable people to do better, to run their lives more successfully, then the case against socialism is definitive. People have the right to make their own choices in life. Socialism denies that in a wholesale manner.

A principal component of socialism is its separation of the aspect of production from that of consumption. Rationally, production is for the sake of consumption; that is to say, of putting the products to desired uses (apart from the important secondary case of "production" for its own sake, as in ballet). If that's why it is produced, you can't just ignore the fact when you turn to the supposedly different subject of distribution. Those who produce would not have done so if they did not think that they would thereby be able to avail themselves of new or more or better things, things that their production enables them to have, and to have in proportion to their production.

Marx correctly distinguished value in use from value in exchange. Of the two, values in use are decided by individuals for their own cases; but value in exchange is, necessarily, agreed by two or more parties. Your interest in how much I want X is that my desire may induce me to pay more; my interest in your desire to sell X is that it may induce you to lower your price. Prices "settle" (for a little while, anyway) as a function of the known general drift of volunteered payments and volunteered productions. If you judge my offer too low, it means you are willing to wait until someone else comes along and accepts your higher price. If I judge your offer too high, it means that I'll go elsewhere, or settle for something a little lower on my scale of intrinsic utilities. Given a certain level of demand, producers will react by ceasing to produce if the price is too low to enable them to profit, or by adjusting their prices or upgrading their equipment to the point where profits are realized. The trouble with central planners, who are not identical with any of the participants, is that they cannot know what people themselves do. They will inevitably misjudge buyers' interests, or sellers', or both. Socialism is economic nonsense. Those who proposed it did not know what they were getting into. After a century of socialism in action, we do: They were "justifying" the taking of enormous amounts of power over others under the delusion that they had the interests of their subjects at heart. It's Aristotle on slavery all over again!

We know that some in the Soviet Union, East Germany, and Byelorussia yearn for the old days when they didn't have much but knew they could expect the same the next day and the next, just as some slaves in the American South regretted the end of slavery. That there was an enormous cost in lives for this supposed reliability is perhaps the worst thing about it. The other is that they could expect it the next day and the next, yes—though the day after that, starvation may await, as in Maoist China, on the largest scale ever in known history.[16]

Socialism claims to turn over the power of production to "the people." There are millions of people, though, and no two think quite alike in regard to what should be done with all this product that has been snatched away from those who created it. How to decide? One thought, of course, would be to go democratic, have an election to see what most people think should be done. The term "democratic socialism" applies to this idea and has a powerful appeal. After all, we all want what is good for society, and we think this is closely bound up with "self-rule."

Or should we? How many ballots will we have, with 30 million or 300 million people? Indeed, what is the use of the ballot? There are hundreds of things that each person is interested in, in immensely varied ways. What will inevitably happen is the only thing that possibly can happen: A small number of people will emerge who claim, whether or not on the basis of an election, to represent the rest. The decision-making power will fall upon these few, and what people want, for their own part, becomes immaterial and inaccessible. The Central Committee will decide what people "want," what they "need," what is good for them. And it will set about trying, with very modest success, to produce this. Meanwhile, it will make many enemies, and it will decree that they are Enemies of the People and have them shot or sent off to prison camps or perhaps to psychiatric hospitals run by the State. That is why I place socialism as a conservative theory.

As against the democratic socialist, there is the possibility that people, given the choice, will vote against socialism altogether. The preceding analysis strongly suggests that if they know what they're doing, they will indeed do just that.

FASCISM

The most denounced among twentieth-century political ideologies is no doubt Nazism. "Nazi" is a contraction for "National Socialist" in fact, and for that matter twentieth-century Italian fascism also had roots in socialist movements. Might it be asked, as one recent writer does, "How can a movement that epitomizes the extreme right be so strongly rooted in the extreme left? What was going on in the minds of dedicated socialist militants to turn them into equally dedicated Fascist militants?"[17] There is an ostensible difference between communism and fascism: In the first, everyone is to sacrifice himself to Society, while in the second, everyone is to do so for the State. The result was "Two rival gangs of murderous politicos, bent on establishing their own unchecked power, each drummed up support by pointing to the horrors that the other gang would unleash. Whatever the shortcomings of any such appeal, the horrors themselves were all too real."[18] In the Nazi case, a bizarre kind of racism was also mixed into the brew, providing additional excuses for enslaving and murdering a sizable portion of its own population as well as a great many neighbors. But then, Nazism's involvement in war cost the lives of many millions of the supposedly superior race as well; the emphasis on self-sacrifice to a supposedly superior cause was quite enough to lead to massive killing all around, including in the end the life of their "supreme leader" who committed suicide at the end of the war when even he saw that all was lost.

If A is to sacrifice his life to B, who is in turn to sacrifice it for A, something seems to be wrong. Presumably neither of these ideologies included the belief that death was preferable to life all around? But if not, the doctrine of self-sacrifice for some supposedly "higher" cause of a distinctively social kind would seem to be lacking in sense. Those who were taken in by such doctrines, evidently, fell prey to a gigantic hoax or to a gigantic fallacy, or both. The hoax was the supposedly superman status of the leaders—who were, of course, nothing of the sort. More accurately, they were psychotics, playing roles comparable to the gods of the Mayans with their unlimited appetite for human lives. The fallacy consists in taking the State to be some kind of superperson, worth sacrificing oneself to.

The American president John Kennedy famously said, "Ask not what your country can do for you; ask rather what you can do for your country." Those words do not sit well with liberalism, which holds that the State, if it's worth anything, is our servant, not our master. If the duties imposed by this servant extend to real self-sacrifice, something would seem to be wrong. What must be shown, given liberalism, is that we all, including the sacrificial lambs, stand to gain by a readiness of each citizen to participate in war (or whatever) to the extent of severely endangering his or her own life. This is imaginable, if threats of external attack pose such danger that life expectancy is worth lowering for the sake of countering it and thus preserving our freedoms. But this should be regarded as extreme, not as typical. Of course, what the German people sacrificed themselves for was hardly freedom, whatever else.

Liberalism maintains that we have the right to our beliefs, however bizarre, and people are apparently capable of believing just about anything. Or does it? But if our beliefs inspire action, as many of them do, and if what it inspires are evils for other people, this right to believe anything has exceeded its limits. What is truly distressing is bizarre beliefs that nevertheless take on cult status, mass delusion. How does it happen?

The answers to such questions must presumably be sought in social psychology. Propagandizing—"brainwashing" as we aptly term it—of very young people is one major factor. In the Cambodian nightmare of Pol Pot's Khmer Rouge, we are told, the killing of about a third of the entire populace was done almost entirely by what we would call "kids"—young people of twelve to fourteen. In the horrifying movie *The Bridge*, an American army unit is held up, at considerable loss of life, by a small number of determined young teenagers, brought up as Hitler Youth. At least equally horrifying is the English movie *Lord of the Flies*, in which a band of school children, left to themselves on a small island, develop levels of savagery of which their middle-class parents would not have believed them capable. These are cases for psychological diagnosis, not candidates for credible political belief. When we ask what there is to be said for these outlooks, the eventual answer is Nothing. We may marvel that so many people were ready to throw themselves under the wheels of these juggernauts, but crediting them with a shred of philosophical plausibility is another matter. Forget it!

IT'S NOT DEAD YET

Ensuing chapters will provide more food for thought on this matter. I have said that liberalism has "won." Yet, the business of exercising compulsion over all in the interests of values that may not be shared by those compelled goes right along. For a current example, consider environmentalism. All of the paper you buy is partly recycled. Why? To save trees? And why save trees, given the incredible capacity for growing more (new trees grow far faster than we consume them[19]). Most countries punish the consumption of "recreational drugs" in draconian fashion, even though those allegedly harmed by such activities are confined almost entirely to the users. People are compelled to send their children to schools, whether they're interested or (mostly) not in what they supposedly learn there. And so on (and on and on). In all of these, the signs of political Platonism are evident. Some people decide how others are to live and are able to wield the powers of the police and the tax collector to see to it that they do. The issue between conservatism, as defined here, and liberalism is not a fussy little academic distinction.

CONCLUDING THOUGHTS: THE TROUBLE WITH CONSERVATISM

The conservative who thinks there is value in his or her society's past, value in stability and order, is on solid ground. Not changing what is good is, of course, wise. But conservatism goes beyond that. It says that these stable good things are good in such a way that present persons who want to do something else may be compelled not to do so. The conservative wants to pass laws to prevent change even when people want it for themselves. That's where conservatism parts ways with liberalism.

The most plausible upshot of liberalism is that mutual freedom, which is equivalent to mutual advantage, liberally construed, is the way to go. The thesis of this book is that for the general case in politics, this bottom line is unbeatable. In a world with diverse people, having diverse interests and abilities, the idea that some should be able to enforce their ideas of the good life on the rest is necessarily unappealing. Perhaps some people like to be told what to do. No doubt many will be in broad agreement with the schedule of values promoted or invoked by this or that conservative. But others will find themselves in broad agreement with different ones, and it is far from obvious who is right, if anyone. In either case, the involuntary submission of some to others is obviously not a prospect that rational people can find attractive—especially if, as is likely, they are among those whose submission is demanded.

What, then, do we do? If we can find no clear ground for appealing to some personal values over others, as is typically true of the many specifically different views of how to live that I am marshaling under the general heading of "conservatism," then to insist, despite this ineliminable diversity, on some favored subset of those many ideas as the one everyone must live up to is not, on the face of it, rational as a basis of political activity.

Our first two general political views were "realism" a la Thrasymachus, and conservatism, understood broadly as Platonism. Generally speaking, the same thing is wrong with both. Indeed, the question arises whether conservatives are not just a classier gang of thieves than Thrasymachus and his buddies. Which is better—to be invaded, despoiled, imprisoned, and killed by a band of robbers, or by a band of fanatical seekers after what they claim to be The Good? In the end, it doesn't matter much. Perhaps the latter is the more interesting way to go. But not having to "go" at all really looks a lot better!

The reader may be thinking at this point, "Well, then, how do we decide who's right?" Ensuing chapters will, I hope, assemble a pretty plausible answer.

NOTES

1. Roger Scruton, in his essay, "How I Became a Conservative," in *Gentle Regrets: Thoughts from a Life* (London: Continuum, 2005), 35.
2. Aristotle, *Politics*, I.2.
3. St. Thomas Aquinas, *Summa Theologica*, II.2.11.
4. This chilling line is from Leonard Bernstein's operetta, *Candide*.
5. John Rawls coins the expression in his *Political Liberalism* (New York: Columbia University Press, 1993), see p. 13 and pp. 58–65, especially.

6. One hesitates to recommend particular books among the thousands on these subjects, but there is a good review of many arguments in David Ramsey Steale, *Atheism Explained* (Chicago: Open Court Publishing Company, 2008).

7. See Noah Feldman, "Islam, Terror and the Second Nuclear Age" in *The New York Times Magazine* (October 29, 2006): 50. Mr. Feldman surveys the prospects for Islamic leaders, coming to the view that no amount of destruction, even of fellow Muslims, is incompatible with the goals of Islam. Those prospects are not dim, it seems. http://www.nytimes.com/2006/10/29/magazine/29islam.html?_r=1&oref=slogin.

8. The classic source for this argument is Plato's dialogue *Euthyphro*. It stands as one of history's monuments of philosophical analysis.

9. Aristotle's *Politics*, Book II, is the general source here.

10. Karl Marx, *Capital: A Critique of Political Economy* [many editions]. The theory is expounded in volume 1, chapter 1.

11. Friedrich Engels, *Socialism: Utopian and Scientific* (Engels, 1880; authorized English version, 1890), section 1.

12. Marx, "General Law of Capitalist Accumulation," in *Capital: A Critique of Political Economy*, volume 1, chapter 25, section 4.

13. See two superb sources on market socialism, one short and one long. The short one is Anthony de Jasay, "Market Socialism: 'This Square Circle,'" in his *Justice and Its Surroundings* (Indianapolis, IN: Liberty Press, 2002), 215–242. The long one is N. Scott Arnold, *The Philosophy and Economics of Market Socialism* (London: Oxford University Press, 1994).

14. For the story in lucid detail, see David Ramsay Steele, *From Marx to Mises: Post-Capitalist Society and the Challenge of Economic Calculation* (New York: Open Court, 1992).

15. Karl Marx and Max Engels, *The Communist Manifesto*.

16. An essential book for our time is Stéphane Courtois, Nicolas Werth, Jean-Louis Panné, and Andrzej Paczkowski, *The Black Book of Communism: Crimes, Terror, Repression* (English translation, Cambridge, MA: Harvard University Press, 1999), which itemizes the death toll from communism's revolutions, deportations, massacres, starvations—an amount estimated to nearly 100 million people.

17. David Ramsay Steele, whose article "The Mystery of Fascism," is found at http://www.freerepublic.com/focus/f-news/916286/posts.

18. Steele, "The Mystery of Facism."

19. See Roger A. Sedjo, "The World's Forests: Conflicting Signals," in Ronald Bailey, ed., *The True State of the Planet* (New York: Free Press, 1995), 177–209. The situation is no different now.

4

Classic Liberalism and the Minimal State

THE IDEA OF A "SOCIAL CONTRACT"

The classic political philosophers—Hobbes, Locke, Rousseau, Kant—held that government, or more generally the basic political setup of the polity, is founded on a "social contract," though this is differently construed by different theorists, and still more differently among recent philosophers who espouse something of the sort, such as John Rawls.[1] Just what is the social contract supposed to be about? Why should we look at society in this way at all?

I will take these in reverse order. People are individuals, each with their own interests, desires, values, or more generally, preferences. Each of us is immersed in society, in frequent contact with other people. We interact with people: Things we do affect them, things they do affect us, and the effects often matter, greatly, to those involved. When we deal with other people, what is our purpose? Clearly, to do as well as possible; that is, that the net effect of their actions be maximally desirable in our view. Some of what they do results in things we'd rather not have (costs), while others result in benefits, and invariably the two go together as a "package" of effects. When we can choose, we choose the package that is maximally to the net benefit of those we want to benefit, typically oneself and some others.

Why shouldn't we say that we want packages to be beneficial to all others? The answer is that it is not obviously true that we all do want this. If we are trying to characterize people as they are, prior to trying to talk them into being more like the way theorists might think they should be, then it is no good reading our desired results into our premises. What does seem true is that virtually all of us select some few others for whom we have affection, and once we get beyond those few, the steadily widening circle of others becomes a circle of total strangers whom we scarcely ever see, know almost nothing about, and have no special affection for. Of course, it is also false that we are all, in any interesting sense, exclusively self-centered. Premises excluding affection are as wrong as premises extending it to all.

Even among those we care about, our observation continues to hold. When you love people, those people offer benefits for you just by being around—which, more or less, is why you love them, after all—and your overall attitude makes it generally and obviously true that your interactions with them are on the whole beneficial, and strongly so, at least on a good day! The same doesn't clearly hold of miscellaneous strangers.

But why "contract"? Does it even make any sense to talk of "contract" with people you never met? We must, of course, understand the notion somewhat differently from the way it applies between two people doing normal business. In those cases, the parties must be in close communication with each other in order to state the terms of exchange and to deliver the goods or perform the other services that are the subject of the contract. If there is to be something like an "agreement" among everyone everywhere, which is the general idea of the social contract in its most ambitious form, then the situation has to be this: that we know the general properties of people, their potential for benefit or harm, and their capability for self-command in response to general considerations about their social environment. We must know them well enough so that we could reasonably set up an inward disposition, a piece of internal software as we may well call it, in advance, for dealing with others, including strangers, when they are encountered. We program this on the basis of assumptions about how others will react. What makes it "contractarian" is that, like regular contracts, it is based on the interests of each party. Thus, our software is "iffy": If you don't injure me, I won't injure you. This "iffiness" is what makes it appropriate to use such a word as "contract." My understanding is that you will do X provided I do Y, and yours that if you do X I will do Y. In the case where what we would see to be the thing to do if the other performs in a certain way is such that we could also realize some gain by reneging on the hypothetical agreement, our software has an instruction to act contrary to our short-term desires. This is what we can call "conscience," though in favorable social climates most of us simply habituate ourselves to avoid wrong things and need no prodding from a little voice in our heads urging us to do so.

In short, the social contract is the set of reasonable terms for dealing with others, given what we are generally like. These terms, known as moral principles, are generally pretty clear. People can help you, and they can harm you, and we them. What we want from others is help, not harm. Harm from them is a cost to me, harm from me a cost to them. The obvious settlement point is, simply, mutual nonharm. It's easy to live up to, usually: All we have to do is nothing, or more generally, to refrain from fairly specific, well-known kinds of harmful activities, notably those that impose physical damage on others or their property.

The major objection to this proposal will come from those who think that it assumes too broadly and too easily the gist of Thomas Hobbes's postulate of general rough "equality of vulnerability," as I called it back in chapter 2. Hobbes, remember, points out that as to strength of body, the weakest has enough to kill the strongest. Even that is not universally true, since there are a few paraplegics and the like; still, all normal people, covering perhaps 99 percent of our adult fellows, do exemplify Hobbes's dictum. But it is reasonable to suggest, in fact, that that really is good enough for the purpose. For the purpose is to constitute a sort of public charter of general criticism of conduct to which any and all may appeal. Now, as Hobbes points out, almost everyone has friends ready to help defend him, if needed. The groups of friends in question aren't equal either, to be sure. But still: Is there any reason at all for building in exclusions in a general code of conduct? For example, should we say that we should all be ready to approve the actions of any group that can manage to outmaneuver or outmatch any other? The social contract theorist's argument is that if it comes to appealing to our fellows at large, to mankind in general, mankind would be irrational to side with aggressors against anyone, provided only that the intended recipient of the inflicted evils is himself innocent of any such tendencies in relation to anyone else. To choose anything else is to ask for trouble.

It is instructive here to compare our situations regarding fellow humans with that vis-à-vis the other animals. Here there is indeed marked disparity. Animals can suffer, no doubt, and are in various ways rational. But we can't communicate with them at anything like the level at which we can communicate with fellow humans. We can't expect animals to learn a code of behavior and follow it, and they can't expect us to treat them like fellow humans in all those ways in which fellow humans can cooperate usefully with others. Our intelligence and ability to build up a mass of useful information, as well as our considerable physical stature, add up to the conclusion that animals are simply not covered by Hobbes's dictum. Animals, in general, are not capable of relating to us as fellow moral subjects. Thus, human treatment of animals is rightly one-sided. Many humans do have affection for certain animals, and most of us enjoy seeing them do their various things. But too, a lot of us like to eat many animals' meat. The facts don't add up to a case for entitling them to the same kind of general respect and rights as our fellow humans.

Once we do get into interactions involving considerable communication, the next thing is to use our capacity to communicate in such a way as not to leave the other party worse off—e.g., in possession of false beliefs where before he had no beliefs. This is the Hobbesian format: There is a baseline of interaction—normally (pending a check on his or her track record to date) the way someone is when we encounter him or her. In general our duty is to refrain from bringing that person below where he is now, given that it is not our doing that he is as he is now. Reckoned in terms of individuals dealing generally with other individuals, this idea looks very good. Indeed, it is hard to see how we could improve on it. Neither of us has any reason to accept uncompensated costs from the other, after all, if we have our choice. And if we do not, we are in a state of war, with all of its disadvantages.

Additionally—and it is a most important addition—virtually any of us is capable of benefiting virtually any other in any number of ways; the social contract makes it clear that we are welcome to do so (again, with the assumption that the recipient will use those benefits for peaceable purposes). Especially, as Hobbes points out (in his Law Four), we should be sure that we don't make the other person's volunteered benefit one he regrets having given us. The payoff from the general respect that the basic restrictions of morals promise from civilized life lies in the innumerable benefits we can hope for from each other once we are secure in life and limb and basic liberty.

That, then, is the social contract for morality. But is it the social contract for government? That question is misleading, actually, for what we are asking about is the underlying morality of politics, that being what political philosophy is about. Hobbes, notoriously, thought that we should accept just any old government so long as it actually governs—indeed, he says we should regard its laws as the laws for our behavior from that time onward, whatever they might be like. That doesn't look to most of us like a good idea at all. But what does, and how do we decide?

A POLITICAL SOCIAL CONTRACT?

The general idea, surely, must be this: Since governments are coercive, we should erect government only if its costs, including its coercive impositions, are outweighed by its benefits. This is a much taller order than the general moral contract, for people do not need to be coercive at all; the costs of coercion with individuals are to cancel out at zero for each, during decent behavior. But it's different with government. To govern is to coerce. How, then, can we accept any government at all?

If there is a good answer, it will have to be that somehow its coercive capabilities are essential to its benefits. That may be plausible in the case where it uses its coercive capacity to deal with the private coercions of individuals in relation to each other. We can then look at government as a sort of insurance scheme: We all pay a bit to sustain it, and it in turn protects us

when needed. If the best way to do this is such that we are all somewhat coerced (e.g., by having to help pay), then so be it, provided that the protection we get is worth the price. (Some will say, "well, then, it's not really coercion after all, is it?" We needn't settle that semantical point: If "justified
coercion'" makes sense, then we'll call it justified coercion. If it doesn't,
then we'll simply say that what otherwise looked like coercion turns out, in
these cases, not to be.)

But there is a hitch. When people come in large groups, their capacity to
present a threat to others, in a way that yields a net benefit for the threatening group, greatly increases. Of course, the size of these groups is enormously variable. It's not hard to find big groups that can beat up on little
groups if they really want to. True; yet, as with individuals, and for that very
reason, it makes sense for the little groups to get together so as to increase
their capacity to deal with the threats from the big ones. Moreover, we may
surmise that every individual is a member of many groups and that all of
the groups to which he belongs that in any way matter to him are in fact
minorities. Even women and men—the two largest subgroups one readily
thinks of—are each minorities, since there are also many children, as well
as many aged people, whose interests and capabilities are so different that
effectively the groups we have in mind under those labels really constitute
quite distinct interest groups. And then, once we go into the differing temperaments of various different women and their very differing views on the
very things that women might try to claim comradeship with respect to, the
point is clear. There are no "majorities"; there are only minorities. Everyone
had better keep this in mind. Any idea of majorityhood is strictly illusory.
The natural conclusion is this: The social contract is among all individuals
as such, and it will underwrite general liberty for all, impartially and universally. Hobbes was right about that. (Disagreement on this is largely confined to the matter of welfare rights. We will discuss this more in chapter 6.)

The idea of social contract is that the total group of all humans can rationally assemble a general platform of prescriptions for all, to be used in
relation to all others at all times. Social contract successfully addresses the
central problem of conservatism, which is that people are different and
their various values incommensurable. For no commensurating is needed
for the social contract. You make your case to me; either I take it or I don't,
and vice versa. At some point, we agree. We are each always working with
our own values and the ways in which they are affected by the impact, actual or potential, of others. If our own values are internally incommensurable, of course, that's *our* problem. We must somehow make up our minds.

The natural point of agreement—so I and the classical liberals agree—is the
Mutual Non-Harm Principle. So long as we can tell where we are now and
whether what I would do would worsen or improve your situation, and you
can make the same judgment in relation to me, then the suggestion is that we

can "agree to disagree" in the sense that we can simply agree to let each other
do as he or she prefers, provided only that this is confined to what has either
no effect on me, or none that matter, or at least no *adverse* effects.

Some modern advocates think the terms would be very different, and it
is an important question whether this is so and if so, what they might be.
But the central issue with conservatism is this: What is this good that the
conservative thinks he knows so well that he can assume that it goes for me
as well as for him? What if I don't accept it? As, indeed, why should I, come
to think? For I am, after all, myself—a different individual. The liberal's argument is: That fact *matters!*

OLD AND NEW LIBERALISMS

Basically, the classic version of liberalism holds that we all have a general
fundamental right to peace; that is, to nonaggression at the hands of our fellows. That right is conceived by these authors as essentially negative: Others are to refrain from interfering, to keep off, to regard fellow humans as
"self-owners" whose property (namely, themselves, and whatever comes
along with that) we are not to touch without the affected individual's permission. The problem now is this: Since States, virtually by definition, do
not respect this law, instead exacting support from all and imposing taxes
on them to support its activities, how can States be justified at all?

John Locke came the closest to appreciating the problem. He lays down
three conditions of legitimacy of the State. The first two restrictions on the
"extent of legislative power" were that government may not be "absolutely
Arbitrary over the Lives and Fortunes of the People" and that it must rule,
not by arbitrary decrees, but by "standing Laws, and known Authorized
Judges."[2] Any sane theorist will support those two restrictions, which appear to be quite compatible with the existence of the State. But then he an-
nounces a third one, about property: "The Supreme Power cannot take from
any Man any part of his Property without his own consent."[3] Well, that
would seem to be another matter altogether. How the State runs on taxes.
(How could it not do so?) And what is a tax, after all, if not a "deprivation
of a part of a man's property without his own consent"?

There are two general ways of responding to Locke's dictum. One, of
course, is simply to reject it and claim that we don't have the general right
to property that he implies. The other is to try to find some way in which
government is compatible with it after all.

There have been suggestions. Ayn Rand, for example, sketches an idea
that there would be a very small charge imposed on contracts, voluntary in
that no one would be compelled to pay it, and this charge would be used
to maintain courts that would adjudicate disputes about contracts.[4] Only

those contracts in which the payment was made would be supported by the government's judicial and administrative systems—if you don't pay, you're on your own, and you rely on whatever help you can get by entirely voluntary means. Whatever the merits of this idea, or others that might be thought up, we will not in this chapter explore further the issue of anarchism, to which Rand's idea appears to tend. Instead, we will consider minimal government, or as some call it, minarchism. This has also sometimes been termed the "Nightwatchman State." We will need to ask what that might be and what there is to be said for it. In subsequent chapters, we will be looking at the "more extensive states" that have come to be advocated by most contemporary writers who consider themselves to be writing in the liberal tradition; but there's a certain point to starting at the beginning, after all. Then we'll follow on, to essentially where we are now.

THE MINIMAL STATE

"That government is best which governs least," said Henry Thoreau. But what is that? When is a state "minimal"? Usually, it is characterized in some such way as this:

> police, judicial systems, prisons and the military, the minimum allegedly required to uphold the law, which is limited to protect individuals from coercion and theft, to remove criminals from society, and to defend the country from foreign aggression.[5]

Why should the State be minimal? Especially, why is liberalism invoked in this connection? The answer to this last question—Why?—is basic and the key to the rest. "Libertarians," as the modern term for classic liberalism calls them, assert as the fundamental principle of morals and politics that no one is to aggress, in this agreeing with Hobbes and Locke. They are not to do so physically—to commit violence, to injure, or to kill—nor are they to steal or cheat or defraud anyone else, except possibly where that someone has himself committed a violation of someone's rights. Previous discussion will have made it clear that this is equivalent to the claim that everyone has a general right of liberty against everyone else. Now, having a right means having a status such that others are required to respect it by doing or not doing certain things, the things it entails as forbidden or required of others. And the logic of liberty appears to require that those forbidden things be the set of positive acts that would interfere with someone else's liberty, insofar as that liberty is compatible with the like right of all others. The libertarian rights are, then, "negative" rights—rights to forbearance, to being left alone—but not, in general, rights to the assistance of others.

According to the libertarian, we become obligated to do things only by enlisting, by making agreements, promises, and commitments. Having done this, it becomes our responsibility to do the things we have thus undertaken. But if we have made no such commitments, then the background covering rule is that of nonharm only. To claim, as contemporary theorists and practical politicians known as "liberals" among today's readers do, that we have many more rights than just that is to go by definition beyond the purview of the minimal state.

Of course, a right is a basis for protection. Here we come to a fundamental issue: Do we all owe this protection—owe it to everyone? If you are under attack, is it the duty of everyone else to come to your assistance? The libertarian cannot say so. For these other potential helpers are themselves relevantly innocent. They have never hurt you or anyone in any way, we'll suppose. How, then, can they be said to owe you this? By not helping you now, they aren't rubbing salt into your wounds, they're just leaving you no better off, though also no worse off, than you would have been in their absence. But no worse off is precisely how, according to libertarianism, we are all required to leave everyone.

Of course, if you do want their help and they are willing to offer it, that's another matter. The libertarian must applaud this. It's partly that he approves of all mutually agreeable undertakings anyway; but in addition, in this case the helpers would be helping by defending the one basic, general right we all have. If it does have that status, then clearly such acts should be singled out for special merit. Moreover, they should thus be singled out by everybody. On the other hand, soccer heroes, contributors to the opera, great poets, scientists, and so on, are people you may or may not have any interest in praising and admiring. In those cases, there cannot, so says the libertarian, be any basis for insisting on public acclaim by all, regardless of their particular interests.

This gets us back to the fundamental issue of how we could justify a State. Such an institution, after all, is inevitably a monopoly. It claims the authority to make laws that are binding on all, to be the ultimate enforcer of those laws and, of course, the ultimate protector of individuals' rights and the last court of appeal on all matters. The minimal state theorist is evidently ready to accept all this. Why so? Because he supposes that this is genuinely the minimum, in the sense that social life, and therefore, realistically speaking, human life itself, would be impossible without it. We would all like to be safe, we would all like to be able to settle our differences peaceably and decisively, and we all need to know "who's in charge" of this or that or the other region of the world. The advocate of the minimal state believes that the only way we can have these things is to have government. But to allow anything more from government would be going too far. Beyond these minimal things, the government is in the business of imposing on some for the sake of others—of curtailing the freedom of some people, then, in order to benefit others. That is precisely what the general liberty principle forbids.

It isn't that the libertarian has something against these others. Consider the familiar recipient classes of the modern state: the unemployed, sick, or physically or mentally incapable; and in a different vein, those previously the victims of injustices, of wrongful discrimination, or previous harassment or repression. The libertarian says that of course we wish all these people good luck, we wish them well, but he denies that we have a duty, one that is enforceable by law, to help them out.

Who would do that? The libertarian's answer is, anyone who wants to. And he might add that in all likelihood you do want to. We feel sorry for those in tough situations or who are born blind, and so on. People who do nothing for such people are hardhearted, uncharitable, unhelpful. Moreover, next time they are in similarly tough shape, are those who have been helpful to others going to help them out? No way! Charles Dickens's portrait of Ebenezer Scrooge is the classic portrayal of the unsympathetic though honest and just businessperson who, upon being exposed to the plight of people in difficulties, has a change of heart and becomes a truly helpful person. The story touches a deep chord of sympathy in human nature, or at least, in most humans' natures. Even so, says the libertarian, we have no business holding up Scrooge at gunpoint, putting him in jail, or forcibly depriving him of a percentage of his income to accomplish these good aims. We are not to do good for some by doing evil to others. (The modern name for this is the Pareto Principle: to interact with others so that we leave no one worse off, in the course of trying to make some, such as ourselves, better off.)

PROPERTY

Obviously, a major concern of classical liberalism is property. The previous discussion assumes that our basic right implies or includes the right to property and income, so long as these are acquired by work, trade, or gift rather than by theft or violence. Whether individuals should be thought to have such strong rights is probably the most disputed subject in liberal political philosophy. Do we really have rights to various bits of the world—our "property"—so strong that our consent to any alterations in it is absolutely required before others may proceed to make them? This is widely denied today, especially by the many philosophers who would identify themselves as "liberal." (It is also not entirely clear what this "absoluteness" really involves. At the least, there is a margin at which interferences are trivial, as when Jones puts one foot on Smith's large lawn. But we can't pursue such things in this brief treatment.)

To help matters out, let's define the notion of property. First, property is a normative notion. A squirrel's tail "belongs" to the squirrel in that it is part of him, but whether the tail is the squirrel's "property" is another matter.

Here is the basic idea: "X is the property of person A" = "persons other than A may use item X only by A's (uncoerced) agreement." [Coerced agreement is a special case, as in negotiations between two countries that may lead to war. It is not relevant here.] An important note: A's lack of disagreement is normally enough to signify "agreement" for this purpose. We need to ask owners in the cases in which the answer is not known in advance.

As is obvious, it would be possible for A and B to have an arrangement whereby B may do some things with a given item, X, but not others. Many writers hold that property is a "bundle" of distinguishable rights. It is true that they are distinguishable, but it is also true that there is a common element. For in every case, what is in question is someone's possible or actual use of something, and the property right holder's permission to use it in those ways is the central idea. The owner is the person you need to clear it with before you use it. But since things can be used in any number of ways, it is of course possible for property rights to be divided: One person gets to do certain things with X, others to do others. Thus, the landlord owns the apartment, but the person who rents it from him has the right to enter and leave at will, which the landlord no longer has once the rental agreement is made. The question is whether there is a reason for a given restriction, as there may well be.

We also have to add, what should be obvious but will always be brought up by someone, that the uses to which A puts X are confined to those that do not involve harm to others, which of course would violate those others' rights, including, usually, their property rights. Any right limits others' activity and limits the region within which new property rights can be established.

Among the various uses to which X may be put, we will want to distinguish these:

(1) A might simply "use" X in the usual sense of the term; e.g., drive a car, live in a certain house, and so on.

(2) A might destroy it, thus making impossible anyone's future use of X in the previous sense to happen at all.

(3) A might give X to someone else, or might give the right to some uses of X, for some time, to someone else, as when A lends B A's car. Although we can distinguish gift from exchange, the two are very closely related. In both cases, one party has the rights of ownership over the item transferred, but he exercises them differently. The gift giver might be said to impose no conditions on the recipient, but that is never really true. Especially, the recipient understands himself to be obligated not to use the gift in such a way as to injure the giver.

(4) The most important case is where A transfers some or all of A's rights over X to B in exchange for some reciprocal action, often B's transferring of rights to some other thing to A. It would usually be money, but that is just one general case of conditional exchange.

Prima facie, when we say, unqualifiedly, that A owns X, we mean that he has the right to do any of the above.

A final observation, of considerable importance, is that property ownership consists of rights, and rights are fundamentally rights to *do*. When we say that people own a "thing," what we mean is that they have the right to do various things with those things. And when (voluntary) exchanges are made, this also means that what is really exchanged are *services*: one person, A, does something for another, B, namely, transfers to B the right to do various things that B previously lacked the right to do; and B, as a condition of the exchange, transfers to A rights that A previously lacked—usually the right to use as he wishes a certain amount of money he didn't previously have.

Our question, then, is whether we should accept that people have property rights, so long as they acquire them in accordance with the restriction that neither the process of transfer nor the use of the items in question once transferred imposes negative effects on the persons or properties of others.

Arguing for Property

Arguments in support of strong property rights have been of different kinds.

(1) We might argue that property rights are straightforward deductions from the libertarian principle, requiring no additional assumptions or information.

(2) Or we might argue that property rights are somehow an especially good thing, in that they express or stem from something very basic in human nature, without which we could hardly—again—function socially.

(3) Or, finally, we might argue that property is a socially useful institution, whether or not (2) or (1) works out.

The "Direct" Argument for Property

Of these, the first would be the dialectically best, surely. If indeed to defend liberty is necessarily and as such, to defend property, then the libertarian's position on property is as solid as his position on liberty—for whatever that's worth. That is to say enemies of property will then say, "well, so much the worse for the libertarian idea!" And they will be referred to previous discussions in this book, which might, I hope, prompt them to reconsider their reaction. But at any rate, what is needed is the deduction. Here follows my shot at it.[6]

When can we be said to be "aggressing" against someone? The basic answer would be provided by the boundary of a person's body: If, without permission, we scratch, hit, break something inside, insert germs that cause sickness, or bind it so that it can't go the way its owner wants it to, we have invaded or aggressed. We always have to add the essential provision that such invasion or aggression could possibly be justified as a measure of defense, because the person being invaded is himself guilty of such an invasion of some other person. But we also should assume innocence until guilt is demonstrated, and so for abstract purposes we should first see how things stand if the parties in question are relevantly innocent.

Self-Ownership

Some property ownership involves ownership of a natural object. Topping the list of such entities is, of course, the person himself. Libertarianism can be, and often is, stated in terms of "self-ownership." To own is to have authority over. One owns oneself in precisely that sense, in the libertarian view: One has authority over oneself. Others who wish to use us must get our permission to do so. Having said this, it will be noted that liberty is not founded on a *prior* idea that people "own themselves." Rather, the point is that the assertion of self-ownership is literally the same thing, said in different words, as the liberty principle.

Some regard it as a vexed question whether one's authority over oneself extends to selling oneself, for example into slavery. There is difficulty explaining just what that would consist of, since it is hard to see how a person could think himself to be gaining anything by consenting to enslavement. But certainly people can, and sometimes have, put themselves quite extensively into the control of others. Now the question is whether the rest of society should allow any such arrangements. What, precisely, is being asked? For example, if it is to do absolutely anything one's "master" asks, and forever, then what if our subject changes his mind a year later? He wants, now, to get out from under the thumb of his master, but his former self, we are supposing, won't let him. Evidently no penalty clause was negotiated against this event, nor was there value given to the new slave, who asked only to become so. What we probably should say is that people may enslave themselves to others for as long as they want to, but beyond that, we should not uphold the contract. Marriage affords a useful comparison. It is typically an unstated two-way contract, in which each both gives and gets. If one partner is not satisfied, reappraisal is possible. If one partner wants out, then they must assess the "bill" for early exit, which the departing spouse needs to settle if all is to be just. That these arrangements last as long as those involved want them to, and no longer, is the plausible outcome. But slavery is unilateral, which makes no sense.

From Self-Ownership to Thing-Ownership

So what does this have to do with owning bits of the external world? There is a natural answer. Ownership is authority over, which is authority to use. In the special case where no previous ownership exists, a person, A, coming upon useful things that A begins to use and intends to keep on using are to be reckoned their owners because now, any further person, B, undertaking to use those same objects, will be invading A—violating the intended, voluntarily initiated activity of person A, who was "minding his own business." That is wrong because of A's general right to do whatever nonharmful thing he wishes. His use of an object not previously used, of course, harms no one, there being no one on the scene to be affected.

Property is exclusive: A's acquisition of X makes it wrong for B to do the same: If A has X, B does not. Joint ownership is possible, but it requires consent of both parties, and we are supposing that A came first, and supposing that A does not consent to the proposed division or sharing or other restriction desired by other persons. The question for theorists, then, is whether this should be thought a violation of B's liberty. But the negative answer is clear. Liberty is a negative right, not a positive right. A has no obligation to make things available to B. Each pursues his or her own way, her own "utility," and in doing so, of course, continually renders unavailable to others certain bits of the world. B has no *claim*; he merely has a desire, or interest. But when interests conflict, they by definition cannot both be satisfied. A's activity creates a situation in which B now cannot have something B might previously have had—if only A hadn't gotten there first. But he did. If this is an objection to A's activity, that will extinguish the possibility of anyone doing anything safe from imposition by others. First-use grounds ownership because those who "come later" harm others if they insist on using what is already in use. But harm is exactly what a liberty principle forbids. Liberty requires that history matters.

The point that it is the firstness of use that grounds rights affords an insight into self-ownership. Why do we own ourselves? Because you, whoever you are, "got there first": Your brain, arms, and so on, being naturally attached to each other, means that *your* (in the psychological sense) connection with them is prior to anyone else's. So if your central decision-making facility issues a command to some part of the body in question, it responds; if someone else does so, it does not. What is called "self-ownership," then, is identical with (social) liberty: your doing as *you* want is the relation between your decision-making capability and the various bits that constitute you being unimpeded by others. (Being unimpeded by nature at large is quite another matter. We talk here only of the rules for governing the behavior of persons in interaction with each other.)

Ownership rights include the right of transfer, of course; transfer is something within the power of someone who currently owns the item in question.

That leads us to the free market, of which we will say much more below. The point for the present is that we need nothing more than what we already have—namely, by supposition, a general right of liberty—to underwrite the right of property. Property, in short, is a clear application of the general right of liberty.

The "Special Effects" Argument

Some have talked in close to mystical terms about property. It is an "extension of the self"; it "realizes our essences"; it is an "expression of our personality." Interestingly enough, these all seem to be true, too. Many people seem connected to certain special artifacts; their lifestyles are considerably defined by their personal possessions. The question about these points is only what they have to do with the right of property. Suppose that Sally sees an item of wearing apparel that would suit her wonderfully, would express her personality, and so forth. Alas, it happens at present to belong to Mary, who is not about to surrender it, even for a good price. But even if it does not suit Mary nearly so well as it would suit Sally, it does not follow that it "really" belongs to Sally. Our first argument is far stronger than this second one. The second does indeed explain why people acquire at least some of the things they acquire, but it does not explain ownership. Property is a social institution for organizing relations among diverse people, and it cannot be justified in this way. To do so would be to put arbitrary power over others into the hands of everyone, making life impossible for all.

The Social Utility of Property

The third argument takes the subject to a new dimension. The idea is that we should have an institution of property because that institution promotes the social good: It enhances wealth, and maybe other good things. It focuses responsibility: It is up to him who owns something to use it with care so as to avoid damage to others, and of course to maintain or enhance its value to himself. It enables people to make effective and efficient decisions. If you own it, you may use it without having to ask anyone else—without having to get a license, as would invariably be the case under socialism, say. And so on.[7]

Adam Smith famously described the operation of private property in a free market as increasing the wealth of nations "as if by an invisible hand." The metaphor has resounded ever since, for good reason. For we do indeed expect, and observe, that the wealth of many is enhanced by the market activities made possible by ownership. A selling X to B increases both A's well-being—since he otherwise wouldn't sell it—and B's, since he wouldn't otherwise buy it. But additionally, the result enables each to turn to others with different and improved sets of resources, enabling still further enhancement in future trades. There is no magic and no requirement that citizens have a view to the good of society. All they need is to be interested in promoting their own situation and be ready to abide by the rights of property in others. Given these very frequently instantiated conditions, the wealth of society is enhanced—hugely enhanced, as time goes by.[8]

The question is, how do these facts matter? Do we adopt private property as an institution because we expect those good results? There is a problem about doing so. For as noted above, the good results flow only if people respect others' property rights. In order for that condition to be observed, it must be meaningful antecedently to the exchange activity that is at the heart of the social argument. And so it appears that the social argument cannot be fundamental. What it can be, however, is a powerful recommendation of recognizing the fundamental liberal right.

It is not clear whether the arguments we have considered settle such important contemporary questions as whether Smith's house may be taken over by the State when it judges that it would be better if that particular bit of the earth were occupied instead by a school, an airport, a hospital, an expressway, or whatever. Pure libertarianism does not allow incursions of that sort. The American Constitution, renowned as a liberty-based document, gives its citizens a right against "unreasonable searches and seizures." It doesn't talk about eminent domain and whether the document would uphold eminent domain is an interesting and difficult question. But one thing is clear: Eminent domain really does curtail the liberty of the individual, at least in the shorter run.

Do property rights curtail the liberty of the people who would like to utilize other people's property in ways that the original property owners object to? The pure libertarian points out that the right of liberty is mutual and that everything must proceed by agreement. The original property holder, we suppose, does not agree: He'd rather keep his house than have a hospital on the spot. While others would prefer the hospital, they need to invade the original person's property to do so. He, on the other hand, does no invading by refusing to allow his property to be taken.

Imagine an old house occupied by two elderly codgers. They are not well off and are sitting on a fortune in real estate. But they like it there and don't want to sell. So they don't, and the parties interested in their property are told bluntly by the courts to go home and live with it. Now, here is a case where many will think that our third argument is in conflict with our first. If property is justified because it makes things so much better, then if in a particular case they would be made still better by exercising a right of eminent domain, why not exercise it?

But would exercising eminent domain in this case "make things better"? Not according to those elderly fellows. The first argument's answer is Sorry, but you must ask the person whose property is desired. That person is the authority on it, and that's that. The rules of ownership are for mutual advantage; they cannot favor someone at the expense of someone else, even if the someone favored is a whole lot of people.

Many modern condominium communities create rules, in advance, that those who join agree to by joining and that specify common property that can't be altered at the behest of one or a few but can at the hands of a majority vote of the residents. That is unproblematic. But shall we say that nonvoluntary communities may have the same structure? The classic liberal says No.

The reader is going to have to make up his or her mind about this one—a crucial case, certainly, for the libertarian view and the minimal state. A State exercising the right of eminent domain is no longer "minimal": It is not merely enforcing property rights, it is using its judgment about when to overturn them. Is that the way we want to go? Many people apparently think we should say Yes. Is society a condominium, in which all have agreed to give up their properties when a "greater social need" is demonstrated? Not obviously. Condominium properties are themselves owned by a corporation or some other private parties, but society at large is not. The only people there are to set the rules are—the people there are! If not all of them would agree to certain rules affecting themselves, why should the majority who do be able, nevertheless, to rule over the minority who do not?

THE FREE MARKET

A free market is a social system in which all respect everyone else's property rights, and only against that crucial constraint do they make whatever exchanges they want to and can. There is no authority external to the particular individuals encountering each other with their various wares and services to do anything more than make sure that no one robs, defrauds, or uses violence against anyone else. (Note that there is redundancy in this list. To defraud or to rob is to use violence against others—those are not different things, parts of a longer list of what is wrong. They are simply the more specific sorts of violences that are more directly relevant to most market activity.)

To understand the free market, we must avoid confusion at the hands of a popular theoretical fantasy: the "perfectly competitive market." In such a supposed market, not only do people own things and seek to improve their situations by exchange but also everybody knows everything about all the goods and services offered. There are no costs of exchange ("transaction costs") other than the values of the items exchanged, and there are no "externalities," that is, side effects such that some people benefit from others' exchanges without paying, or pay without benefiting. There are so many sellers of anything that no one can alter a price by unilateral say-so: If you raise your price, your market vanishes; if you lower it, your costs exceed your income.[9]

"Perfect competition" is impossible; we always have limited information, transaction costs, imperfect competition, and externalities. But the perfectly free market, on the other hand, can happen, and is often approximated. Of course, the chief causes of departure are taxes and regulations, which artificially impose restrictions on market activity. Force and fraud do happen but are comparatively infrequent. But limited information, transaction costs, less competition than someone might like, and many externalities are compatible with freedom. You are allowed to be ignorant, to refrain from jumping into a market just because there aren't very many already there, and to try to charge higher prices than people would like. The only feature of the many stipulated by the "perfectly competitive" model that is importantly present in the free market is respect for property rights. When we list the attractions of the market, we assume compliance. We know that it does not always happen, and among the major problems of society is that of dealing with thieves, liars, forgers, and other frauds as well as people willing to murder others for money. Classical liberals do insist on government's dealing with these. But abandoning capitalism goes too far, insists the liberal. After all, the alternatives we know of—socialism, for example—do not so much solve these problems as institutionalize them. Twentieth-century socialist States, for example, were prize polluters, and its chiefs wholesale thieves of their citizens' money. Plenty of self-described dictators are among the world's richest men.[10]

What has the free market to recommend it, then? The whole point of the free market is indeed freedom—to decide what you shall produce, if anything, and what you shall buy, if anything, and always to have the right to say No. This, so the libertarian proposes, is a social good to be cherished above all. Indeed, the libertarian claims that it is the precondition of all other good things in society. This last claim is strongly denied by the modern liberal, who will also claim that the more extensive welfare state actually enhances freedom. We will be exploring the latter's case later (chapter 7).

To be sure, feedom would be an odd thing to value "in itself." We want to be free because we want to do various things and therefore want not to be prevented from doing them. When we have liberty, we can act, and we can hope to gain from those actions. That freedom enables great wealth is, of course, one of its selling points. But much more important than that is the fact that those who make this great wealth make it in such a way as to benefit a great many of the rest of us. On a free market, that is the only way we can gain: by selling to others who don't have to buy, and therefore who may be expected to be gaining, in their own view, from the transaction.

The attractions of the free market above are striking, and well recognized. Why, then, is it so unpopular among social theorists and practical politicians alike? The reason, I think, is that there is one immediate and important phenomenon to be concerned with, creating an issue that takes us very directly to the heart of the matter. In the free market, what people have the right to is freedom. They do not have what we have identified above as positive rights. Someone with a flourishing business has the right to the profits he may make from trade. He also runs a risk of losing his shirt if his customers decide to go elsewhere. They just may do that, for competitors are often lurking around the next corner, ready to pounce with superior products or lower prices. Those competitors may be turning out products very much like yours for a quarter of the cost because they have invented fantastic labor-saving devices or because they have been able to hire production workers in far-off places at 15¢ per hour instead of $15. At this point, the well-paid local workers will complain. They are used to this job at this wage, and now, suddenly, it promises to evaporate before their very eyes. The cries for protection will go up.

The free market doesn't guarantee anyone anything except freedom: You may take any offers you can get, and make any offers you like. But you never have the right that somebody else must accept your offer, or make you a better one. The "local workers" referred to above are the ones who haven't learned that. And it certainly isn't just "workers," for as Adam Smith also complained, business executives are forever turning to government to give them an unfair advantage over possible competition. They want a big tariff on foreign goods or subsidies for their industries. But the free market theorist points out, for example, that the very reason why current jobs pay so well is that ingenious people in the past have devised the machinery, or whatever, that we work with and that enable us to be so productive, and in developing it, they in turn put out of work many who were using methods too inefficient to be competitive. In short, the free market is a scene of constant change, constant revolution, for that matter. First it's megamachinery able to do ten times as much, then it's computers, now it's robots controlled by computers—and who knows what lies ahead?

All of these expected improvements make for new things we want or reduce the prices of things we already use; in either case, all who buy are better off. Meanwhile, if you become unemployed at job X, someone will come along and offer you job Y, or you can become self-employed. The new job Y might turn out to be better than X. Further, the effect of the competitor's improvements will be that their customers now have more to spend on something else, creating a challenge to more entrepreneurs to invent products or dream up services that will now attract their attention. Of course, this also creates new employment. Increased efficiency does not reduce employment overall; instead, it makes us all wealthier, in the longer run. That is a hard lesson to learn for those who lose well-paying jobs they liked. It is understandable that they worry—but intervention to prevent it is worse yet.

REAL INCOME IS THE POINT

One of the most elementary lessons of economics—but one that continually needs to be relearned—is that the point of working is not to accumulate piles of little green pieces of paper, but rather, to be able to acquire things one likes or needs, that others will provide in exchange for some of the income you get for making the things they need and like. To know about someone's "income," we need to know not the number of units of currency he commands but what he can do with it. If we compare the wages of worker A in 1990 with the same worker's wages in 2000, merely comparing the figures does not tell us enough. If A in 2000 earns the same number of dollars but his costs have gone up, then his real income is less; if they have declined, then his real income has gone up. Correcting for inflation helps, but there are problems it can't cope with. For the worker in 2000 can buy things that simply did not exist in 1990: cell phones, DVD players, superfast computers, and dozens of things that were not available at all in 1990 or were ten times the price. All of these products will be due to many people's ingenuity and hard work, and all of their effort will have been expended in hopes of making money—hopes that the more successful ones will have realized, sometimes to the extent of immense fortunes. We read now[11] that 1 in 800 American households has an income of more than $2 million per year, and 1 in 300 or so a net worth over $10 million. Meanwhile, the typical American "poor family" owns a sizable house, two cars, three TVs, and worries about overeating.

How could we have a "right" to a certain particular kind of job, employing a certain particular technology? In order for anyone to have such a right, people who offer that job would be liable to be compelled to offer it. That obviously violates the freedom of those people. Further, most jobs have features that simply did not exist a century earlier. How can we have a right to what doesn't exist? How is it that the "right" to do precisely that, and have other people subsidize your practice of it, began suddenly just when that job came into existence, even though it had been unheard of before?

The sort of rights that this kind of critic of the market calls for amounts to rights to technological ossification. We may be sure that farmers in the Egypt of 3000 B.C. used almost exactly the same tools and tilled their fields in the same way as their successors of 2000 B.C.—and, of course, that they were precisely as poor. A "guarantee" of this or that job is an incursion on the freedom of someone else. The society that keeps everything the same does so at enormous cost to the many people who would be improving their lives if only they could. Perhaps the conservative will maintain that the ancient Egyptians were better off than we are. They lived a third as long, ate exactly the same thing every day of their lives, and never traveled more than ten kilometers from home, but they were living the good life. Or were they? If we ask the peasant, we are likely to find that he'd prefer the life lived by those who rule over him, if he could, or the life lived by his descendants of four millennia later, who travel the world, eat well, and attend interesting entertainment events three times a week.

And finally, if there are some who still prefer stability and poverty, the free society says that they are welcome to form their own closed communities in which they have virtually no contact with outsiders. If those who do this also complain about their poverty, the reply is that they have but to emerge from their ghettos, taking their chances but in all likelihood surging very far ahead of where they were before.

The reference to "getting ahead" requires a note as well. Talk about the "Rat Race" of the free market is familiar—about how it corrupts people's souls by compelling them all to "get ahead" and that the free market exalts competitiveness and smothers cooperation. But this is a misunderstanding. Workers in the free market society are indeed trying to "get ahead," but not ahead of their neighbors; rather, they hope to get ahead of where they were yesterday. There's all the difference in the world. People will sometimes, no doubt, be competitive in the other sense as well, but nothing about the free market requires this. In the nature of the case, indeed, the free market doesn't require much at all, only that you refrain from making your way by fraud, theft, or violence. What you want to accomplish is your business. But how you do it is not: Always, you are restricted to the methods of peaceful mutual benefit. Given that, then anything goes, including the choice to prefer a life of indolence and nonproductiveness.

The market is also in fact cooperative, even if it may not at first look like it. We cooperate when we refrain from using force and fraud; we cooperate when we buy products that are the result of thousands of persons' efforts, coordinated by the pursuit of income. Every market transaction requires cooperation in the form of respecting the rights of those with whom we interact. Bad luck does happen, but unless the effects of innovation are clouded by bad policy, anyone should expect to benefit from the free activities of others, in the not very long run. Prudence, of course, recommends saving in any case, and millions of people have retirement schemes or stock portfolios with the same effect. But in general, increasing wealth makes for increased security as well.

EFFORT, WEALTH, AND REWARD

By now, it is generally agreed that capitalism is very much superior to socialism. Why so? Basically, it is because capitalism is simply the systematic, institutional recognition of the fact that people are individuals, with interests and intelligence and energy that they direct to the pursuit of those interests. All effort is somebody's effort, the effort of some particular persons interested in achieving something. The returns awaiting those who do this well are intrinsic to the activity. It is misleading to say that profits are "rewards," as though a committee somewhere gets together and decides to pin a medal on this or that entrepreneur. That image is entirely wrong. People who buy do so because they like what they see at the price asked. They have no intention of "rewarding" anybody: They simply make a good purchase. The entrepreneurs who pay their employees do not "reward" them either; rather, they buy their services, paying them the agreed wage or salary for doing what they were hired to do. Those who go to the trouble and expense of investing in productive enterprises that meet success, in that this particular organization of production enables them to make a profit from sales, realize the favorable results of their efforts, and that's all. But it's enough.

In today's complex world, capital is considerably and increasingly international—"globalized" as we now say. The reasons for this are familiar. A large company can separate the different portions of the productive process, putting some operations in country A, some in B, some in C. It can even have employees in, say, India, doing some of the work while production-line workers in Singapore do some more, and sales people and managers work back in Toronto. This enables them to locate each part of the enterprise in the part of the world where that part can be done most efficiently, thus reducing overall costs and so lowering the price of their ultimate products. The result is to spread the benefits of enterprise around the world, to the advantage of all. (We return to that subject in chapter 8.)

INEQUALITY OF WEALTH

The free market permits all voluntary exchanges (provided, as always, that those exchanges in turn respect the freedom of others). Many of these will render some parties markedly more prosperous than others. I noted above that in the United States, 1 in every 300 or so households has assets worth over $10 million. We also read that "the richest 2 percent of adults own more than half of global household wealth . . ." and that 27 percent of the wealthiest 1 percent are Japanese.[12] Such figures disturb many people. Should they? The free marketer says that they should not, or at least that the disparities are no ground, in themselves, for forcible intervention, such as by government or thieves, to do something about the situation. But because of the way market fortunes are made, such interventions make everyone else poorer, too. If they reduce the spread from rich to poor, they also further impoverish the poor. So insists the classical liberal. Perhaps no one issue is more typical of the distinction between the classical liberal and the contemporary writers broadly termed "liberal," whose ideas we will be considering in chapter 6. These "new" liberals, as we might call them, call for government-compelled equalization, social security, medical care for all, and so on—a very great departure from the free society as understood by classic liberalism.

THIRD-PARTY EFFECTS AND PUBLIC GOODS

There are two very different kinds of criticisms of the market. One comes from the egalitarians, who think there is something wrong with the situation in which some do better than others. We will address that kind of view later. The other comes from the general category of "externalities." This is of enormous importance and is the subject of this section.

Broadly speaking, an externality is an effect on nonconsenting parties that matters to them. Everything we do has some effects on others, of course, but most such are completely trivial—the alteration by a few blocks, as I walk to work, of the distance from me to someone in Shanghai is of no interest to anyone. Economics in the liberal vein is concerned with transactions, specifically voluntary transactions, done with eyes open and a view to benefit for each intentional participant. But it can happen that although the central event is A's getting x from B, and B's getting y from A, yet some other party C is also affected for better or worse, even though C didn't ask for this. In the case where the effect on C is desired, it's called a "positive" externality, and in the case where it is undesired, it's "negative." We should also perhaps include the extremely important case in which A's effects on B are negative and undesired by B but deliberately administered by A in order to be so. B can do nothing about them at the time. This too is an externality, but in a quite different way, and not our subject here: violence, fraud, injury, and in general the intentional worsening of someone's situation by someone else have been the object of our main attention in earlier chapters. Those externalities are the direct enemies of freedom. But our interest here is in the side effects of market activity. These are important because insofar as they occur, they may upset the normal presumption of market activity, which is mutual benefit for those involved, while those not involved are presumed to be unaffected. But in the nature of things others are often affected nonetheless.

Public goods are a special kind of externality. They are goods whose producers cannot confine their production in such a way as to benefit only voluntary purchasers. Sometimes it is said that they are goods such that either "everyone" gets them or "no one" gets them. There are no such things, though; but if there were, the difficulty of making money by transferring them only to those who will pay would be enormous. Theorists tend to invoke the State as a way of controlling what are claimed to be such effects. Thus, the State might tax people so that no one can be a "free rider"—one who benefits from others' efforts without paying. Otherwise, their existence creates a disincentive for the would-be producer, who can't make a profit if his intended customers can get it for nothing anyway. As noted, nothing is such that either everybody gets it or nobody does; always, there is some control by producers and consumers, as well as considerable variation in degree from one affected person to another.

The other effect is the "assurance problem." Suppose that A proposes to create a public good, and B is deciding whether to pay to help produce it. But, B reasons, if enough other people pay, B will get it anyway. And if not enough do so that it is not worth A's while to produce it, then B would have wasted his money. What to do?

There is a widespread tendency to assert that we must resort to the State at this point. Those who say this, however, speak too quickly. Assurance problems can be solved without recourse to the State. For example, would-be supplier A starts a list of subscribers, and if enough people subscribe, he supplies the good. If not enough do, he promises to refund the ones who did, or alternatively does not collect in the first place. By contrast, with taxation, all are compelled to pay, including many who wouldn't buy if they had their choice. Advocates of government action in such matters need to ask whether the evils presumably done by public goods are so bad that imposing the costs of prevention on everyone is justifiable. The classical liberal argues that the answer, virtually always, is in the negative.[13]

A NOTE ON UTILITARIANISM

One of the standard theories in moral philosophy is known as utilitarianism, the term coined by John Stuart Mill to designate the theory that the fundamental criterion of right conduct or good policy is the maximization of utility. There is considerable disagreement about just what "utility" should mean for this purpose, but none about maximization. We sum the gains and losses of everyone affected by the actions or programs or institutions being considered, and account those that yield the highest net sum the best—"net" in the sense that losses and gains are completely integrated, so that an action causing A a gain of ten and B a loss of five gives a net gain of five. If the utilitarian criterion is allowed in our discussion of public goods, then an easy way (theoretically) to justify the interventions so often used to cope with third-party effects is to hold that those who lose less than those who gain, so that the sum of good is maximized after all.

This "easy way" is, as I parenthetically noted, "theoretical," for in the first place, interpersonal comparison of utility, no matter how that notion is construed, is a major stumbling block for the theory. Can we really say that Jones has advanced six units while Smith has been set back but four? Taken literally (with talk of "units") the answer, of course, is in the negative, as all serious students of the subject agree. But this doesn't stop people from being utilitarians; there is often a kind of gut sense that something near enough does obtain and that sustains hope for the theory.

Second, however, a different problem stems directly from the nub of our major issues, which concern the relation of the individual to the group, and thus to the State. For if we take it that the point of State action is the common good, so that all must agree—no individual being sacrificed for the sake of any other—then the problem with utilitarianism is one of simple irrelevance. Individual Jones is typically not mollified, when visited with a loss, by the fact that somebody else has gained more than he, Jones, has lost. Classical individualism is founded on the social contract idea, not on the aggregate-good idea. If anyone is hard done by, without compensation, then the game is off.

There are various possible responses to this by those inclined to see more in utilitarianism than I do. (The reader is warned that I was once a utilitarian, and I rank as an apostate in their ranks: I came to see, as I would put it, that the doctrine is fundamentally flawed.[14]) One respectable response is that utilitarianism will, if well applied, work out for the benefit of each individual anyway, for in the longer run, the number of times the individual wins from this procedure exceeds, or exceeds in total degree, the number of times he loses. A problem with this response is that, first, it's very difficult to do the sort of arithmetic that would be needed to confirm any claims of this kind, and, second, that for the people who, for example, lose their lives early in the process, it really doesn't look very promising.

Another response, less respectable, is simply to pooh-pooh the individualist critique. Now, each of us is an individual, and we do have only one life, and it is uniquely ours. If those points do not give us a strong basis for rejecting theories that see us as pawns or cyphers, those who want to take this line have their work cut out for them. Speaking as one of the 6 billion individuals on the planet, I am inclined to be dubious. At any rate, the point of view of this book is that utilitarianism as a fundamental theory is hopeless, and we will pay no further attention to it at that level. Occasional resort to sum-of-utility talk can be useful, but not as a fundamental theory.

"PUBLIC GOODS": AN AMBIGUITY

In fact, the term "public goods" is used ambiguously today. Its "official" sense, introduced by economists a century or so ago, is as discussed above. But it is also widely used, simply, to refer to whatever goods are in fact being managed by the public, that is, by the State, whether or not they are public goods issues in the first sense. Roads and schools, opera houses, welfare, and the many other things that contemporary governments have gotten into are called "public goods," along with the former sort. Of course, the effect of this is to confuse issues. For the claim that something is a public good in the first sense is plausibly employed as a reason why government should involve itself in them, but that sense does not in fact apply to more than a very small proportion of what the public actually does. Health, education, and welfare, to take three major areas, are not intrinsically public goods. You can be healthy while I am not; measures to improve Jones's health may have no effect whatever on Smith; one person's education or welfare does not entail another's, and so on. If these latter things are to be defended on some kind of public goods grounds in the first sense, then subtler arguments are required—not just question-begging labeling.

INFRASTRUCTURE AND "NATURAL MONOPOLY"

An interesting example for analysis is what we now call "infrastructure"—roads, gas lines, bridges, canals, and many other of what are sometimes called "public works." Most important, perhaps, is the supply of money, to which we'll devote a separate section. These are almost universally accepted as proper subjects for government supply. Should they be? The arguments used in support are generally public goods arguments. The argument is that these things are natural monopolies, in the sense that competitive supply is impossible: just one electrical grid in an area, just one bridge over that river, and so on.

The claimed natural monopoly is never perfect, of course. Any and all of these things could be and all have at various times and places been supplied by private initiative. And then, the claimed publicity of the service is also imperfect. Does everybody use the roads? Not quite. But the individual who doesn't drive or possess a car nevertheless gets whisked to the hospital in a motor vehicle when he suffers a heart attack, your groceries are much cheaper and much easier to acquire because of the vehicles that bring them to the store, and so on.

While all that is true enough, it is also true that even roads don't have to be under the control of governments. Public appropriation of this category is easy. It would, arguably, be inefficient to be charging particular users for using particular roads. But this isn't conclusive. Private roads have existed, still exist, and were once frequent, we are told. Even in the case of long-distance superhighways (expressways, motorways), private ownership is possible, and happens. Ingenuity has enabled modern toll highways to reduce the transaction costs of toll collection to modest levels; frequent users buy a device that records onto a sensor as they enter the highway, and again upon leaving, the user then being billed for that session onto a credit card. These are technically soluble problems, and solutions are even now coming into widespread use. The capital investments required for major roads are very high, true—but then, modern corporations command huge sums.

Even neighborhoods in cities and towns could operate streets in a different way. Each homeowner, for example, might also own a fraction of the street out in front. User policy has to be set by someone, but it is easy to see that systems would rapidly emerge for the purpose. The main difference between public and private ownership would be that the private citizen would make his own decision about costs, in consultation with the most relevant others (fellow residents of the block, to start with), rather than having some external committee make his choice, and his cost assessments, for him. And in all likelihood, the private option would enable both cost savings and considerable variation in the level and type of maintenance and even the visual attractiveness of the streets and roads thus administered and produced.

We read of an interesting experiment in several cities of Europe in which all traffic signs are abolished in certain urban areas where automobile travel is substantial. This is reported to be having good results, as individual motorists watch out for each other, take care, and take turns all on their own.[15] This will astonish most readers, who probably think that infrastructure without government, including government supervision and control, is impossible. But any number of examples show that that is simply not true. The arguments for government involvement are strong, yes—but the claim that they are strong to the point where the alternative is simply out of the question is not true, and in fact there is a good deal to be said for private ownership. If you survey the skyline of Manhattan and realize that overwhelmingly what you see is private property—not public—then surely the idea that what you see at street level could be so as well should not be dismissed. It does not follow from the fact that streets and the rest could be privately owned that they should be, but neither should the very possibility be rejected out of hand.

In Adam Smith's time, in fact, bridges and most other "public" constructions were in fact capitalized by private companies but with loans underwritten by the government. Even today, of course, all "public" construction is by private companies working to contract. An important issue in many of these cases is whether the contracts were tendered fairly, and town councils or citizen groups worry if the lowest bid is not taken and want to know why. We will say more about such matters below (see equality and fairness, in chapter 6); the point here is simply to put on the reader's agenda the possibility that many current public services could be provided in a very different way and that it is not simply obvious that the other way is not better. The argument against public ownership and management is elemental: It necessarily involves compelling some to support what they would prefer not to. Private ownership, by contrast, is inherently voluntary. The classical liberal infers that we should have a strong general bias against making anything public if it can function privately instead.

Whatever we conclude about private ownership as a possible method for providing infrastructure, the further question is whether we can include it under the "minimal state." It is obvious why we need police, whether private or public. It is arguably obvious as well that we need roads and other such things. But is that enough to qualify them for inclusion in the minimal state? If so, the question arises: minimal for what? And where would it end? This is a serious question, not a rhetorical one. Suppose we could show that State provision of some such service as health care would actually benefit us all. Will the classical libertarian still object? But, on what ground? On this point, I side with Everyman. I don't think Everyman has a sense of individual rights of such a kind that we should prefer the heavens falling to the violation of even one of them. I do think that Everyman wants the system that works out best for him, given that it also works out best for everyone else, and whatever the look of that system may be.

Even so, the case for individualism is extremely strong, in part because the cases for social intervention are so riddled with problems. One recent writer says,

> there are grounds for believing that today's welfare states have done more harm than good to their intended beneficiaries, at least in part because high social overhead costs have priced low marginal productivity workers out of employment, fostered a dependency culture, and broken the ladders of opportunity through which poor people self-improved in the past.[16]

He is addressing the welfare state in particular, but the charge is generalizable. Precisely because we are all individual people, with a huge variety of specific interests and needs, it is extremely difficult for a centralized political agency to refrain from using its vast powers in ways that work ill because they do not need to secure the agreement of each and every person affected by their actions. That is what the classical liberal is worried about, and he is right to worry.

SOUND MONEY

One of the tasks that has fallen to government, even in the classic view, is that of establishing and maintaining the monetary system. Almost all economic activity takes place via the medium of money. Rarely do we exchange goods or services directly—"barter" as it's called. Rather, we use money, the medium of exchange. Historically, money has often been embodied in bits of valuable stuff, especially gold. But gold is a bit of a nuisance to carry around, and of course there isn't nearly enough of it either, for the modern world's extremely high level of economic activity. For a long time, paper money has been employed, but maintaining the value of those pieces of paper turns out to be both extremely important and very tricky. The cost of gold production is enormous; the cost of printing one more dollar bill is virtually nil. Thus the temptation, with a government-produced currency, is always there—to solve its problem by simply printing more dollars. And that is a disaster for any monetary system.

What is especially important is that the same face-value lot of money will continue to have the same value; that is, be exchangeable for the same lot of goods or services from one day to the next. How to measure that, however, isn't so easy, for one thing, in part because modern economies continually produce new goods, not easily comparable to the old ones. We can't here go into the complexities of banking theory. We can, however, again point out that it is not actually a matter of necessity that this be done by governments. It is one of the many functions that the State has assumed to itself, and in the process has managed to convince almost everybody that it is the only institution that could possibly do this. It is simply not so.

The importance of this function can be appreciated when we contemplate economic history. Above all, there is the Great Depression of 1928–1941, during which unemployment in the United States shot up into the two-figures category and stayed there for more than a decade, while economic activity ground to its lowest comparative level in history—and any number of people solemnly concluded that this demonstrated the inadequacies of capitalism. What it did demonstrate, as it turns out, was the extreme incompetence of the new Federal Reserve Board, supplemented by wrong-headed policies by the governments of the United States, both the Hoover and then the several Roosevelt administrations. Between one policy and another, an enormous amount of suffering, quite possibly including World War II, can be laid to the door of bad government management of money, though some lay the blame more, or at least equally, on fiscal as distinct from monetary policy. We now know, pretty much, what we did wrong, and those particular errors, we can hope, will not be repeated. But it is also fairly clear that the whole thing would never have happened had the money supply not been in government hands but instead been a function of competing private suppliers of money, maintained in value by market forces. "What failed in the 1930s were governments, in their eagerness to direct activity to achieve political ends—ends that were often contradictory."[17]

That is a large subject that is only mentioned here. What is perfectly clear, however, is that if government is going to manage money, then it must do so with a view to maintaining its value as steadily as possible, never succumbing to the ever-present urge to solve government deficit problems by simply printing more money. Without that reliability, the private market will function badly (and the "public market" will become oppressive and dysfunctional). To invest money—a rather long-run involvement—when you can't be sure that it will have nearly the same value a year from now, is to take a risk that can easily be seen as unacceptable, thus inhibiting that investment, even if it would otherwise be sound. Meanwhile, the temptation to turn to the printing press, on the part of politically powerful persons, is enormous. It's much easier to tell people that they are doing well since more "dollars" are flowing into their hands than to admit that things are going badly and that those dollars are not real dollars but, increasingly, just pieces of paper. "Easy" money is an economic catastrophe.[18]

PRODUCTIVITY

Capitalism has been celebrated, including by its famous critic Karl Marx, for its productiveness. And it's true, of course. But productivity is an easily misunderstood virtue. The prior question is Just what should be produced? An economic system that produces vast amounts of useless stuff is not what we want. When capitalism is celebrated, it is because it produces so much of what we do want, rather than what we don't. True, it produces a lot of what some people don't want others to have, but why is that a relevant complaint? And sometimes the production in question is claimed to be not "needed." Critics often deplore the dozen different brands of identical stuff to be found on the grocery shelves in capitalism's domains. In doing so, they cross the line from liberalism to conservatism: They claim to know what you and I should want, and when we purchase in such a way as to call forth seemingly pointless variety, they deplore its pointlessness, but they don't consult us on the point. If my neighbor pays $1 for a bottle of Aspirin while I pay 30¢ for a bottle of no-name but otherwise identical ASA tablets, these critics lament the capitalist system. But neither I nor my neighbor does so. And of course, when it comes to things where there is a difference, though subtle, the critics need to be shown the door. To some of us, it matters that the item looks like *this* rather than (yech!) like *that*, and we are ready to pay for the difference.

Capitalism is productive because people have their choice; they can say "no!" and you, the producer, can make money satisfying their wants, even when they are whimsical. However, doing so will require careful attention to those wants. The ones who get it right can make fortunes because they are making a lot of people happier than they would otherwise have been.

Or are they? Well, at least, they will have more nearly satisfied their desires. If this is not the same thing, the question is, what to do about it? Should we appoint a committee of experts to tell us what makes us truly happy? Do we need to do more than mention the possibility to see that we will reject it? Nowhere is the battle line between liberalism and illiberalism more clearly drawn than here. Capitalism requires respect for property and individual choice. The consumer is monarch, indeed emperor. Capitalists make money if and only if they give the consumer what he or she wants, but if they do hit it right, the sky is the limit. To this the classical liberal says, "Go thy way in peace, brother!"

In so saying, classical liberalism has the distinction of, very nearly, modeling politics on economics. The point of politics is to supply the goods and services people want. Classical liberals are impatient with governments that try to tell the man on the street what to do or to inspire him with vague ideas of the "nation" and patriotism. If he is grateful to the State, it will be because the State gets him what he wants. What he's really grateful for, therefore, is freedom—insofar as he gets it. That freedom inspires many people not only to practice variant religions, or none, to create idiosyncratic works of art, and so on, but also to go into business, providing people with the many things they want, and no doubt stimulating new desires as well. But each thing that people buy is paid for, and so the customers really owe nothing to the businesspeople who provide it. We all owe major thanks to the system that allows all this to happen.

The classical liberal points out that everything that government claims to do for us is done at a price: taxes, and a great many impositions. The effect of these is to subsidize some people at public cost so that they gain at the expense of others—the very thing that individuals are properly forbidden to do and that it is a large part of the point of the State to prevent. Classical liberalism throws down a challenge to those who think of government as a great good.

In recent times, the word "liberal" is typically used in such a way as to imply a very much more extensive range of involuntarily supported services than the classical theorist would allow. Is this new version of "liberalism" called that only by mistake? Recent governments undertake a great deal: education, health, welfare, safety, the regulation of almost everything, and the pursuit of what is claimed to be justice, fairness, and equality. Why is this called liberal? The short answer is that it still claims to be giving us what we want, although the line between liberalism and conservatism is worn very thin in the process, as we will see. This new version of the liberal state is the welfare state: Government claims the right to promote the goal of increasing the welfare of its citizens by its special methods of taxation, regulation, and control. We consider it in chapter 6.

OTHER LIBERAL RIGHTS

Liberalism is typically characterized in a much more elaborate way than it has been so far in this book. For example, it will be said that liberalism involves "autonomy, guaranteeing that every citizen can choose her own reasonable conception of the good . . . a commitment to moral equality and tolerance . . . [and to] uphold basic rights and freedoms, including freedom of conscience, speech, movement within the state, the rule of law and democratic institutions. Finally, most liberals take pluralism to be basic to contemporary states: Reasonable people disagree about substantial moral and ethical issues."[19] To the above we should add freedom of lifestyle (currently a major example being gay marriage), and of association.

These more elaborate characterizations tend to ignore or attach no importance to the distinction between negative and positive rights. But that distinction is absolutely crucial to the classic view. On that view, the citizen of course should be able to enjoy all of the things on that list—construed as negative rights. To do what we wish so long as we refrain from injuring others in the process is to have freedom of conscience, speech, movement, our choice of "conceptions of the good," and more. It of course requires, as a fundamental feature, tolerance and respect. Does it require the rule of law? Recalling our discussion in chapter 1, it is based on a wise understanding of what the rule of law is, but it does not permit States to make a huge range of laws such as they do now.

Much space could be devoted to these freedoms taken as separate items. For example, what is freedom of speech? Not, certainly, the right to say whatever you like, anywhere you like, any time. Consistently with classic liberalism, this right must be the right to say whatever one likes to whomever is willing to hear under the circumstances, but even then, we have to worry about conspiracy. Do we want to say that the members of al Qaeda have the right to talk freely about their next terrorist event, with no fear of interruption by outsiders? Presumably not. Similar things need to be said for all of the others. Freedoms may be abridged when they enable their possessors to abridge the legitimate freedoms of others.

Do freedoms need to be itemized? The classic view is not really. For general freedom, always with the same restriction that what one does is not to impact negatively on others, implies all more specific freedoms. And after all, we differ. One liberal freedom will mean little to Smith, a great deal to Jones. If we have an itemized list, what about items not on the list? The liberal formula, on the other hand, takes in them all. The "list" view is currently popular, but not, I think, for good reason.[20] But we'll return to that, a bit, in chapter 6.

What about democratic institutions? These new functions are closely associated with the rise of democracy. Indeed, no one today advocates a nondemocratic welfare state, even though that would not only be perfectly possible but also has actually happened. (The welfare state was initiated by a State that would hardly be considered a democracy today, and certainly not initiated by democratic means—instead it was imposed by the German "Iron Chancellor" Otto von Bismarck in 1883.)

Laws are good only if they allow us to do as we want; democracy is not obviously a good in the same sense. It is a very special case. Whether and why it should be thought a good thing, then, is what we will consider next, in chapter 5. We then return to the welfare state in the following chapter.

NOTES

1. John Rawls, *A Theory of Justice* (Cambridge, MA: Harvard University Press, 1971), which has become a modern classic.

2. John Locke, *Second Treatise of Civil Government* (1690), 138.

3. Locke, *Second Treatise of Civil Government*, section 138.

4. Ayn Rand, "Government Financing in a Free Society," in *The Virtue of Selfishness* (New York: Signet Books, 1961), chapter 15, 116–120.

5. This familiar characterization comes from the Web: http://en.wikipedia.org/wiki/Night_watchman_state.

6. In this I am much helped by many others, notably Jan Lester. See his *Escape from Leviathan: Liberty, Welfare, and Anarchy Reconciled* (New York: St. Martin's Press, 2000).

7. This aspect of property was emphasized by Aristotle. See his *Politics*, Book II, especially chapter iii.

8. For a more thorough account of why it works that way, see Jan Narveson, "The Invisible Hand," *Journal of Business Ethics*, vol. 46, no. 3 (2003): 201–212.

9. For a typical characterization of this "ideal market," see Allen Buchanan, *Ethics, Efficiency, and the Market* (Totowa, NJ: Rowman and Allanheld, 1985), 14–15.

10. As a delightful example, Forbes lists Fidel Castro's wealth at over $550 million: www.forbes.com/billionaires/2005/03/07/cz_bill05_royalsslide_6.html?thisSpeed= 40000.

11. "Now" was 2006 when this was written.

12. As reported in the Toronto *Globe and Mail* (December 5, 2006): A12–A13.

13. A superb general discussion of public goods effects is found in David Schmidtz, *The Limits of Government: An Essay on the Public Goods Argument* (Boulder, CO: Westview, 1991).

14. For my earlier efforts, see Jan Narveson, *Morality and Utility* (Baltimore, MD: Johns Hopkins University Press, 1967).

15. http://www.spiegel.de/international/spiegel/0,1518,448747,00.html.

16. David B. Smith, *Living with Leviathan: Public Spending, Taxes, and Economic Performance* (London: Institute of Economic Affairs, 2006), 18.

17. Gene Smiley, *Rethinking the Great Depression* (Chicago, IL: Ivan R. Dee, 2002), 162. His book makes a readably short summary of the extensive research supporting that general conclusion.

18. The reader may benefit greatly from consulting one of several fine, clearly written books about economics, such as James W. Gwartney and Richard Stroup's *What Everyone Should Know about Wealth and Prosperity* (Vancouver: Fraser Institute, 1993); pp. 53–58 are about money supply.

19. Taken from an anonymous paper under referee. I choose it as being perfectly typical.

20. One of the most influential among recent writers along this line is Ronald Dworkin, whose "We Do Not Have a Right to Liberty" is widely anthologized. See Ronald Dworkin, *Taking Rights Seriously* (Cambridge, MA: Harvard University Press, 1977, especially chapter 12, "What Rights Do We Have?," starting with "No Right to Liberty," 266–272. See the same author's "The Place of Liberty" in *Sovereign Virtue* (Cambridge, MA: Harvard University Press, 2000), 120–183.

5

Democracy

All Power to the People?

"DEMOCRACY" DEFINED: DIVIDING POLITICAL POWER

Democracy has been the subject of a great deal of interest, and not a little of alarmed concern. Among the subjects of current debate is whether it is either possible or useful to define a term like "democracy." As usual, my answer to that question is in the affirmative. In fact, I think it is essential to produce a definition that gets to the basic features, for the things denoted by the many other "definitions" are so significantly different that very different considerations would apply to what they denote. So here is my general definition: Democracy is *the equal division of fundamental political power among all the governed.*

As we noted earlier, the ancients discussed constitutions under the headings of "the one, the few, and the many." The term "democracy" has a remarkably clear derivation in this connection: It means rule (the "cracy" bit) by the many (the "demos"). Ancient Athens is cited as a classic example of democracy, yet we are told that perhaps 10 percent of its inhabitants were citizens entitled to vote. Plato regarded democracy as a particularly degenerate kind of system, irresponsibly turning over political power to the "mob." All this points in the right direction, though. If democracy is to be rule by "the people," then it would be misleading to say this unless what was meant was all the people—the "mob," then. No way around that. The Athenians may have regarded the 90 percent excluded as not exactly "people." But it's better to say that they are wrong about that, or more precisely, that democracy comprehends all those above childhood, possessed of the minimum amount of experience and reason necessary to get into political matters. Better still, we can recognize that democracy is a matter of degree,

Athens being fairly low down on the scale, contemporary democracies very high up on it. (In saying this last, I do not mean that Athenian society and civilization was inferior to ours. I mean that it was less democratic.)

The division of this power must be equal, too. Why equal? Because that's the point: If we don't want to entrust power to some one or some few, and we all want it, then turning it over to "us" in such a way that a few have most of it would be defeating the point. The logic of the situation points us overwhelmingly in the direction of equality of power.

The sort of equality in question for this purpose is happily easy to realize in concrete practice: one person, one vote. There are other conceivable ways in which we could share political power equally. Imagine instead that each citizen is the sole ruler for $1/n$ of the time, where n is the entire population: Queen for a day! Except, of course, that with many millions of citizens, it wouldn't be a day, but more like a few seconds, thus dramatically illustrating why government by taking turns is not a practicable proposition any more. We could also imagine a lottery in which the prize is dictatorship and the mechanism a perfectly fair lottery in which everyone participates equally. That result is perhaps worst of all. Such thought experiments support the voting mechanism as the way to go, if we are going to try to be democratic.

LEVELING SOCIAL CLASSES

One thing we expect of democracy is that it will not be a "class" society, in the older sense of the word in which there were aristocrats and commoners and maybe some other sets of people, each with their own special privileges or restrictions, and perhaps a bottom class with no privileges to speak of. But in democracy, everybody gets one vote, nobody gets more than one, and it doesn't matter what you wear or the size of your purse or whom you know at court, because what's going to happen is what the majority of all these miscellaneous people vote for—and that's it. That is how democracy is a kind of equality: equality, as I put it above, of fundamental political power.

The word "fundamental" here is essential. For government in all cases above the level of small villages is carried out not by all citizens, but by a quite small subset of them. In democracies, though, the main ones among those few persons—presidents, members of parliament, and so forth—are elected. Whether this leaves us with the society of "equals" hoped for by many enthusiasts for democracy is another question. Elective offices are rather few—few enough so that they can get "the job done," that is, the job of grinding out the laws, and then setting up and overseeing the administrative machinery by which those laws are carried out.

In the end, out from the legislature comes one single set of presumably consistent rules or laws—just one. The legislative buck stops somewhere, and that "somewhere" is the law. That's why a device such as majority rule is required. There has to be some way of going from the process in which legislators, typically a few hundred, deliberate, discuss, and then vote, to a single output that they have "decided" despite all their individual differences. We can be certain that those differences will be both numerous and deep.

Nor is that all. All democracies have not only legislatures but also executive branches of government, and whatever the process by which the executive comes to be selected, the people in it have, functionally speaking, much more power than ordinary citizens. What makes it a democracy is that all of those with more power have it because of the actions of many people who have the same amount, by use of their one vote each.

Now, the elected officials do in fact have more power than you or I. But they are not a "social class" in the old sense of the term, for it's not hereditary, and moreover, exists only by virtue of the power of the "lower" one. Still, if you point out to the officer that you have a vote, he is unlikely to be deterred for a moment from writing your ticket.

Many thorny questions of relative detail arise. Should incarcerated criminals get to vote? What do we do about people who do not vote? (At present, the usual answer is, Nothing: The offices go to those who get more votes than any other candidates, no matter how few of the electorate vote. But there are other options. In some countries, voting is required, like it or not. Or perhaps we should take seriously the wag who suggests that a non-vote should be considered a vote to abolish the office in question: If less than 50 percent vote, then we do without it!)

Another more serious problem is what to do if the winning candidate gets less than a majority, as is typical in modern countries, where three or more candidates for an office are typical. Do we simply select the candidate with the "plurality;" that is, more votes than anyone else? Or do we hold a "runoff" election? Again: Do we divide the country up into districts, and hold an election in each one, winner take all? It is well known that this could have the effect that a political party comes to power with less votes than its rival obtained in the election overall. Is that antidemocratic? Or not? Arguments can be given for both sides on this. Our definition of democracy does not settle those matters. But we must content ourselves for the present with the realization that there are problems of this kind, that they need solutions if democracy is to go forward, and that, as we say in academia, much work remains to be done. Still, they are questions of detail. The basic idea, that who governs is determined by (all) the people, remains the core idea.

UNLIMITED DEMOCRACY: THE "AGENDA" QUESTION

Does a democracy need anything else than the vote? "Having the vote" actually takes in quite a bit, when you think of it. Having it means being oriented toward abiding by the outcomes of elections. When side A wins and side B loses, B, after all, could take up arms and try to subdue the A side by force. It happens. But a country in which that happened often would have to be said not to understand what democracy is about. To have a real democracy is to have a set of citizens who are going to accept the results of elections, at least so long as the proclaimed election results are perceived to have been an accurate summary of what happened rather than marred by vote frauds.

But what else? If there is nothing else, then anything whatever can, in principle, come up for a vote. This should give us pause. Consider Hitler's Nazis, who won by plurality in the German election of 1933. Once in power, they abolished further elections. Can a democracy commit democratic suicide? The Nazi case illustrates a central question for democracy: Just what is a democratic electorate or its elected legislature to be permitted to consider? Is everything really available to be on the agenda? Is it consistent with democracy to vote on the proposal to flay John Jones alive for the general amusement? What is a 50 percent +1 vote to be allowed to bring about? What are those elected by such procedures permitted to do? On even the scantest consideration, we can see that the interests we hope will be served by democracy require restrictions on what we can vote about, well beyond the basic requirement that those who rule should have been elected first. Let's review some of those.

THE DEMOCRATIC CONSTITUTION

Answers to that question might be written up in a set of constitutional restrictions on the operation of the vote. This may seem paradoxical: How can democracy be restricted and still be democracy? But actually, there is a pretty good answer to that. The idea of democracy is equal fundamental political power, yes—but when? The unlimited agenda democracy might last a day. But one major set of restrictions could be aimed at making sure this continues over time; that is, at making democracy a stable, enduring system of government. The trouble with electing a lifetime dictator is that once he's in, we're out! If we are to continue to have this basic equality of power, a restriction on that would surely be necessary.

Here is a list of the main things needed for the preservation of democracy. Most democracies in fact do have most of these in some way or other, and all, I think, understand these rights to be implicit in the democratic system. Some of them may also be regarded as really ensuring the more basic idea of the rule of law. Aristotle, for example, regarded respect for the law as what divided acceptable democracies from sheer mob rule.[1]

The Right to Vote

To avoid the problem of self-extermination, we make voting a right, one that is *not itself subject to voting*. Whether you have the vote or not is determined solely by whether you are a competent member of the community (perhaps we exclude felons).

As we already saw, the prior question of just who is a "member" is an important one. Minimal competence, such as the ability to read the ballot, is a plausible criterion. That in fact raises a fundamental issue: If we thought, for instance, that political power should be proportional to intellectual ability, then we would already have departed from democracy as understood here and moved instead in the direction of intellectual aristocracy. John Stuart Mill's proposal to give plural votes to the intellectually or otherwise more capable would do this, for instance.[2]

Periodic Elections

Suppose that we elect the government, but once in, it's for life: we would have "democracy" for the time it takes to count the votes. But a government with no controls by the people after election is scarcely better than hereditary monarchy—the very thing we were trying to avoid. Clearly if democracy is to be realized, elections must be frequent enough so that if the people do not like what is going on, they can change it. How often? That is another important question of detail. Periods range from about one year (many village councils) to seven (the president of France). What determines it? Roughly, we may suggest, the probability that the government will have had time either to prove itself or to go wrong, in the eyes of its electorate. Two weeks is too short; in a modern society, it would be impossible to say that soon whether things were working out. After two years, though, the chances that things aren't going right, if they aren't, because of what this government has done, are quite good. After five, they are excellent. This is not decidable by purely abstract considerations independent of local peculiarities, and variations are only to be expected.

Freedom to Run for Office

Even if everyone has an equal vote, what about the determination of whom we may cast those votes for? Suppose that some people are not allowed to run for office at all. In that case, it is clear that, contrary to the democratic idea, those who are allowed to run have more power than those who are not. To equalize power, we must say that in principle, anyone may become a candidate for office. In ancient Greece, sometimes offices were filled by lot or by rotation. That is eminently equal in this respect. But of course, if the office requires ability and effort, such democratic rotation could easily lead to disaster. Concerns about such things are crucial to democratic theory. We hope that majority determination will have better results. In modern times, most candidates for office do so as members of a political party, a sizable set of people who think in similar ways about some sizable range of issues. Party backing, we might hope, carries with it a likelihood that their candidates will not be ignorant or incompetent. Nevertheless, imposing a restriction, such as that no one may be a candidate who is not a member of some specific recognized party or one from among a select few, reduces the democratic character of the system to that extent. If the machinery keeps Jones from running when he wants to, that is, so far as it goes, antidemocratic. (But if Jones didn't have a prayer of winning anyway, it perhaps doesn't matter as much.)

Freedom of Political Speech

Another factor that can have major effect on the distribution of power is control of political information. Suppose that some candidates are permitted to have the ear of the people, but others are not allowed to. Those who do then have a major advantage. In Canada recently there has been a Supreme Court–upheld law forbidding substantial criticism of political parties during the period in which federal election campaigns are run. This greatly improves the likelihood that incumbents are returned to office, which seems a clear violation of the intent of equal political power since the unequal power of those in office is being used to continue it into future governments.

In any case, affecting the will of the voter must mean the voter's bringing it about that what happens is what that voter wants—certain results or outcomes. But what is the connection between the voter's vote and such outcomes? To know this, the voter needs information, which requires communication. Moreover, she would like good information. Let us admit, in the first place, that the probability of getting information as good as we would like is zero. The world isn't predictable enough, for one thing. In any case, how do we know which information is good? One party says such-and-such, another, so-and-so. Is there any way of guaranteeing that one is correct?

The short answer to this is: No. A longer answer would envisage procedures of various kinds, say, certification by experts. But then, who decides who is an expert? Under the circumstances, there is no good alternative to freedom. All candidates must be allowed to communicate as they like, to criticize the other candidates, or whatever. And unless each has the same right to do this, equality of power is, again, compromised.

Criminal Procedures

When the police come for you, the first question is whether you did what they claim you did. If all we need is a majority to convict somebody, evidence or no, then another way the government could solidify its power is to throw suitable members of the minority, in suitable numbers, in jail—a device widely employed. Again, majorities as such should not be able to determine these matters.

As with the other freedoms, this one is much more important than only as a device for maintaining democracy in workable condition. If the official agencies of society are to be able to throw us in jail or execute us or take our money, then procedural safeguards that hopefully increase the probability that we are punished if and only if we are guilty of something that is against the law are obviously important. Still more important, of course, is that the laws themselves be good ones, and decent criminal procedures aren't going to be enough to ensure that. We return to that basic theme below.

Other Freedoms?

The short list we have just run through concerns provisions for the preservation of democracy. But it does not concern provisions for anything else. Should it? Or are there connections between other freedoms and democratic ones? On reflection, there would seem to be one, at least. The citizen's political power is the power to get his way—the "way" he favors, being the individual he is. But what if the way he votes is determined not by this but by threats of gross physical harm if he does not cast his vote the right way? One remedy is the secret ballot. If the bully cannot know whether the citizens voted as the bully prescribed, that effectively reduces the likelihood of this happening. Whether it eliminates it entirely depends on circumstances. In a small constituency, a gang of efficient bullies could threaten to murder everyone if the vote didn't go the right way. Secret ballots won't cover that case. It seems that we need something else here: a guarantee that citizens will not abuse each other in such ways. Something like a general right of personal security from politically motivated coercion is needed—not merely on paper, but in the souls of the citizenry.

But is it not absurd to think that such a right is needed only in the interests of *preserving democracy*? It may have some bearing on it, to be sure. But the aforementioned possibility, for instance, is not only remote, it also pretty well depicts a situation in which democracy would not obtain anyway, for the mob who can control the community no matter what it does at the polls is in effect the sole possessor of political power. Such a community has a more serious problem. Yet, no matter what kind of government we have, the citizen has a major interest in personal security. Democracy, as such, no matter how well preserved otherwise, is neither a necessary nor a sufficient condition for having such a right. The citizens will vote for measures to promote security, very likely. Will they get what they voted for? The persons they voted for may turn out to be unable to provide it; or if they voted directly for measures to that end, those measures might turn out to be ineffective.

Which brings up a question: If it is really possible to have effective constitutional-level restrictions, then a constitutional restriction on interpersonal violence and coercion itself looks to be the way to go. Why should we take the roundabout route of ensuring democratic rights in the hope that the majority will be nice guys and not vote to beat up on the minority?

PROPERTY: THE CHALLENGE

No democracy has taken seriously John Locke's insistence that a government does not have the right to deprive people of their property without their consent. (Some say that if it is taken without consent, the citizen is due "compensation," with the State, of course, deciding in the end what level of compensation is "due.") Those who have done anything at all about property confine themselves to talk about real estate and the like—safe enough, since wages and salaries are by far the most typical source of income for people, and those are never seriously included in any practical political discussion of property rights. Yet income from work amounts to rental of one's own personal property, viz., one's body and mind, one's person. The claim of a person to be the owner of that is more basic than his claim to be the owner of stocks, bonds, or real estate.

These "economic" issues are, it is clear, the bottom line. Does the State get to take your money at will? It does so now, and democracy doesn't discourage that—indeed, quite the reverse, for in fact it encourages it, immensely. Modern democracies take far more of our money than any previous State. How does that come about? The short answer is that with the misguided idea that democracy is a fundamental right comes also the rather less misguided idea that democracy affords the opportunity to take from our neighbor without having to do anything to merit it. That may be the whole story, indeed. If it is, that's very bad news for democratic theory and for democracy as an institution. The cynic holds that government is a gang of thieves. If the cynic's view is right, then with democracy the gang becomes huge, and the theft astronomic.

A BUDGET OF PARADOXES FOR DEMOCRACY

Careful students of democracy have formulated many puzzles and paradoxes stemming from its basic structure. Here are several, of different kinds.

Voting Paradoxes

Suppose we have three voters choosing among three alternatives. A prefers them in the order x, y, z; B prefers them in the order y, z, x; and C prefers them in the order z, x, y. Now which has the majority? In the most obvious way of answering that, every one of them does. Two out of three prefer x to y; two out of three prefer y to z; and two out of three prefer z to x! What do we do now?

This interesting little problem has extensions that are no longer just abstractly cute. We could fix it by always limiting the alternatives to two. But in real life, there are always more. How, then, do we pare them down?

Every student of democracy also knows the answer to that. There will be a smoke-filled room (no longer, of course, now that the majority has seen to it that smoking in the back room as well as the front is prohibited), and in this room, a small group of pundits, silver-tongued, well-heeled, or otherwise possessed of a considerable inequality of effectual political influence despite their possession of the same number of votes (one) as anyone else, will whittle down the agenda, or the list of candidates. In the course of all this, of course, there will be some question just what has happened to the original ideal of democracy. It is not altogether lost, to be sure; but surely it has become obscured, at the least.

Strategic Voting

Suppose that in polity P the system is that if no candidate gets a majority at the first round, then a run-off election is held between the candidates on a new, shortened list, arrived at by dropping some of the losers on round one; for brevity, we'll make it the top two in the first round. Knowing this, the supporters of candidate A throw their weight behind candidate C so that C will get more votes than B. Once the voters are faced with the choice of A and C, A will win; had they instead faced A and B, B would have won. What is to prevent this? Democracy is inherently incapable of ruling that all citizens shall vote for their "real choice" rather than for strategic reasons. As with the first problem, this is no laughing matter. Major political changes can be due to precisely such manipulation of the vote. And given democracy, it surely looks as though we are stuck with it.[3]

The Conscientious Democrat

When we vote, why do we? Suppose it is because we believe that the person or policy we vote for is the right one—a reasonable supposition, in the case of those who vote for any reason at all (which is by no means all, to be sure!). But now suppose, as often happens (perhaps especially often in the case of those who do vote their "consciences") that the Good Guys lose. Now what? We are asked to go along with a policy that we know in our hearts is wrong. Yet if we are committed to democracy, we will have to go along with it, and do so not as a matter of knuckling under to superior force but rather because of the claim that democracy is right.

How seriously we should take this problem is an interesting question. All we need note here is that if you think that democracy really is some kind of morally preemptory system and you have any other moral beliefs about who should be elected or what should be done, then you will very likely have this problem. If the majority party should be Nazi-like as well, then the problem will be serious indeed.

WHY VOTE AT ALL?

This question is not just a curious little puzzle. The point of voting, one presumes, is to get the candidate of your choice into office. But you are one among many voters, typically, 100,000 or more. If your preferred candidate is also that of a majority of others, then it seems there is little point in your voting, for she will get elected anyway. If on the other hand your heroine is unpopular, there is again little point in your voting, since she will not get elected anyway. Putting some figures on this will firm up the point. It is rational to vote on that basis only if your vote will make a difference. The probability that it will make a difference is the probability that the election will be a tie if you don't vote. Then and only then will your vote make a difference. And the probability of that happening is, of course, extremely tiny.

In a recent flyer in my mail, a brochure from the government informs of the date of the next provincial election, which includes a referendum item; the brochure says, "Don't Let Others Speak for You! Be sure your voice is heard."[4] Well, who will "hear" me, and so what? If I vote, the vote whichever way will be about 1/20,000th different from if I didn't vote. Why on earth would one bother to go down to the polls to exert so tiny an influence?

Take this point a bit further. Suppose it costs you a half hour of your precious time to vote. Let the importance of the election be ever so great—it would be much better if Ms. Goodsoul got in instead of her awful rival, Mr. Dufuss. Yet, the expected value of your voting is not simply the value of G getting in, but of that, weighted by the probability that she will win only if you vote, and that probability is vanishingly small. The likely result is that even if the matter is very important, there will still be no point in your voting. The half hour lost is real and important; the expected gain is vanishingly close to zero. Now what?

RATIONAL IGNORANCE

We can up the ante on the previous point. Getting informed on the issues in elections is no easy matter. Who can claim to know all that is relevant in a given election? How much work would it take to become that well informed? And how much, frankly, is it worth to you to do all that work? Well, given that your vote is not going to make any difference anyway, the answer would seem to be none, or near enough. Remaining ignorant seems the rational decision.[5]

This result is devastating to the idea of democracy, insofar as the idea was that democratic government will give us the government we want. For getting such a government by democratic means is evidently all but impossible. Plato complained that democracy involved "giving a strange sort of equality to equals and unequals alike."[6] The equality democracy gives to all is that of political power. But on no account of the matter from anyone's point of view is it rational to think that we are all equal in the one thing that counts for responsible use of such power: knowing what's relevant to the issues. John Stuart Mill, indeed, hoped to stave off the unsavory prospect of government by the ignorant by giving plural votes to those who were smarter, did more important work, or were more knowledgeable.[7] But doing that surely moves us away from the central democratic idea. Democracy, necessarily, is rule by the "mob"—the rabble, the ignorati, the scruffy. For it is rule by everybody, and they, of course, don't know what's coming off. What now?

This is not a cynical claim, but a sober and obvious truth. Governments get into all sorts of things, and vast amounts of information are relevant at almost all points. Who knows all of this? No one, of course. But more to the point, only a few know enough about even a very few of those things to claim the kind of expertise that we would allow as sufficient to qualify that person to make that kind of a decision. And when we consider Mr. or Ms. Ordinary Voter—forget it! There is no way that we can acquire enough information to make rational decisions on more than a tiny handful of matters that we are asked to decide about, or that would be relevant to our choice of candidates.

Consider opinion polls such as this: "Is there global warming of a level, and due to causes, justifying action to try to remedy it?" Hardly anyone can plausibly claim to know, and even their claims are well short of authoritative. But in democracy, it is beliefs about such things that are at stake in elections, and people vote on the basis of their beliefs despite their obvious lack of qualification to have any beliefs on the point. The suggestion that democracy pools the wisdom of the many is not credible. It pools the ignorance of the many, and what that will do to resulting decisions of government can be imagined.

Modern writers have catalogued the extent of voter ignorance even on obvious political matters. Half of Americans do not know that each state has two senators, and three quarters do not know the length of their terms. Over half cannot name their congressional representative, and 40 percent cannot name either of their two senators.[8] And so on and so on. Things like that, perhaps, don't matter much. But if voters are ignorant about such things, their ignorance about elementary economic theory is profound, and that does make a difference. Voters kept Franklin Delano Roosevelt in office for thirteen long years, during ten of which his policies prolonged an economic downturn into the worst depression America had ever seen. Voters elect lawmakers who make marijuana illegal, outlaw abortion, keep slavery in power (in the American South, prior to 1865), and any number of other things that one can reasonably argue are manifestly unjust, or catastrophic, or both. Defenders of democracy have a lot to answer for. On the face of it, rule should not be by the ignorant; yet democracy enshrines the ignorant, in spades. Is that a good idea, really?

The big problem with democracy in this crucial respect is easy to identify. Your vote is virtually certain to make no difference to the outcome, and so the cost, to you, of voting on the basis of irrational folly, malevolence, or innocent ignorance is practically nil. "When a consumer has mistaken beliefs about what to buy, he foots the bill. When a voter has mistaken beliefs about government policy, the whole population picks up the tab."[9]

"PARTICIPATORY DEMOCRACY"

It might be thought that we can help matters out by invoking participatory democracy. Everyone, in this view, will not just vote but will also discuss, and maybe campaign, do extensive study, and so forth. It is, to be sure, very unclear just what the ideal of participatory democracy intends. It can't intend that we require all citizens to do these things, on pain of disenfranchisement; to do that is to flush democracy down the drain, once again. And it can't mean that citizens do do this, because most of them don't. Moreover, they act wisely; thereby, the ignorance in question, as we saw, is perfectly rational. It is hard to see how participation could be any more than a palliative—and one that more than likely will put political power into the hands of those who are best at political rhetoric—at words that sound good but make no sense. (We will have occasion to mention several such in the ensuing chapters.)

All of these things mean that democracy is a problem, to put it very mildly.[10]

MAJORITARIANISM

Standard writings on democracy identify one special problem under the heading "majoritarianism." This is where some sector of the voting public is in a position of perpetual, or at least ongoing, minority in relation to the rest. Quebec in Canada, at about a quarter of the entire Canadian populace, regards itself as a permanent standing minority, even though Quebeckers don't by any means think as a bloc and there is a substantial Anglo minority in Quebec as a whole. The point is that insofar as they do "think as a block" and differently from the rest of the country, they are doomed to minority status indefinitely. And this is perceived as unfair.

But if it is, the claimed unfairness is really an instance of a much more fundamental problem. For democracy is inherently and necessarily majoritarian. Democracy fundamentally makes everyone subject to the rule of the majority, always. If that is a problem—and it surely is—then it is the fundamental problem of democracy, not some kind of sideshow.

APOLITICAL DECISION-MAKING

Is it a problem with a solution? At least in part, it is, and we all know what it is. It is generally claimed that unanimity is an impossible, utopian method for politics. Even if we accept that, we need to realize that we rarely need to resolve problems by voting or any other political procedure. Instead, we can divide things up so that those involved in a given problem are few, and they can then operate on the rule that who wish to do X, do X, while those wishing to do Y, do Y. Law is the imposition of a uniformity on the community, as Aquinas puts it. But as he also points out, that uniformity is to be for the common good. When there is no common good in the larger community, we can go for liberty, which permits each to go his own way so long only as he does not thereby inflict injury, damage, harm, or in general costs or avoidable restrictions, on others. Indeed, we may say that liberty *is* the common good. Within that general rule, people with issues resolve them by negotiation and agreement, against the background of the property rights of those concerned.

There are specific associations of people who often do adopt the rule of majority for some purposes. But they are associations and not societies;

recall that distinction from the beginning of this book. Its members all agree on certain general things, namely the purposes for which all who belong joined the association in question. There is no problem in using democratic methods for those purposes, then. But note how limited they are. No voluntary association can compel its members to remain members; none can compel others to join if they don't want to. Government is entirely different. It rules over all, like it or not. Emigration is difficult, expensive, and hardly amounts to a reason for claiming that the State really is voluntary after all.

Some indeed do claim such a right. The Muslim religion, for example, alleges that no one may leave that religion voluntarily. But if it does say this, then it must be seen to be seriously in error. So far as the wider community is concerned, all religions are and absolutely are required to be voluntary. No organization may threaten to shoot people wanting out. The government of England spent a lot of money protecting Salman Rushdie when a "fatwah" was issued against him for writing heresies. They were right to do so. That membership in a religion should be voluntary is not a "majority" rule: It is an absolute rule. It is the rule of the moral constitution of humanity—so says the liberal.

When there are matters on which we do not and cannot reasonably be expected to agree, interpersonal decision-making requires that agreement on the practical matters in dispute not be contingent on agreement on the matters that are impossible to resolve by reason. Thus, each religion can recognize the right of practitioners of other religions to have their own places of worship, and those places can be bought as an ordinary real estate transaction from people with no particular religious interests. You pay the rent, you can worship there, no problem—that's what the nonreligious real estate owner can and does say. In similar fashion, at least almost all other problems in a community can be resolved by appropriate bargaining among the specifically relevant parties. What democracy does is to abolish the distinction of relevant and irrelevant: Everybody has a vote, on all issues. Not surprisingly, the resulting decisions are likely to be bad ones.

GOVERNMENT BY SPECIAL INTEREST

The idea of democracy is that everyone has the same amount of basic political power. One might suppose that this makes it unlikely that laws will be biased or rigged in favor of some special group. The supposition, alas, turns out to be altogether wrong. In fact, democracy turns out to be the most efficient device in history for incorporating special interests into the law.

Here's how. Some group, suppose, would benefit considerably if a law is made providing it with a special advantage. But those who would lose by it—say, taxpayers—lose only a little each. The costs are diffused, while the benefits are concentrated. Now, the legislator is extremely interested in getting reelected. If the special-interest group's members all vote for him, while other people's propensity to vote for someone are unaffected, then the group is very likely to attract the support of that legislator for the proposed law. The results are manifest in democracies everywhere. Special laws to help out local manufacturers, milk producers, cab drivers, and so on and on and on—the law books emerging from parliament or Congress are sure to be filled with them.

If that bothers us, then democracy should bother us. For it is all but impossible for democracy to happen at all without this tendency being realized to a very substantial extent.

WHY DEMOCRACY?

What this all means is that there is a very great problem in justifying democracy. The superiority, even the acceptability of democracy, is not at all obvious. How could people have ever thought it was, as so many seem to? An implausible answer might go like this: "Democratic procedures are uniquely fair means of arbitrating among competing views or interests."[11] The trouble is that the claim is prima facie unbelievable, unless a great deal more is wired into the notion of being "democratic" than either the majority principle or even that plus the several further rights listed in the preceding would sustain. Competing interests are fairly adjudicated only by finding out who is imposing on whom and then insisting that the person imposing stop it, or compensate for his impositions if already committed. Finding this out requires, often, considerable knowledge and careful reasoning. We can't expect either from a mass of voters.

Only in the case where this procedure won't work because the interests don't have a structure of a kind that makes it determinate whether someone is in the wrong, might it be plausible to settle the matter by voting. If no one is imposing on anyone and it's just a matter of deciding which to select among several reasonable possibilities involving cooperative activities among those concerned, then the democratic principle looks pretty good. If 55 percent prefer driving on the right and 45 percent prefer the left, with the "rights" then winning out, who really cares? Yet that is so rare a case as hardly to make much difference. Much more typical is this one: When 51 percent prefer that no one be permitted to smoke marijuana while 17 percent strongly prefer being so permitted, then a lot of people do care, and care a lot. And then the possibility that the "nays" are simply muscling out the "yeas" rather than being in a genuine situation of "competing interests" comes to the fore. Democracy is not what we should be employing there.

What we must remember is that democracy is plausible only when there needs to be a uniform decision by the community. But that is rare. In almost all cases, it is possible for the Fs to do things their way and the Gs to do things differently. When this is done, the Fs and the Gs both pay for what they get. The very large sports facility built in my town recently at considerable public expense serves a small fraction of the populace, but the rest all pay (a great deal). Why? For that matter, why not have those interested in sport S1 build a facility for themselves, while the S2 people build a very different facility, and the indolent simply go to the movies? Democracy enables a smallish constituency to get its way at public expense. This is hardly a matter of adjudicating conflicts of interest, for there is no conflict about the primary matters. There is only "conflict" if the question is Which subset of the people will get its goodies at the expense of the rest? The proper answer surely could be None.

DEMOCRACY IN ASSOCIATIONS

For a relevant comparison, we might well go to the governments of associations. These, remember, are groups formed by voluntary means: The members join this group, and do so because they have common ends that the organization of the group (in the cases where it is organized) is intended to promote. Frequently such groups do have democratic structures. They perhaps elect chairpersons, or assorted other functionaries, to represent or act for the whole for various purposes. Should we appeal to this as a source of support for political democracy?

There are two crucial reasons why the answer is in the negative. In the first place, it is not true that all associations have democratic structures. There are many where such structures not only don't obtain but also where the members understandably don't want them. Roman Catholics don't typically think that the Pope should be elected by the general membership of that church. (He is elected by a small body within the church, but it in turn is not elected, or anything like it.) And we can easily imagine that no sincere adherent of a religion would think that its fundamental doctrines should be decided by majority vote. The prospect of infiltration by perceived enemies who join in order to alter the association beyond recognition would be frightening to most such members. We are often voluntary members of associations without democratic structure, and we prefer it that way.

And second, and most fundamentally, we just have to remind ourselves, once again, that the State is not an association. Maybe we'd like it to be. We might well agree that the ideal model for a State would be the association: It would be an institution such that anyone would want to join it, given the way it is. But as we have already seen, this is an ideal model that never obtains, whereas the State's power over us real people here and now is precisely what is in question. It is not at all obvious that making the State democratic makes it more attractive. It could easily make it less so, at least until numerous restrictions and safeguards are in place.

Thus the people of Hong Kong, over a long period, prospered mightily under British "rule." They did not have the right to vote, but they did have economic and other liberties in abundance. Before its mandatory return to Chinese mainland rule, Hong Kong was a world's showcase of a peaceful, liberal, and very prosperous society. Would frequent elections have made things better? That is very doubtful.

DEMOCRACY BY FALLACY?

The plausible answer, then, to the question how it could have been supposed that democracy is a superior system of government, is: by fallacious assimilation of very different cases. Democracy makes sense only for a very circumscribed set of problems. Selection of leaders might be among those, once it is clear what the selected leaders are and are not to do.

The preceding takes what we may call the "high road." But democracy hasn't happened in the area traversed by that road. Democracy emerges, instead, from the politics of the jungle. Strong men want to push us around. We want not to be pushed around. If we are going to be so, by whom, then? Now it becomes plausible to say, in the words of a late colleague, "All that Democracy determines is, who would win in a fair fight." He meant to imply that that's all it does, and that it can hardly be thought much of a compliment to it that it does so. But, to be sure, there is much to be said for avoiding fighting, and one way of doing so is to count up our forces in advance and then cede victory to the greater numbers. Even that we will do only if the consequences are not horrible. We can invoke constitutional restrictions first, to constrain the options within a narrower area, and then go to democracy as the only option giving us all the optimal chance, abstractly speaking, of getting our way. This seems to do the job, but it's not a "high road."

In short, the opinions of the "many" among political writers nowadays that democracy is a uniquely just system of government seem far-fetched. Much better simply to say, along with Winston Churchill, that if we are going to have a realistically available government, and once all the ifs, ands, and buts are taken care of, democracy is probably better than its alternatives. Or at least, better for otherwise pretty savvy and advanced societies.

In Churchill's accounting, the options don't include anarchy—an option we have tabled mostly thus far, and will remain tabled until the end of this book. But the chips are not all in.

DEMOCRACY AND WAR

One important point about democracy—and it really is important—is that it appears that widespread democracy is likely to reduce the incidence of international war. Kant thought of it first (to my knowledge): Make all the nations in the world what he called "republics," which for this purpose are fairly close to democracy, and there will be "perpetual peace."[12] He thought this was so because once wars are fought only if they have popular support, then the only wars that would get it are wars of self-defense. That was rather too quick, as it turns out. But there seems to be a very robust finding in social science to the effect that democracies do not make war against each other.[13] Sometimes democracies will be found on opposite sides of a war, but that is always because they are united by treaty or the like with some nondemocracies, which are responsible for the wars in question.

This finding looks promising, and if so is certainly a very strong recommendation of democracy, so far as it goes. And after all, it is a very important aspect. Wars have a way of killing a great many people, and if democracy can do something to reduce their incidence, then huzzahs are in order. (We'll say more about this in chapter 7 on international matters.)

CONCLUSION: LIBERALISM VERSUS DEMOCRACY

Liberalism is the view that government (and morals) should be for the common good of all, where that good is understood as what the persons in question will accept as good, each in their own cases. The classic liberal argues that the most plausible way to incorporate the ideal of liberalism is to adopt a general right of all to the maximum liberty compatible with the same right being extended to all. So understood, the cherished Western freedoms—security of person, property, and lifestyle, including religion and expression—come rapidly into view. Yet democracy threatens all of these freedoms. In the absence of constitutional constraints, the rule of law, and settled habits of tolerance and fair dealing among the populace, political democracy can easily be a disaster, as has been amply shown in the history of the past century or so. Democracies without these essential further restrictions turn into tyrannies of the most oppressive kind. Even short of such disasters, the panoply of counterproductive pieces of legislation steadily emerging from the halls of democratic legislatures ought to give us pause.

We could "solve" this problem by simply incorporating a bunch of cherished rights into the very idea of democracy, so that a State in which people vote for leaders but otherwise lack the full range of valued liberties is not called "democracy." But though that is often enough done, to do it is to sweep the issue under the carpet. That issue is that the liberal freedoms are altogether overwhelmingly more important than democracy as narrowly and literally defined, if a straight choice between them were possible. But realistically speaking, it is not. Democracy is the political juggernaut of our time. It is all but irresistible, for better or worse. Hopefully it is going to function in a way that generally supports these liberties. But at the margins, that's wishful thinking. For democracy encourages, indeed positively invites, the syndrome of government by special interests, with the politically correct suppression of individuals minding their own business(es) and the endless regulation, restriction, and dabbling with our lives and money that has become the day-to-day gestalt of modern government. Democracy has become a sacred cow. It may be a false god.

NOTES

1. Aristotle, *Politics*, Book IV, chapter 4.

2. It was advocated in John Stuart Mill's classic work, *Considerations on Representative Government*, chapter VIII.

3. The Marquis de Condorcet (1745–1794) is credited with being the first to see and seriously discuss such anomalies. There is now a Web site devoted to this work: Condorcet.org. See also Robert Abrams, *Foundations of Political Analysis* (New York: Columbia University Press, 1990), especially 28–36.

4. Elections Ontario flyer, September 5, 2007.

5. See Russell Hardin, "Street-level Epistemology and Democratic Participation," *Journal of Political Philosophy*, vol. 10, no. 2 (2002): 211–229.

6. Plato, *Republic*, Book VIII.

7. Robert Paul Wolff makes much of this aspect: *In Defense of Anarchism* (Berkeley: University of California Press, 1998).

8. For an account of democracy that is both sympathetic and yet shows awareness of many of its problems, see Robert A. Dahl, *On Democracy* (New Haven, CT: Yale University Press, 1998).

9. Cited in Bryan Caplan, *The Myth of the Rational Voter: Why Democracies Choose Bad Policies* (Princeton, NJ: Princeton University Press, 2007), 8.

10. Caplan, *The Myth of the Rational Voter*, 14. For further on the points made in this paragraph, see more generally chapter 2 (pp. 23–49).

11. L. W. Sumner, *The Hateful and the Obscene* (Toronto: University of Toronto Press, 2004), p. 74.

12. Immanuel Kant supports the general idea in his famous little book, *Perpetual Peace*, section II, First Definitive Article.

13. For a modern empirical update, see Michael Doyle, "Kant, Liberal Legacies and Foreign Affairs," *Philosophy and Public Affairs* (1984): 204–235 and 323–353.

6

The Modern Regulatory
Welfare State

WELFARE AND THE STATE

Modern governments do a great deal more than their predecessors did, and a great deal more than the theory of the "minimal state" would allow. Indeed, they do much more than any government in history did before the twentieth century. In addition to providing "law and order" and national defense, the State nowadays takes upon itself the tasks of overseeing education, health, welfare, regulation of almost everything, operation of railroads, electrical generating and distributing facilities, and far too much else to list here.

In addition, there are many levels of government: local or even sublocal (wards, say), regional, county, and provincial or state. All of these levels provide suitable examples of the problems of politics, and I will assume that the differences among them do not matter seriously for discussions of philosophical principle. We can at least plausibly assume that all persons have a common interest in protection against crime, along with facilities for fair trials and other procedural matters. Whether even those interests justify the State is the challenging question of the anarchist, which, again, we will table here. But when we get beyond the narrow sphere of classical liberal government, hope of virtual unanimity recedes quickly. Why should all be herded into state-provided schools, and why should all be required to help pay for those schools even when they do not send their own children to them? Why should Smith and Jones be compelled to help pay for Robinson's medical care when needed? These are the serious questions discussed in the remainder of this chapter. We will select only a few, though very popular, ones of these further areas of State action and see that all is not smooth sailing for the State.

HOW DO WE JUSTIFY STATE INTERVENTIONS?

A perception very widely held about government is that it is a creative agency that provides all sorts of things for us, the people. We no doubt believe this for two reasons. One is that the State appears to do so. Certainly it busies itself with all sorts of projects. The other is that it keeps telling us so. But the perception is misleading. Perhaps we should instead compare it with the member of the Mafia who brings home a nice new car for his wife. The fact that he bought it with money recently robbed from a bank is not mentioned. Similarly, the fact that all these things the State does are done with money taken, without asking, from the people who created the services now curtailed peremptorily by the government should, surely, matter. Normal people do things by working or selling things or at least investing in enterprises. Not, however, the State. It spends its days fleecing its subjects, as Thrasymachus held. The people who "do" the things the State does are actually us, except that unlike in the rest of our lives, we didn't have any individual choice whether to do them. We work under compulsion. It is not obvious that this is all right. We loudly decry slavery, after all. There would seem to be a real question as to how this is different. (It's more comfortable, certainly. Better "chained" to my computer with 50 percent of the proceeds being siphoned off by the Internal Revenue folks than being chained to a galley. Agreed!)

In the previous chapter it was noted that in a democracy, the people calling the shots are the majority, more or less, though in a very indirect and unreliable way. Even if it were perfectly direct and reliable, we surely don't want to say it's all right for the majority to enslave us. What, then?

Much of what the State does would in some way have happened anyway. But it would be something else, and so the question would naturally arise whether these other things are as good. Those other things have the advantage that they would have happened in accordance with the wishes of the concerned parties. The question whether what the State does is better compares with the question whether what the robber does with your money is "better." Doesn't the fact that he's doing it with *your* involuntarily extracted money matter? Some libertarians think that it matters so much that it isn't even legitimate to go into the question of comparing the one set of actions with the others. If they're right, the argument against the State looks pretty strong.

An argument to counteract this appearance is seriously required. There are two to consider.

(1) The money you and I earn isn't ours anyway, really. This option really denies the right of private property. If the reasoning in chapter 3, about Marx, is right, then the socialist arguments against this will not do. If the arguments of chapter 4 are right, then to do that is to deny the general right of liberty and replace it with a conservative view. Since liberalism is being presumed here, and is shared by virtually everyone, that is a measure of desperation.

(2) The other idea is more promising. It could be argued that what the State does with your money is so much more effective and efficient than what you would have done that it's worth it from your point of view, even taking its involuntariness into account. For one thing, since the State simply takes our money without asking, collection costs are fairly low—to the government, that is. Of course, we citizens spend agonized hours filling out tax returns, keeping extra accounts that we wouldn't have had to keep, and so on. "True, the cost to the IRS of collecting taxes is relatively trivial, at about six-tenths of 1 percent of venue. But this is simply because nearly all of the costs of taxation are imposed on the taxpayers. . . ."[1] We must factor these costs into the total. But still, perhaps it will work out that if you did for yourself what the State does for you, the cost to you would work out to be greater than if the benefit is supplied by involuntary means? Maybe.

The burden of argument for the State on this latter, more reasonable view, is very strong. To be sure, it is far from obvious that the State is efficient in anything like the sense specified. Critics, indeed, by and large argue that it is far less efficient than private sources would be for just about anything it does, including protection, health, education, and welfare. Who is right about this would seem to depend on the facts, of course. The point at this stage is simply that this is the burden it needs to meet and that it won't be easy to meet it. (According to the same author, roughly two of every three dollars collected for purposes of transferring to indigents and other needy people by State agencies is absorbed by the administrative staff. This compares with less than 10 percent in the private sector.[2])

We should note a variant of this argument. Suppose, as some claim, that there are things that simply can't be done at all except by the State. If so, of course, the efficiency argument would go through by default: If agent A can do X, and agent B cannot, then if we want X done, the choice of A is clear. Unfortunately, there appear to be literally no cases of things that simply can't be done except by the State—unless we cheat and say that if we didn't have the State do it, we couldn't have state schools, for example. But in that case, the question is whether it would be better not to have state schools at all. Begging the question, as usual, is unhelpful.

Thus the serious issue is whether, for each and every citizen, that citizen prefers having the State do whatever is in question, at the cost of having it do so, to having it done some other way, given the costs of having it done in that other way. An important issue, of course, is presented by the possibility that some people would indeed prefer the State action and others would not, in the terms just set forth. Then what do we do? The short answer to this is that we have lost the "social contract" with this result. That contract is between everybody and everyone, not some and some. If we insist on the common good, then this result shows that we have not achieved it. What would have to be shown is that the ones who prefer the State could find some way to compensate the ones who do not.

There is a simple solution to that, too. The ones who prefer the State can simply sic the police on the rest and compel them to go along. This, indeed, is the standard procedure. But our question is whether this is morally right—and our answer, thus far, is that it is apparently not. Are we arguing here, or are we skirmishing? If we are serious, these points are important.

Perhaps the most obvious candidate for something that the State "does for us" would be the establishment and maintenance of law and order. Surely this is something only the State can provide, and surely it is of enormous value. Isn't it?

The State certainly makes laws, that being its defining function. But the claim that that fact is of immense value, just as it stands, is questionable. For everything depends on whether those laws are any good. A law requiring everyone to wear green shoes at all times is not a blessing. If laws generally are like that one, then law is a curse, not a blessing, and what the State does for us is to make our lives miserable. The alleged blessings of "law and order" need to be taken with several grains of salt.

Well, but is law and order not a product of the State, then? In one obvious sense of the word, that would be true by definition: Something is a "law" in this sense only if some or other government "passes" it, gives it its imprimatur. But as we saw earlier, legislated law is not all there is to law. There is custom, common law, contractual law, and ultimately moral law. If we think of law as essentially enforceable, then too it is possible for people to think they are enforcing a law that has not been legislated by anybody in particular. We saw reason to think along Lockean lines in this regard: People living in fairly close touch with each other evolve rules having the status of law, enforcement of which will happen.

Thus we have two very different notions of the "rule of law" as:

(1) the rule of the basic moral law(s) of human interaction; and
(2) the rule of *laws*; that is, the imposition on the community of the particular laws enacted by the regime in force.

The distinction, then, might be put this way: it's the *rule of law* versus the rule of *laws*.

Now if the claim is that governments govern rightly when it is only the second of these two ways that is in question, that implies that political might makes right. This lets in the Nazis and every other government there has ever been. But if we instead insist that law must be "an order of reason for the common good," we will then have a critical idea of considerable power.

GOOD LAWS

Hobbes provided an attractive analysis of "good laws": laws that are useful for enabling people to live their various lives, and, most importantly, are "needful" for that purpose.[3] When is a law "needful"? When, that is, is an imposition on somebody's voluntary behavior actually needed in the particular case? The case is strong when the individual compelled is out to injure someone. But when else? The purpose of government is to enable people to pursue their lives in their own ways, not to tell them how to live. The common good of liberalism is liberty: an environment in which people can pursue their projects without compulsive interference, either from their neighbors or from the government itself.

The rule of law as a principle protects the individual insofar as it imposes as a condition, before the government can be justified in descending on the individual with force of arms, that at least there must be an enacted statute on the books saying that individuals doing these things will be treated that way. That at least helps us out toward the goal of meeting Locke's stricture that government is not to be by "arbitrary decree." It enables the citizen at least to know how to keep out of harm's way. But if there are 10,000 laws on the books, knowledge of all of which by any individual is absolutely impossible, then this protection becomes pretty scant. Few of us can be sure that we are in fact violating no law in a modern State. And when the laws themselves may be as arbitrary as you like in the respect that they could impose restrictions on person A in the interests of person B, whose interests the government of the day has decided to promote at the expense of A, then the "protection" that the individual gets at the hands of the law has turned into arbitrary tyranny of the very type that we might have hoped government would function to prevent. The noble ideal of the rule of law has then turned into a refuge for tyrants—the rule of whatever laws the tyrant happens to want to enact.

Anyone claiming that the rule of law is a blessing for which we should all be grateful, and one which can be supplied only by government, has therefore to make some important distinctions. Just because a law is general and is passed by the legislature or other official body is no guarantee that it will truly be for the common good. The wrong laws can kill us, and certainly impoverish us, at least as effectively as no law at all. We will see some examples shortly.

HEALTH

Suppose you don't feel well. Someone claims to be able and ready to help out, for a price. You go to this person, accept the proposed terms, are treated, and pay the bill. One might have thought that this is how the supply of medical services would proceed. But in modern democracies, that description is very far from the reality. I recently heard a description of a visit to an American clinic by someone who, having been seen, took out his wallet and asked what the tab was. The person at the desk hadn't the faintest idea! Where was his insurance card? Who was his employer? Was he on Medicare? Invocation of the familiar model of exchange of services between voluntarily acting individuals, it seems, was not what this institution was ready for.

Almost every government of the day asserts that it will provide for the medical care of its subjects, in some measure or other. Most claim that they will guarantee meeting the individual's "basic health needs," defined somehow by some committee. In Canada we read that "Health care in Canada has long been a source of national pride. Known as "Medicare," the system is publicly financed but privately run; it provides universal coverage and care is free at the point of use."[4] Government intervention in this otherwise peaceful scene is responsible for the imposition of approximately $3,000 per Canadian per year in taxed medical costs[5]—collected quite irrespectively of whether the individual in question has actually seen a doctor about anything in that year. The State exerts a medical monopoly that extends to almost all corners of the health care area. Not surprisingly, the effect of all that is that Canadians must wait inordinate lengths of time for operations and the like; the average waiting time from initial visit through to surgery was sixteen weeks in 2001.[6] A side effect is that a great many Canadians fly to the United States where such things are still legal. An operation for which you will wait several months in Canada can be had in a few days in the United States, if you have the money to pay. Many people conclude that extra weeks and months of intact life and limb are worth the price. Meanwhile, the cost of health care in the supposedly free-market American medical system has skyrocketed, owing largely to extensive interventions by all levels of governments there—about half of all medical payments.[7]

The story is similar with minor variations all around the world. The government claims it will guarantee basic health care to all, but what that generally means is that it will tax everybody, regardless of their actual use of medical services, and beyond that exert innumerable restrictions on who can offer what. If it allows private practice, as most do, those who get it have paid for the public system whether or not they avail themselves of the private one, and thus pay twice over for health care. Altogether, the net effect for the citizens of such countries—almost all—is that health care is the most expensive of all services that most people use, and, taking into account its effect on the individual's longevity and general health, probably several times as costly as it would be if left to the devices of voluntarily acting persons.

What is the basis for this widespread imposition? Of course, it is grandly proclaimed that health care is a right, possibly because *health* is a right. Is it supposed to be, perhaps, a human right? Well, not exactly. For no government undertakes to provide health care to all who need it wherever they might be—no matter how human all those other people are and no matter how much they need it.

Notice that the libertarian has no problem asserting a right to health, in the negative sense; namely, that nobody else is to damage your health without your permission. But the welfare state version of this right converts it into a positive right to health services, a right against their own governments, which means their taxpaying neighbors, to be supplied, free of charge at the point of supply. As such, of course, it is really a right to compel one's fellow citizens to provide medical services at their expense. There is no use trying to make philosophical sense of the principle on which these manifold interventions into the lives of people are allegedly based. It is much more helpful simply to point to the fact that in a democracy, it is easy for a politician to get elected on a platform offering to provide something for nothing—the overall result of the government's intrusions into this area being a huge increase in costs.

What is the ideological issue? It is whether health care should be understood as anything further than a negative right, in the terminology explained in preceding chapters. That it is a negative right is immensely plausible. A wants help and is willing to get it from B for a price proposed by B. Should anyone be allowed to interfere in this exchange? The case for denying that is very strong; the negative right in question is, then, generally accepted, in a sense.

But welfare states need to claim that they will do better for our health than individuals acting on their own. The claim is in almost all instances going to be false. Where does the supporter of public health measures go from there?

THE NEEDY

A familiar argument for public health care monopolization is that if it weren't for that, some individuals would not have their health needs adequately provided for. Now, no health care system does or can live up to any such general promise of service, as is common knowledge among health care workers. Few people's health care is "adequately provided for" by the standards nominally enshrined in such legislation. For that matter, it is impossible even to define the objective of perfect health. Just what is a government supposed to be providing if it is to live up to the promise to look after everyone's basic health? No doubt anyone, however healthy she or he may be right now, could possibly be still healthier. The net effect of these questions is to sharpen up the point here, which is, Why is it an argument for government compulsion in health care that some people might not otherwise be as well supplied with it? For certainly millions and millions will be less well supplied for the same reason.

The question at issue, remember, is whether everyone in country A may legitimately be compelled to assist in supplying the medical care of everyone else in country A, though not in any other country. The answer is offered in the affirmative by the proponent of Medicare. If we inquire on what this answer is based, we are very likely to be told that if people did not have this right, then it might happen that somebody would die or be sick when somebody else could have been compelled to assist him. But how is that an argument? It appears to be simply a repetition of the very claim in question here; namely that, somehow, citizens of X all owe each other support for health care. That claim, in addition, is only made on behalf of an arbitrarily designated subset of humans—those selected as being in need, in that country.

Meanwhile, the proponent of Medicare takes on an empirical claim that they rarely try to provide any real evidence for; namely, that if we did not have government involvement in medicine, then a significant number of people would die or be less healthy than they otherwise would be. That is to say, the claim is that if medicine were entirely carried on by the usual voluntary means—the market, plus charitable activities—then a significant number of people would be less well taken care of. In Canada, which is undoubtedly typical, it is well-known that many people are direct counterinstances to this claim: They voluntarily go, in thousands, to places (the United States especially) where they can get private care at great expense, despite the fact that they have already paid for the promised public care back home. Only, they aren't getting it to their satisfaction. The Medicare enthusiast ignores this. He or she insists that the system is justified by the fact that some poorer people who wouldn't be able to afford care in the United States would be worse off here (in Canada) if it weren't for the Medicare system. But why would they be? Presumably the claim is that if they can't pay themselves, then no one else will help. Yet, no proponent of Medicare offers any genuine evidence for the proposition that so few Canadians (or others) are generous enough to be ready to help supply medical care to needy poor persons that in fact, if we had such a voluntary system, then a significant number of them would be badly off or dead.

Much the same will be found with almost everything else that modern governments do. A claim is made that some important service can be provided only by the government, and this is used as an excuse for preventing anyone else from trying to provide it. As a result, of course, the claim becomes self-confirming. Then the service is more or less provided by the government in question at enormous cost to the citizen and with little recourse for the innumerable misapplications of the service in question. The many people who do get treated in a health care system are pointed to in self-congratulatory terms by the government that provides it, and the fact that almost everyone is treated at much greater expense than he or she might have been treated in the absence of the government's intervention is ignored, as also is the number of people who die or whose diseases go untreated for much longer, enduring weeks and months of unnecessary pain waiting for the government's ministrations.

Notice that the proponent of voluntary care does not need to prove anything here anyway, since his position is that our basic duties to each other do not include taking care of each other's health; thus, if someone does die for lack of care, there is not necessarily anyone to blame for this. Nevertheless, most libertarians will in fact take on this further, though strictly unnecessary, burden of argument. Their perception of people is that, by and large, most are pretty helpful to their fellow men: When some people get into a serious scrape due to no fault of their own, others are ready to volunteer assistance. That perception looks pretty plausible to me, and should, I would think, to anyone who has been around much. Human generosity and helpfulness are matters of common observation. Bill Gates and his wife created a charitable foundation with a capital of $30 billion, the purpose being to improve health in Africa—more than any government contributed. While the most spectacular case, the Gateses are one couple among millions who give to charitable causes, including care of the poor or sick. Despite very heavy and nearly ubiquitous taxation, people do in fact contribute considerably to charitable causes. Wealthy people, as we might expect, often spend a great deal of money on them. These levels are such that the libertarian can plausibly suggest that in the absence of government monopolization and imposition in the health care field, people's levels of medical care would be, both in general and in the case of the especially "needy," at least as good as it is now.

The general upshot of this is that the case for government intervention in the health care field is essentially nonexistent. This will be found typical as we look at further areas into which modern government has extended itself. The proposal is made in the absence of any even remotely respectable abstract arguments and accompanied by self-serving refusal even to bother collecting the empirical evidence that would be needed to support the claims on the basis of which the intervention is thought to be justified.

EDUCATION

In the late nineteeth century, politically active people in Great Britain (especially) began to call for getting government into the education business. They succeeded dramatically. Everywhere today, young people are more or less required to go to school, and their parents are taxed to support school systems whether those parents use them or not. Today education is spoken of as if it too were, somehow, a human right or at least a human need; and when it is said to be a need, most leap directly to its being a right. As usual, people fail to distinguish between the right in its negative form, which is common ground, and in its positive form, which definitely is not—yet the latter is what the whole debate is about. Moreover, what is meant by "education" in this debate is the services of a professional teacher. Yet we spend our lives learning, and most of what we learn is not acquired via teachers. Even the kind of learning done in schools can be had without professional educators. Of course, within that context, education can be private rather than public.

In the previous 10,000 years of human history, education was not regarded as a need and certainly not as a right in the new, positive sense of the term. Once writing came onto the human scene, by and large, it was a rather esoteric skill taught only to some priests, princes, and businesspeople, though the circle grew wide enough that the ancient philosophers appeared to be able to depend on a readership for their treatises. Industrializing England created a rising demand for reading and writing, to the point where we are told that, despite the absence of public schools, literacy in that country was pretty close to today's levels—before the rise of public schools.[8] Education is a classic example of government invading an area that was already in good shape before it came on the scene. Governments note which way the troops are marching, then dash to the head of the column to lead them on. They raise prices for their services, and they cut off or undercut competition.

Why should government be involved at all, let alone to the extent to which it actually is nowadays? The usual view is that it's simply obvious—case closed. Occasionally a doff of the hat is also made to the idea that education is a public good. But it's not, in the normal understanding of public goods: A can be educated while B is not, or vice versa. That we all benefit from other people's education is plausible enough. All, at any rate, except those who are subjected to an educational regime they don't want. But these benefits are realized in ordinary relations and especially in the marketplace, where the exercise of skills by those who provide special services is compensated sufficiently to cover the costs of acquiring them and inducing them to exercise their skills in the pursuit of profit.

Is private education, as it is often said to be, "expensive"? That depends. Again, the usual view is that education is of necessity provided by educators, and they of course must be paid to supply this service. Undoubtedly many people do learn much from teachers. But then, they learn a lot more on their own, or from readily available sources such as newspapers and, nowadays, the Internet and from their friends and from books. In fact, much education today consists of getting students to read certain things and then trying to find out whether they have read and understood those things. There's nothing surprising about this. But it undermines the case for treating education as something that can't happen without a well-paid coterie of professional educators to do the educating.

Among the manifold counterinstances to the standard claims, standing out conspicuously, is the phenomenon of home-schooling. The number of Anglo-Americans in home schools is difficult to get, but figures in the neighborhood of a million or more are common, at a median cost of about $450 per child, though that is highly variable. The main cost is that one parent normally stays home to do the schooling, though usually only part-time. Whether he or she would be working outside the home otherwise varies—many do not.

The public schools are used as child-care services at public expense. The expense is pretty substantial, certainly. The cost per child in public schools in North America tends to run about $8,000 per year and up. A parent who would otherwise be working might not make a lot more than that cost for two children, especially after taxes and the expenses associated with working are deducted. There are also, of course, any number of private schools, and again we are told that the average cost of educating children in such schools is somewhat less than the public school figure.

The real question is why education for children should be compulsory. It will familiarly be said that if we didn't have public schools, "children would be running around illiterate"—a view known to be false insofar as empirical evidence is available and also misleading in that the implication is that public education will fix this unhappy condition. Yet a sizable fraction of children who finish compulsory schooling are illiterate anyway, despite the many years they have sat disconsolately in their classrooms.[9]

A plausible analysis of the public education movement is that, first, it represents an effort to socialize and indoctrinate children so that they will "fit in" with the society to which they belong. This is a vague goal, of course, and insofar as it is not vague, it is mostly one we might well regard with suspicion.

Most of the great universities in the United States are privately funded, though increasingly they accept students with government scholarships or government research funds. Meanwhile in Canada across the border, private universities are mostly illegal. Research funds are carefully controlled and devoted exclusively to projects with the imprimatur of the politics of the day. Meanwhile the faculty associations jealously guard their academic freedom.

What, it must be asked, is really the point? One might have hoped that the point of education was to enable people to learn interesting things they might not otherwise know. But governments mostly emphasize such "needs" as to enable the country, as a country, to "compete with" other countries. What the point of that competition is, is left unsaid. To talk that way is to treat the country as a team competing against the other teams for something. But what, and why?

WELFARE

The production of food, one would think, must be the most important thing in any society. In the upper echelon states of today's world, with their generally free-enterprise farmers and entirely free-enterprise grocery stores, it is all but impossible to find anyone in serious danger of starvation. Why is this? If it's so important, and government provision is necessary for basic needs, shouldn't government be doing it?

Certainly government doesn't stay out of the business altogether, by any means. But governments, contrary to what you might expect, do not mostly come down on the side of us consumers. On the contrary: Most contemporary governments subsidize their farmers. The European Union pays European farmers to grow sugar, though Brazilians could do it for one-sixth the cost. Canadian milk producers get licenses giving them the right to produce, thus making its price more than twice what it would be on a free market. And so on. Yet all these are manifestly unnecessary if the point is merely to enable all to eat. Indeed, the most significant agricultural interventions in the twentieth century were in the Communist countries, where they led to massive starvation—notably the thirty-some million who starved in Maoist China as the communal agricultural system went from bad to worse.

This is all a prelude to the government concern with "welfare," a concern that has mounted up as the decades have gone by and as, one would think, claims of need have grown ever less plausible. In recent times, the familiar practice has been to erect standards for estimating poverty. These are specified at some level of income, and the figures are frequently adjusted to ensure a plentiful supply of people needing "welfare" assistance. In Canada in 2001, for instance, a large family living in an urban region of over a half-million population was deemed to be living in poverty if its income was less than $47,988. A single individual in a rural area, on the other hand, would have to make do with $13,021. These, it should be noted, are incomes that in most parts of the world would count as high. How, one might wonder, did it come to be thought that our fellow citizens owe it to us to have an income of some particular size, and a fairly good size at that?

Certainly many philosophers have thought that they do. St. Thomas Aquinas, notably, was of the view that the very poor were welcome to take from the rich, and that it doesn't even count as theft if they do.[10] Considering the agricultural/political situation in Aquinas's day, we may suspect that St. Thomas would have turned his nose up at the suggestion that any of today's "poor" count as genuinely needy. Thomas Hobbes, John Locke, and Immanuel Kant all agreed that we had a duty to help our fellows in need and that one of the legitimate functions of government was to make sure that it was carried out. Of course, this again was a duty that stopped at the borders of one's own country. It wasn't part of the bargain that we are to help feed everybody everywhere.

Part of the motivation for the welfare state seems to have been that if we didn't do this, the poor might get uppity and start using violence against the rich. It was not made clear why the rich shouldn't arm themselves against these enemies rather than turning their pocketbooks over to them. After all, making war on others isn't cheap, and the rich would seem to be able to make a pretty good go of defending themselves if it came to that, not to mention that in making war on the productive, the unproductive are cutting off their own hoped-for source of livelihood.

But presumably these rather morbid arguments are not what they had in mind. Presumably, many who support the welfare state are sincere. They do so because they believe we do have this duty. The question is, why? It is one thing to appeal to human sympathy, which undoubtedly will touch a chord, as Hume puts it. Few lack such sympathy; almost any of us is ready to help a fellow human in real need. But it is one thing to act from sympathy and quite another to exert compulsion on people to do these things—and compulsion is what is in question here.

There are two large questions about the welfare state. First, of course, is whether it's necessary. Second is whether the kinds of measures that governments take can be expected to work very well, or at all. Opinions differ about both. There is considerable reason to believe that the answers to both questions are mostly in the negative.

The reason for a negative answer to the first is, again, that noncompulsory measures are adequate for any genuine "needs" in this area. Everywhere, at least in North America, there are many welfare suppliers that are not government agencies—churches, community groups of various kinds, and of course relatives and friends, all ready to lend a hand. Second, one suspects darkly that the need for welfare is generated in considerable part by restrictions on employment and housing. Minimum wage legislation, for example, ensures that those who could work for a low wage will not be employed since the government will forbid offering that wage.

The reason for a negative answer to the second is that the measures taken tend to do more harm than good. In his classic study of the American "War on Poverty," Charles Murray found that over the twenty years in which those programs had been in operation, the groups whose assistance was the object of the programs were worse off in every respect than at the beginning.[11] It seems that state-sponsored compulsory charity tends to be self-perpetuating and counterproductive.

Hobbes's primary criterion of good laws is that they be necessary. Those that aren't, he complains, are "traps for money" rather than genuine contributions to the public weal. There is ample room to suspect the welfare state along these lines.

PARKS AND SYMPHONIES AND SUCH

Modern democratic states operate a variety of facilities for the public, such as parks of various kinds. In the United States, national parks occupy an area equal to that of a large state such as Colorado. In addition, there are state and local parks. All of these are kept in more or less virgin condition, except for the roads and camp sights enabling the public to have convenient access to the wilderness so that they can enjoy nature. Some also preserve historically interesting sights. A fraction of their cost of maintenance is met by user fees; for the rest, the public maintains a considerable and rather expensive benefit for a relatively few heavy users. Light use is different. Perhaps in the end nearly everyone uses at least some parks on some occasions (I, for example, walk through one on my way to work). If parks had to be paid for entirely by users, there presumably might be fewer and smaller parks than there are. In the view of park users, this would be very sad—but then, they are the very people who are enjoying the free ride. What about all the people who would be living in the areas currently covered by parks instead of residential buildings?

Again, we note that there are private parks. Presumably all parks, of whatever size, could be operated by Park Co-ops consisting of interested people or by neighborhood associations, and many more. They could even be bought by Parks, Incorporated, and run as businesses thereafter. Many wouldn't like that, of course, but that hardly shows that the idea is impossible. It does indicate how strongly many people would resist the idea, however. One might, again, wonder why. Normally, putting something into the hands of those who care about it is a good idea. Putting it into the hands of civil servants is not obviously as good, though modern governments do often command the services of talented and sincere people—along, of course, with others not quite so talented or sincere and a great many who are just doing their jobs, well or badly.

A somewhat different case is the support of high culture: symphony orchestras, art museums, ballet companies, theaters, and the like. The problem is that a quite small fraction of the populace—unless it's a very unusual populace—is likely to use any of these facilities. The rest do not care about them. So, why are we permitted to descend on the uncultured in order to help support expensive productions for the interest and enlightenment of the cultured?[12]

The main answer to this would be, no doubt, In Order to Promote the True and the Good. I'm all for that, but the trouble is, it seems that only a modest number of us are interested in that, and what about the rest? If we say, "Well, serves them right!," then we have departed from liberalism. If we don't say that, we can quote various and sundry town councilors who will say that it's good for tourism and that will benefit another handful of merchants at the expense of all the merchants who would have been patronized by those whose money is taxed from many people who don't attend the symphony, and so on.

Putting public money into culture, in short, assumes and invokes a "common culture" which, generally speaking, doesn't exist. Again, there is no real question of this being a public good. Certainly it is not true that X hears the symphony only if Y does, except in the irrelevant sense that we aren't going to have a symphony orchestra if its concerts are attended by just one person.

We can also surely ask whether culture is really all that great if the people who get it are unwilling to pay for it.

Can't we?

REGULATING ANYTHING AND EVERYTHING

Not for nothing has the modern State been referred to as the "regulatory state." Why regulate? Well might we ask. According to the official theory, regulations are to protect us. Here's one of my favorites. In my town, if you should be affluent enough to have two sinks in your bathroom so that you and hubby can both wash at the same time, then the good town leaders have decreed that you will have to run two separate plumbing lines all the way down to the basement, thus doubling the expense, instead of only up at the bathroom sink level. It is not clear what this protects us from—certainly not from the rapacity of plumbers. Or here's another, due to the European Common Market: "[A] spicy sausage known as the Welsh Dragon will have to be renamed after trading standards' officers warned the manufacturers that they could face prosecution because it does not contain dragon. The sausages will now have to be labeled Welsh Dragon Pork Sausages to avoid any confusion among customers."[13] Clearly this is an important protection to all the several hundred thousand people who have been buying those sausages for many decades under the illusion that they were eating genuine dragon meat!

American regulation sees to it that new drugs come onto the market only after many years of extremely expensive testing. In the meantime, many people die of the diseases that the new drugs will save others from when finally it makes its way through the regulatory procedures—at several times the price it would otherwise be able to be sold for.[14] It also makes life impossible for small companies, since they are incapable of maintaining the capitalizations necessary to cope with ten-year waiting times before their products can start earning anything. This reduces competition for the big companies, enabling them to charge yet more. It is odd that democratic government works out so well for the interests of the big at enormous cost to the ordinary consumer.

There is no end of regulation, and the story is always the same. The regulators make sure that the consumer buys a more expensive product than he or she otherwise might prefer and that other suppliers could and would supply at competitive prices. The regulated products may also be safer—or, quite possibly, not—but at least it will be the same for all, like it or not. The requirements imposed will see to it that small producers of the item are at a disadvantage; another side effect that also has the predictable effect of raising prices. Whatever else, regulators are in the business of not letting customers have what they want. This should strike us as odd in a society dedicated to the proposition that The Customer Is Always Right. But the regulatory apologist will respond, righteously, that the regulations are designed to promote certain important values, such as safety and fairness. You may not think that what they claim is safe is so, and you may not be as interested in your own safety as the regulators. Fairness seems to be a matter of making sure that we all get the same thing, like it or not, and that people willing to settle for something lesser, for a correspondingly lesser price, will not be able to get it, while people willing to pay more for a better product won't be allowed to do that either.

According to a recent study, "By 1990, 25 years of regulations enforced by the U.S. Environmental Protection Agency had cost the U.S. economy an estimated 22% of the manufacturing output that otherwise would have been produced."[15] In the meantime, people have been deprived of their property, prevented from taking useful business opportunities, and sometimes wound up in jail in the interests of regulation. It is hard to see how all this is in the interest of the public.

EQUALITY AND FAIRNESS

Political philosophy these days is dominated by a claimed interest in equality, or fairness, or the one because of the other. Not very much has been said about these notions in this book as yet, apart from the central role of one kind of equality in the theory of democracy. This will be thought strange by many: those topics are at the top of many philosophers' agendas in this area.

What is the proper role of these notions? There is considerable confusion about them, which I will attempt to do something to clear up here—at least to the extent of seeing where these notions fit in the political scheme of things.

First, it will be well to recall that the basic concern of politics and morals is with adjusting the software of society in such a way as to enable us all to get on. They are, then, notionally universal. We seek principles for all.

Second, our fundamental methodological idea is that the principles of morals and politics are to be such as to be acceptable to all, given that they must also be acceptable to all others—working from a starting point or "baseline"of no rules at all. We want, then, that these principles will look good to everyone: They are to be such that if followed, each is to be enabled to do as well as possible given that the others are doing likewise, insofar as the person's situation can be determined by moral and political arrangements as distinct from personal capabilities and fortune. For this reason, these principles to which we all are to be able to appeal when things get sticky are, by their very nature, impartial. Impartiality is a matter of these principles' not preferring anyone, as such, to anyone else. That, however, is not at all the same thing as (what is usually intended by) *equality*.

Third, equality is conceptually a relation holding between two things that are being compared in some respect that is (a) variable in *degree*, and (b) *commensurable*. Height, for example, readily affords such comparisons: Jones and Smith are of equal height when the number of units of height that measures the height of Jones is the same as the number measuring Smith's. There are innumerable variables in respect of which two things, or in this case two persons, can be compared, and for this reason there is also simply no sense to the question, asked without specification, whether one person is, without further specification, "equal to" another. People are different—they are distinct individuals—and they are similar or dissimilar in no end of respects. But being a person is not something that is variable in degree and commensurable. So if we are to talk of "moral equality" we are going to have to ask just what that is. The most meaningful answer is that it is not really equality at all, but rather, that each is being treated *in the same way*, that is, the same principles apply to all, despite their differences. Some call that equality. But it is not literally any such thing. The more appropriate name for this is *identity*, that is, all coming under the same concept or, as in this case, rule. That is not necessarily a matter of degree of comparable things.

When are we entitled to equality of any kind, properly so called? The egalitarian is the theorist who claims that there is, despite all these de facto differences among us, something commensurable about people such that morals and politics should be concerned with getting each of us the same amount of something—whatever it is the egalitarian claims we should be getting; at least, that they should be concerned to reduce disparities in that respect. "All men are created equal," in the most obvious understanding of this claim, is obviously false. People are "created" at birth unequal, not equal, in innumerable ways, both genetically and otherwise, even if equal in many respects as well. And in all sorts of ways, this inequality will also ground relevant inequality of treatment. Milo the wrestler, as Aristotle observed, should get more steak than you or I.

You can, however, jury-rig things so that what Milo the wrestler gets and what I, of ordinary physique and energy, get is describable as "the same" after all. For instance, we could suggest that what should be the same for the two of us is the input of calories per unit of body mass, adjusted by our level of physical activity—or some such thing. The fact that such things can be done should warn us against employing notions of equality as if they were perfectly clear.

Meanwhile, the question now is Is there anything such that you and I or the State should be trying to bring it about that all of us has the same *amount* of it? Theorists have answered this in the affirmative with assorted candidates. Perhaps the most popular nowadays is equal opportunity, but there have been many others: equal resources, equal welfare, equal income, equal respect, equal chances at living a good life, have each been advocated.

Should we add "equal freedom"? But is *freedom* a commensurable variable of which we should all be getting the same amount? There is, again, a tricky way in which we can make this true. Freedom—that is, the sort of freedom with which politics and morals are concerned—consists in noninterference from others. So we might say that what we all deserve an equal amount of is, indeed, violence or interference: We should all be getting the same amount at the hands of others—namely, *none*. But of course this isn't at all what egalitarians have in mind. They want us all to help bring about an equal amount of F, where F is some positive amount—(with the right values of F being supplied by his theory).

Hardly anyone literally believes that, however. To be real, we need to back away from the goal of literal equality and instead say that we may all be compelled to do something to, say, narrow the gap between the most and the least in the respect this theorist is interested in. Thus, government should, say, tax the rich and redistribute the resulting income to the less well off. How much? Well, good question! But anyway, some.

If that strikes the reader as not much of a theory, well, you're right. Indeed, it is difficult to think of anything such that we all have a duty to equalize it, and so may be compelled to try to decrease any and all disparities among people in that respect. How about income, say? The idea, popularized by assorted theorists, that justice calls for all of us to have, or nearly have, or have approximately, the same income is quite a lot too absurd to be worth more than a casual mention as an example of a cracker-barrel theory that seems to have been held by some romantic theorists in times past. Each individual is, and should be, doing his or her best—trying to live the best life possible for that person. Many among them will include the goal of making as much money as possible, though many others will make that a lesser goal or disown it. Doing that by legitimate methods only—hard work, discovery, ingenuity, creative thought and effort, together with a good deal of intelligently guided voluntary exchange—is manifestly beneficial to others as well as to the agent. Thus we should all be in favor of people doing this, too. But, obviously, we have no business exercising compulsion here. Egalitarianism in that respect, for example, is so far from being required by justice that we should instead say it is *forbidden* by it. No one may intervene in order to prevent someone from increasing his or her income by any legitimate means simply because of the relation it bears to someone else's income, and if the person does so in the name of egalitarianism, then that's precisely the trouble with egalitarianism.

More generally, there are no significant independent variables (that is, such that one person's exemplifying any given amount does not entail anyone else's exemplifying any particular amount), and such that more is better, so far as a given person is concerned, and yet such that we should be limiting the amount one person has in light of how much someone else has. As one wag put it, "I used to think that equality was the geometry of justice; but now I see that it's merely the arithmetic of envy."[16]

FAIRNESS AND JUSTICE

But shouldn't we be fair? Doesn't fairness require equality of some sort? The trouble is that the idea of fairness can be used in various ways—so many that it is not even clear whether we owe everyone any general duty of fairness.

(1) One legitimate meaning would make fairness simply another synonym for justice and the right. To treat someone fairly in this most general sense is to treat him the way he ought to be treated, or the way he "deserves" to be treated. But that takes us in a broad circle. We must then ask, deserves how? If the answer is, "deserves, in justice" then the circle is closed and we have gotten nowhere. Of course, we all want justice. But fairness in that general sense is not here being used as the name of some kind of independently specifiable mode of treatment that we ought to engage in, but rather as simply a name for whatever kind of treatment would be right. Since the question is, what is that kind of treatment?, this is hardly helpful.

(2) Still, we sometimes do owe some people a duty of fairness in a narrower sense. In this sense, fairness requires a background set of relevant rules, normally rules that all concerned do accept. A familiar example in the writings of recent moral and political philosophers is that it is fair, at the party, to divide the cake equally. But even that example is satisfactory if generalized much. For any given person, A, and any other, B, in any circumstances, C, it is obviously not true that it would be fair for a given piece of cake to be given half to A and half to B. Suppose, for example, that it is A's cake. Or if it's a birthday party, suppose that B wasn't invited? Among the invitees, should each get an equal amount of something—cake, wine, TLC? Sometimes, but usually not. Rather, each should have what he or she likes, if there's plenty, and if not, then dispensations such as one piece per person may come into play. If you invite them to the party, you treat them well— what would be the point if you didn't? Meanwhile, however, the State is not a party, and we were not "invited" by anyone, so the famous analogy is inapplicable from the start.

We should treat our employees fairly. Meaning what? And, why? It does not mean paying them each the same—indeed, that could well be unfair, and usually would be. But fairness here is going to shade rapidly into impartiality. The company isn't here to advance the interests of one employee against another, but rather, to make as much profit as possible, with each employee contributing to this goal in whatever way that person is hired to do. Other respects in which employees may differ, as for example in age or sex or race, are usually irrelevant or at best partially and indirectly relevant to that central factor. Accordingly, the wise company will ignore these irrelevant features and pay in proportion to the contribution made by the employee in question to the firm's profitability. Fairness here consists in attending only to the variables made relevant by the general purposes of the association, and ignoring others.

In a competitive sport such as hockey, say, it is quite possible to be unfair by violating the rules, subtly or otherwise. We shouldn't do this because we all came here to play, as defined by common acceptance of the rules of hockey. We all want to win if we can, but what we may do to achieve that is limited by those rules. It is an injustice to the other players to cheat. The cheater is making an exception of himself, holding the other players to the rule but not himself. That indeed is unfair. There is perhaps no better field of application of the notion of fairness: you're fair if you don't cheat, and to cheat is to go against the rules defining the game we all came here to play or enjoy.

In life, however, we mostly aren't playing anything, and there aren't any "rules" in the sense in which games have rules.[17] And this, in the end, is what is wrong with thinking that fairness is both an interesting and a fundamental idea in political and moral philosophy. Once we distinguish universality and impartiality, which of course are central and crucial, from equality and fairness, it is clear that the latter are relatively special matters, rather than being the fundamental concepts in the field, and that they often do not apply.

RAWLS

No book on this subject in contemporary times can avoid saying something about the celebrated philosopher John Rawls (1921–2002), whose book *A Theory of Justice* is by academic standards an all-time best-seller.[18] The influence of that book is so far-reaching that one hesitates to criticize, and far too few do so. But we must make our peace with it here, however briefly.

Rawls supposes that the fundamental principles of justice are objects of choice or decision by everybody, thus putting it into the social contract category. Unfortunately, the idea becomes rapidly less clear as we read on. We are to choose under a "veil of ignorance" which denies us information about ourselves in particular, though we are to know general facts about people. Just why we would be very interested in principles that "we" might choose in a condition where we literally had no idea who we were is less than clear. Perhaps the thought is that there is a core of common humanity left after blanking out all information specific to oneself. But then there would surely be room to ask why our individual differences, which are many and profound, should not get their "due" as well.

The choice is conceived as an exercise in distributive justice, the theory of who gets what. What is to be distributed are things that society makes. But this raises the point that society doesn't make anything, in one sense; only its members do that, and different members make all sorts of different things. There seems to be a presumption that somehow individuals' products are "social" in a sense that implies their availability for handing out to whomever we please. And there is a very strong presumption that somehow it is wicked to be born smarter or more talented than somebody else. We are to "adopt a principle which . . . mitigates the arbitrary effects of the natural lottery itself."[19] One cannot, of course, help being born the way one is born, but it takes a deft twist of the semantic dagger to convert that into an excuse for appropriating the output of the more talented and redistributing them to all and sundry on the ground that the producers didn't really "deserve" to be so capable. Society should not, of course, go out of its way to reward the talented just because they are so, independently of what they do with those talents. But we should "reward" people who do us a good thing, and that's what the productive do. How is there anything wrong with that?

Rawls holds that we would emerge from our theoretical sessions behind the veil of ignorance with two principles:

(1) An equal liberty principle: "Each to have the most extensive liberty compatible with a like liberty for all" in its earliest versions. These give way to a more convoluted principle as follows: "Each Person is to have an Equal Right to the most extensive total system of equal basic liberties compatible with a similar system for all."[20]

(2) The "maximin" principle, which says, "Social and Economic Inequalities are to be arranged so that they are (a) to the greatest benefit of the least advantaged, and (b) attached to offices and positions open to all under conditions of fair equality of opportunity."[21] The word "maximin" means "maximum of the minimum," as in clause (a).

A major claim, reiterated often enough, is that the first principle is to be "lexically prior" to the second. This, as we will see shortly, is not really adhered to.

Regarding the definition of social and political liberty that looms large in this book, Rawls is not helpful. The normal one is this: You are at liberty to do X, socially speaking, when other people do not prevent you from doing X. If you can't do X anyway, the liberty may not be of much use to you, as Rawls agrees. An idea that we have a positive right to liberty in general is complete nonsense, as the reader will have discerned from our earlier discussions. But an idea that we have a positive right to protection in respect of our liberty is not; it was explored in chapter 4. But what does Rawls mean here? We don't know.

Whatever he means, the question arises whether he wants to include economic liberty in the scope of the first principle. He seems not to, but one must wonder why not. He wants the liberties covered to include the familiar ones—freedom of conscience, speech, assembly, lifestyle, and also to hold strictly personal property—but when it comes to making a living, earning the income by means of which one would acquire that property, he's not so sure.

What about the second principle? There is a spectacular unclarity about the meaning of the maximin idea. Are we to redistribute benefits so that the least advantaged have as much as possible? If so, we will have to distribute them equally, since otherwise, the less advantaged will not, of course, have the "greatest" benefit they can have, in respect of whatever it is that is so distributed. If something is supposed to block that redistribution, it's unclear what it is. Rawls mentions incentives, but he can't mean this, for if my incentive is that I get more than you, which is an inequality, then his reply should be that I can't have it, because equality is supposedly required by justice. If I can, though—well, what's left of the principle?

In any case, if the first principle is literally prior to the second and the first does include economic liberty, then the second principle would be useless, since we would not be allowed to take from the better off in order to bene-fit the worse off in whatever way the murky second principle is thought to require. As to part (b) of the second principle, it is not clear, first, which offices it is supposed to apply to: political ones only? Or all "offices" such as personnel manager of my hardware business? (Or, husband? Are we to be "fair" regarding all possible candidates for that post?) What is "fair equality of opportunity" for hiring? Must I advertise to the whole human race before I hire? If not, why not?

In any case, the snag with all this is that opportunities are created by the activities of people. If they are free to create those opportunities or not—as the first principle seems to imply—then why are they not free to extend them to some people but not others, as they choose? Note that the constraints of the market will push them very strongly in the direction desired by postmodern liberals anyway. If you want your good employees to stay, you'd better not pay one of them a lot more for the same work, and in any case you'd be wasting your firm's money if you did. (But what about seniority?) Would you discriminate against women, black people, white people, or whatever? You do so at your own peril, in the business world—discrimination is expensive! And so on. Market freedoms, in short, do everything that it is reasonable to insist on doing, and nothing that it is unreasonable to insist on doing.

If Rawls thinks that market liberties are not enough and we owe much more, of course, he needs to explain why. But there are, I think, no useful answers to any of these questions in the pages of *A Theory of Justice*, nor in the extensive literature to which it has given rise.[22] (Since many thousands of articles and dozens of books have been written on Rawls since *A Theory of Justice* first came out, I must obviously add, "so far as I know" to this last statement.)

RACE, GENDER, AND OTHER VARIABLES: DISCRIMINATION

Modern governments pay a great deal of attention to the subject of discrimination, in particular as it applies to certain large groups in society, notably as distinguished by race, gender, ethnicity, and perhaps religion and national origin. Now, the general notion of nondiscrimination is roughly this: to discriminate is to favor on the basis of some irrelevant characteristic. That uses the word "irrelevant," which requires some background principle to tell us what is and what isn't relevant. Sometimes the word "morally" is inserted: We are not to treat people in ways that are morally irrelevant. But again, to say this is pleonastic. Of course, we should treat people only in the ways that morality says we may, but which are those?

There is one good answer to this. Morality forbids harm: It forbids making people worse off as a result of one's intentional actions. But that doesn't imply that we must treat people equally, in any number of imaginable ways. We should not treat our friends merely equally with others, we should and do treat them better. Should we even treat all our friends equally? No: Some are better friends than others, closer, say. What we should specifically do for them varies hugely from one friend to another.

Should we say that it is morally wrong to discriminate in hiring? That is perhaps the most popular single context for the application of notions of discrimination. It obviously presupposes some notion of how we *should* treat someone in regard to employment. But just what is that notion? How should we treat them? The plausible answer is that we hire in order to enable the firm to make more money—if it's a profit-making firm. (And if it isn't? Then we'd need some other purpose of the firm, such that we would take on employees [or whatever] as a function of that purpose, whatever it is—saving souls, for instance, in some evangelical undertaking.) Hiring someone because she is a woman is perfectly reasonable in a women's club, for example, but not in many other establishments. And so on.

The modern State presumes to supply all with various goods: health, education, welfare, and a few others that have been commented on here. If indeed it should be doing that, then it should also be trying to provide those goods equally to all, somehow. Or at least, it should not be doling them out only to the black people or the white people or the female people or, etc. In this book, much doubt is shed on the claim that the State should be "doing" all these things. If it shouldn't, then does that mean it's OK for it to discriminate after all? No. What it means is that it's not OK for the State to be imposing on anyone, of any color or sex or whatever, for the sake of promoting those objects, whatever they are. (For example, programs of "affirmative action," where the government positively requires the employer to hire on the basis of irrelevant criteria, such as race or sex, clearly are aimed at promoting some people at the expense of others.)

All of which is to say that fairness in the sense of equality or nondiscrimination cannot rationally be regarded as fundamentally significant notions in political theory. Once we do know what the State should be doing—even if it's nothing—we also know what it would be for it to "discriminate" or "treat unfairly" in those respects and that it should not do such things. Those who think that fairness or equality are fundamental notions have a problem. A "fundamental" notion is so called because it is not derivative, not based on anything else. Someone who advances a major political or moral proposal that he can't offer any reasons for, however, is in a very weak position to respond to anyone who rejects the proposal. Considering the nature of egalitarian proposals or proposals to make some kind of "fairness" the fundamental consideration, we may be sure that such proposals will run into flak, very quickly.

The views advanced in this book differ in that no such controversial notions are taken to be fundamental. Our interest in individual freedom, for example, is based on our other interests, whatever they may be, on the sheer fact that we have them, in general. It is not a "fundamental" value. If you are interested in having x, y, and z, then you are interested in not having other people prevent you from getting them. Or if you are, that is odd, given your claim that you were interested in x, y, and z. But it is, indeed, all up to you. That's the strength of liberalism. The other strength is that it makes the existence of other people a highly relevant factor in our lives. Others are able to affect our own lives, drastically. We had better accommodate ourselves to them, as effectively as possible. Should we be "fair" to others, or treat them "equally"? Once we have settled the more basic question of just how we are going to relate to them, then fairness and sometimes equality can often come into play. But also, often not. Contemporary philosophy tends to fail to come to grips with this variability. And that in turn is because so many philosophers seem to think that we can't really give any good reasons for basic proposals in these areas, in which case—well, anything goes, right? Or, more likely, they think that their proclivities on these matters are somehow "knowledge" that should be accepted by the relatively less articulate people they are addressing. I don't buy that, and I'm sure you don't, either. All of which leaves us with the question of what the modern State is really for. Why has it got into so many things, despite the inefficiencies and evils that its efforts invariably entail?

The answer to the last, of course, is depressingly easy to come by: the State gets into whatever it thinks it can get away with getting into, in order to expand its powers. In a liberal society, such ambitions should be regarded with extreme suspicion. As P. J. O'Rourke puts it, "giving money and power to government is like giving whiskey and car keys to teenage boys."[23]

THE STATE AS FUN

Another answer to this last question that should be taken slightly seriously is: It's more fun that way. Politics is, in its way, interesting, and it has that unpredictability and arbitrariness and potential for drama that reflects Life. People are often willing to go out and take huge risks, including the risk of death, for their country. They should be compared with contemporary terrorists who, as of this writing, are one of the world's major political concerns. Terrorists are willing to blow themselves to bits, along with as many other people as possible, for the sake of vague political and religious ideas and ideals. The fact that people can do things like that is interesting, in its macabre way. . . . Interesting, yes—but, of course, it really is evil, and paradigmatically unjust. No doubt injustice is interesting, in its way. But the

interest in question comes at a high price. It is not easy to think that inter-
estingness really does justify all the bad things done in the name of the
State. They may be interesting because they are bad, but their interesting-
ness doesn't excuse their badness.

NOTES

1. James Rolf Edwards, "The Costs of Public Income Redistribution and Private
Charity," *Journal of Libertarian Studies*, vol. 21, no. 2 (2007): 8.
2. Edwards, "The Costs of Public Income Redistribution," 9.
3. Hobbes, *Leviathan*, chapter XXX, numerous editions.
4. From a general description of the system by the Civitas organization:
http://www.civitas.org.uk/pdf/Canada.pdf.
5. The per capita average of $2,931. Health care spending will account for 38.6
cents of every dollar provincial and territorial governments spend. www.cbc.ca/
canada/story/2006/11/01/health-costs.html.
6. This article from *The New York Times* explains how things are changing and what
the problems have been: http://www.nytimes.com/2006/02/26/international/americas/
26canada.html?ex=1298610000&en=c2dd6e7e8f107208&ei=5088&partner=rssnyt&
emc=rss.
7. See David Gratzer, *The Cure: How Capitalism Can Save American Health Care*
(New York: Encounter Books, 2006), 25–44 and more generally, the entire book.
8. See James Tooley, *Education without the State* (London: Institute of Economic
Affairs, 1996), 31–48.
9. See, for example, James Bartholomew, "Education: Eleven Years at School and
Still Illiterate," in *The Welfare State We're In* (London: Methuen, 2004), chapter 4,
151–224.
10. Regarding the poor, St. Thomas Aquinas, *Summa Theologica*, II.2, 96.7.
11. Charles Murray, *Losing Ground: American Social Policy, 1950–1980* (New York:
Basic Books, 1984) is the classic study in this field.
12. Tyler Cowen, *In Praise of Commercial Culture* (Cambridge, MA: Harvard University Press, 1998), details both the extent and high quality of nongovernment cultural initiatives here and elsewhere.
13. Reported in *The Times* of London, November 18, 2006. http://www.timesonline
.co.uk/article/0,2-2458696,00.html.
14. Robert Higgs, "The U.S. Food and Drug Administration: A Billy Club Is Not
a Substitute for Eyeglasses," in *Against Leviathan: Government Power and a Free Society* (Oakland, CA: Independent Institute, 2004), 59–75.
15. Robert Higgs and Carl P. Close, eds., *Re-Thinking Green: Alternatives to Environmental Bureaucracy* (Oakland, CA: Independent Institute, 2005).
16. Passed on from a friend, who doesn't know where he heard it either.
17. The notion of a game is beautifully explicated in Bernard Suits, *The Grasshopper
—Games, Life, and Utopia* (Peterborough, Ont.: Broadview Press, 2005). It is also, by
the way, one of the most delightful philosophical works ever.

18. John Rawls, *A Theory of Justice* (Cambridge, MA: Harvard University Press, 1971).

19. Rawls, *A Theory of Justice*, 74.

20. Rawls, *A Theory of Justice*, 302.

21. Rawls, *A Theory of Justice*, 302.

22. A more extensive criticism in some of these respects is found in Jan Narveson, "A Puzzle about Economic Justice in Rawls' Theory," *Respecting Persons in Theory and Practice* (Lanham, MD: Rowman & Littlefield, 2002), chapter 2, 13–34.

23. P. J. O'Rourke, *Parliament of Whores: A Lone Humorist Attempts to Explain the Entire U.S. Government* (New York: Atlantic Monthly Press, 1991), xviii.

7

War and Peace, Immigration and Trade

A main cause of States is other States. If the folks next door have a State, there's a good chance they'll take a notion to move over and beat up on or take over the locals here—and, as they say, there goes the neighborhood! So we make a State over here to counter them. International war is a frequent occurrence and obviously a main issue in international politics. But alongside it is international commerce, which has been going on for a very long time, too. In this chapter we will briefly ponder these subjects, which can hardly be dispensed with, given their importance. Why, you may ask, group the two together? The prima facie liberal answer is that just as war is a violent incursion against other armies, so restrictions on commerce are (always potentially, and often actually) violent incursions against individuals trying to make a living. The two are also interconnected in that restrictions on commerce are often done in the name of national security.

WHEN IS A STATE? THE BOUNDARY QUESTION

A question not even skirted in the foregoing chapters is How is it to be decided whether a given stretch of territory with a given set of occupants is, or, if it isn't already, should be made into a "State"? If we look at a political map of the contemporary world, we see many boundary lines that have been redrawn in recent times, and much more of that in more remote times. And we read, quite often, of groups within some existing State who think that they should constitute a State of their own, sometimes complaining loudly, or violently, if they are not given their way in that regard. How are such questions to be decided? Or can they be?

We generally take our State for granted. It had some historical origin, various wars perhaps were fought resulting in the drawing or redrawing of borders, and here we are, inside one particular set of them; usually by being born there, though occasionally due to immigration or happenstance. It is usually possible to track how a given State came to be what it is. But there is more than a little difficulty in trying to justify a given State's being what and where it is.

Is it even possible? On some occasions in the past, important political figures have assembled to address the question of just what should be the boundaries of certain places—Poland, for example. When some committee of potentates is able to address the question of where to draw boundaries, then some kind of criteria are called for. Among famous examples are the Fourteen Points proposed by the American president Wilson in 1918 for post–World War I Europe. One of its general conclusions: "An evident principle runs through the whole program I have outlined. It is the principle of justice to all peoples and nationalities, and their right to live on equal terms of liberty and safety with one another, whether they be strong or weak."[1] But unfortunately, those criteria cannot settle the question of where State A should end and State B begin. Wilson treated "nationality" as a relevant variable, but which variable is it? Doesn't nationality just take us back to statehood—the very thing we are trying to decide about? Or if not, does the aspiration to statehood by some group of people claiming to be a "nation" justify its being promoted to statehood? As to living on equal terms, let's hope that applies to all of us in relation to all of us.

A reason for getting into this subject is that every now and again, some part of an existing State becomes the subject of an aspiration to secede from the larger State it is a part of. Then what? Should we always accede to such a request? Historically, they have often been put down by force, as in the American Civil War. Is that ever right? Is the initial rebellion ever right? The American War of Independence, for example?

Of course, such questions basically arise only if the State is legitimate. But even if we think it is not, there sometimes will be a serious question of what to do. For example, if the area and people aspiring to independence would form a much worse, or a much better, State than the one they are part of now, then resistance, or acceptance, as the case may be, would surely be advisable. It is easier to have criteria for answering such relative questions than for the "absolute" question, whether a given area should or should not be a State at all.

Probably the only thing to say about this absolute question is that States come into existence when some politically ambitious people see, and seize, an opportunity to establish a State. Once they do, we will have to decide whether to knuckle under or not, and if not, just how to resist or otherwise to adjust one's reactions. If you are a member of such a set of ambitious people, will you have a philosophical view about what your shiny new State should be like? Maybe, but more likely, the upshot will be settled by power politics. The American Constitution of 1787 stands out as having been crafted by very thoughtful people, with pretty clear and relevant ideas of what they wanted, and not much personal, e.g., economic, interest in the outcome. Yet the American founders already had their territory established. They weren't making States for uncharted wildernesses of people. (They were, on the other hand, making a State that would oversee the taming of uncharted wildernesses beyond their existing frontiers.)

We may also predict that if the set of persons inhabiting the territory in question speak the same language and have a considerable history of dealings with each other, preferably friendly, then the chances of success are much better than if they are a more or less random collection of the earth's people. Those chances are yet more improved if in addition the territory in question has "natural" boundaries: e.g., if it is a large island, or there are mountains, rivers, deserts, and the like between this territory's population centers.

And finally, we can say this, following some very interesting recent work by Russell Hardin.[2] Likely the territory in question will have a population that divides more or less naturally into certain interest groups, and these in turn will likely have natural leaders or representatives, whether by an election process or something else. What matters is only that they are in de facto positions of leadership. Then if the set of such leaders of major segments—the "politically effective groups" in the community—can just agree on the general outlines of the new State, its success is close to assured. If they can't, failure is more or less certain. So the thing for the aspiring State-builder to do is to get these people together and find a formula for a State that's going to work for them.

The preceding discussion may be viewed as a cop-out on our original question. Alternatively, we may view it as all that is possible in the way of an answer. The fact that we can't do much better is, I think, significant, and reflects what we may call the factuality of the State. The State is just *here*. Or more precisely: Particular actual States have histories, and those histories tell us how they got here; but there's little that's normative going on in these histories and probably nothing of the philosophically interesting kind that would be needed if a high-level normative theory were to connect with that history.

This includes the case where a constitution comes about by virtue of a convention such as was held in Philadelphia in 1787. Is there something privileged about that story? We may like to think so, but it cannot be claimed that the Philadelphia convention had a claim to a new and re-markable kind of legitimacy. For one thing, that convention was charged with refining or revising the previous arrangement, which was thought not to be working very well but which did serve as an in-force backdrop for the new document. Only if we can find a good argument as to why we should all acknowledge the work of a few dozen people in 1787 as normatively pertinent to the State we have will that 1787 meeting have any status. But then, it will have that status because of the rational, high-level theory, whatever it is, from which it emerges that it would be a good idea to go along with the results of such a meeting as that one. Still, that same theory could well advise us to go along with the results of an entirely different history. Hobbes, indeed, thought we should go along with just any history.

What to do with the State we happen to have is the question. That depends on what's possible, which in turn depends on just what exactly is here—as well, of course, as on what kind of leadership potential the new guys have. If they're Alexander the Great and his teammates, we may be sure they'll have considerable success. If they are ordinary people, they probably won't.

There is a sobering thought arising from the general liberal view about these matters; namely, that it is unclear why it matters which State we belong to. If all States proceed on the principles we have surveyed, then people in one of them will be able to relate to people in other States with as much ease as they relate to their neighbors. If governments are not allowed to pocket our incomes to spend as they please, my State won't be able to pocket yours either; no one would be preferable to another, politically speaking. It looks as though particular States are irrelevant: Given a successfully liberal set of regimes, people can relate to others in multifarious ways, none of which are significantly affected by politics.

WAR AND THE STATE

If we cast an eye over world political history, what we will probably see above all else is war. We will see conquerors and defenders, squabbling neighbors, empires on the upswing and on the way out, kings attempting to preserve their power against challengers, and a whole lot of nameless people getting themselves killed in the process. ". . . [T]hirty years later, the main result of Alexander's conquests is that all the people he killed were still dead," so one wag put it.

Is it true, though? Do all these wars make no serious difference? Focusing on our own day, it is hard to deny that they do make a difference. Life for a great many people would have been very different—and for a lot of them much shorter and much worse—if Hitler had won, or if a world war between the Soviet Union and the NATO powers had happened.

Among things we can certainly say about war are these:

(1) there is an intimate connection between war and the State
(2) wars are in general fairly close to unmitigated evils
(3) wars, in modern circumstances, are basically pointless

Why (1)? We should distinguish between miscellaneous interpersonal violence, gang violence, and the political kind. The latter in general is by orders of magnitude greater in its impact on society than the other kinds and requires such a level of organization, material arrangements, and therefore financing that only States are capable of carrying them on. Very large armies with very sophisticated weaponry are generally regarded as being beyond the means of anything except the State. This is not quite altogether true, to be sure: If there were any feasible occasion for doing so, the General Motors Corporation would be up to the job of assembling and equipping a sizable army. What GM lacks is, especially, two things: First, the sort of political power and authority necessary for ordering large bodies of troops here and there (as well as for raising those troops in the first place; States can resort to conscription, which no private organization can do); and second, any need or rational motivation to do this.

We need scarcely dwell on (2) except to note that there have been persons who gloried in war activities. For example, "The pleasure and joy of man lies in treading down the rebel and conquering the enemy, in tearing him up by the root, in taking from him all that he has. . . . Be of one mind and one faith, that you may conquer your enemies and lead long and happy lives" or ". . . The greatest joy a man can know is to conquer his enemies and drive them before him. To ride their horses and take away their possessions. To see the faces of those who were dear to them bedewed with tears, and to clasp their wives and daughters in his arms" (Genghis Khan).[3] Temperaments differ, but beyond doubt some people have enjoyed battle and the disciplines and discomforts of military life. Meanwhile, however, as that little extract illustrates, their favored activities are very hard on the people they conquer, as indeed on the civilians in the populations who support the war efforts in question. It is, in short, absurd to rate war as a positive human accomplishment at any important level. To those who glory in war, we say, "Oh, come off it!" And if they do not, there is nothing for it but to assemble an army led by normal, bourgeois generals who frankly would rather be home playing golf, and compel the would-be heroes to, indeed, come off it. Or perhaps better, to take up hockey or football, sports in which their violent tendencies can be well fulfilled but which leave them and their opponents to live another day and providing safe amusement to the spectators in the process—instead of misery and poverty.

Point 3 is an extension of point (2) in that wars, in modern times, are strictly pointless. If what is wanted by the conqueror are the goods and resources of the enemy, then his method of acquiring these, is strictly speaking, stupid. Buying those things is a lot cheaper than murdering huge numbers of people in order to get them, not least because murder has a way of making the victim not very useful for further production. Production, after all, is what is needed in order for goods to exist so that they can be used. War, on the other hand, is also, of course, likely to make the friends, relatives, and fellow citizens of the victims hopping mad, probably for many centuries.

In point of fact, modern armies are needed, if they are, only because other States have armies that are thought to be intended for conquest of the first parties. Defense is the only acknowledged legitimate cause of war. Often those other States' armies are not intended for conquest, and the whole thing is a mistake. But when the reasoning is not wrong, and there really is a threat, then the basic absurdity of warfare is clearly revealed. If the war is fought, both sides will end up worse off than they were at the start, whereas if it is not and instead a decent level of trade and other kinds of intercourse prevail, that same period will bring prosperity, or at least slow progress, for both sides.

This brings up a point about anarchy, which is often criticized as being quite unable to cope with the need for military defense. The point is that if it weren't for the bellicose activities of others, armies would not be needed anyway, and inability to raise them hardly a point for censure. True, for some time to come, there will be power-hungry nations that contemplate conquest. The modest level of intelligence necessary to see the basic absurdity of warfare is readily masked by ignorance and passion, and wars go on. For awhile. But there has been progress. No important contemporary thinkers hold that wars are a fine idea as long as one wins. We know better now. (It would be interesting to estimate what the gross domestic product of the United States would be now if it had been involved in no wars since the World War II!)

CAN WARS BE JUST?

We owe a remarkable set of ideas about the possible justice of wars to many philosophers in the medieval period. So strong have these ideas been that they are still pretty much the reigning paradigm today. These ideas are known as "Just War Theory."

The main features of the theory are these:

1. War can only properly be declared by a (legitimate) government.
2. War is only permissible for "just cause." (Defense is rightly prominent among the acceptable causes—are there, indeed, any others?)

3. War should be a last resort: Peaceful means of settling disputes come first.

4. In the carrying on of war, the damage inflicted on the other side must be confined to what is necessary for the military objective of winning the (by hypothesis) just war.

5. In particular, killing the other side's civilians for its own sake is unacceptable, as is killing them, just as such, as a means to any end including the successful completion of the just war. This is the restriction known as "discrimination."

6. Such damages are permissible even if they are foreseeable, as long as they are not intended as such, are unavoidable, and are proportional to the just military objective. This is the restriction known as "proportionality."[4]

All of these depend on the second, however—"just cause." Are there any just causes for wars? As noted, there is one that is all but universally accepted: self-defense, or more precisely, defense of someone who wants to be defended by the parties in question. (The "all but" qualification is intended to take note of pacifists, who profess that war is never justified on either side. That it is our duty to roll over and let the bad guys have at us seems to most people incredible—even if you're preaching steadily at them as you fall. I think we should agree with those who find it incredible— see "pacifism," below.) Meanwhile, the question is whether there are any other legitimate "causes" of war. At this point, a problem arises—a very big problem.

REVOLUTIONS

Many revolutions in history have been violent. Among those are some that have been well received by a great many quite sober people: the American Revolution, for example, or the French until it got out of hand (which was early on). We can adapt the question of just war to that of revolution: When is it just?

When the existing government is reckless of human life, what is one to do? The logic of just war surely seems to apply. If someone insists on using force against innocents, they may defend themselves. If that someone is the government, then citizens can only defend themselves by going against the law and using violence against the violent. If this is correct, though, then point (1) will not do as it stands: Some wars will be legitimately carried on by non-States.

Some people think that this is a very bad idea (St. Thomas was one of them). Such people, I think, normally endow governments with an aura of moral rectitude, and the question is, how did it come by that aura? Governments are extremely concerned to justify their own existence, which they do by copious efforts at self-congratulatory propaganda. Perhaps we have all been conned, and it's a case of the emperor's new clothes. As we should know by now, governments are prima facie bad, not good; far from us having to justify ignoring or flaunting them, it is they who have the burden of proof, who need to justify themselves.

Still, the reaction that all governments are, as such, legitimate targets for violence at all times will not do either. It's partly that governments consist of people, most of whom are usually decent. Not only that, but governments, at least in the currently best-case places like Canada, tend to attract goodhearted people who are genuinely interested in promoting the public good. Or at least, they think they are. (The fact that they are trying to promote it by means that are basically bad is the problem.) But meanwhile, we can use objective criteria. A "proportionate" response to government action whose evil consists in being a nuisance and an unnecessary expense would not consist in killing the miscreants. It should consist, first, in evading the law, and second, in trying to get things changed by peaceable means. That is far from easy. (As a thought experiment, imagine that you are totally convinced by this book—you and maybe two others. That isn't much of a base for starting the mass wave of rejection required to get anywhere in a democratic state!)

But when governments murder their citizens, that is another matter. When it becomes the norm, as in Stalin's Russia or Mao's China, then revolutionary violence may seem to be the only way, in which case we are back to Just War Theory. That said, however, we must remember that in fact the Communist governments of both the Soviet Union and of China were changed by almost entirely peaceful means. The Soviet Union collapsed under the weight of its manifest inefficiency as compared with the capitalist states of the West and under massive public protest against a regime whose armies were in no mood to kill thousands of their fellow citizens in order to sustain it. Maoism collapsed when insiders in the government had the wisdom to see that economic communism was a miserable failure. They converted overwhelmingly to capitalism, though without calling it that—a nifty, if confusing, political maneuver.

An important implication of this story is that the last-resort status of violence should be taken seriously: Peaceable methods just may work better. Contemporary readers recall the Ukraine's Orange Revolution: Tens of thousands of people camped for prolonged periods in the public squares, making their protests perfectly clear but threatening no violence. With brilliant coordination by experienced and dedicated fellow revolutionaries, nonviolent methods can work, and when they do, are surely preferable in general to violent ones. For with violence, we may be sure, it is all but impossible to confine the slaughter to the Bad Guys. Soldiers whose job it is to kill upon command but who are otherwise decent people, civil servants who happen to be in the wrong place at the wrong time, and any number of civilians who are also at wrong places at those wrong times, will be predictable casualties of political fighting.

It has become standard to proclaim that governments must regard other governments as sacrosanct. Only if the other country is attacking us do we get to defend. But this drastic restriction on the use of force strictly implies that no matter how horrible a government is being to its own people, only the victims themselves are allowed to resist. And who is in a worse position to try to resist than the subject of a totalitarian tyrant?) But it is, on the face of it, incredible that some people should be allowed to get away with murder simply because the people doing the murdering claim to have a right to do so and because the only people who are in much of a position to help live on the other side of a line.

This being incredible, we are led to the uncomfortable conclusion that the standard view must go. Indeed, it should never have had the acceptance it has. Government is for the sake of the governed, not vice versa. Evil governments are legitimate targets for other governments as well as their own subjects. Note that war's only legitimate purpose is still defense. It's just that the people needing defending are on that side of the line, while the defenders are on this side. But at this point, we also need to bear in mind that culture is a major factor in politics, and country A may not in fact be able to do much for the people in country B, even if those people are being tyrannized by their governments, big time. The case of Iraq comes quickly to the contemporary mind in this context.

The solution to this as to all government is to have the government do a great deal less governing and the people being governed do the things that matter: commerce, culture, and in short, life. Telling this to a high-testosterone young fanatic thirsting for power is not easy, and until the lesson is learned, we will continue to have trouble.

What else is new?

PEACE AS THE INTERNATIONAL NORM

The main lesson of this book has been that the only credible version of the common good is general liberty, which is equivalent to general peace. How do we apply this lesson to States? Those entities are accustomed to thinking that they have something called "sovereignty," which is thought to entail the general right to do, in a word, whatever they please. But this leads to war. War is a problem in the sense that virtually all parties to it lose, by comparison with possible peaceable alternatives. A good many people get killed, and virtually everybody gets robbed. War is expensive, governments are terrible at managing other people's money, and assorted financial disasters follow in war's wake, not to mention hideous restrictions on the liberties of citizens as well as the deaths of many.

A main apparent motive of war in past times—"imperialism" as it came to be called—is founded on economic fallacy. States went forth to conquer new markets and new resources: That was the idea. What actually happened, often enough, is that they went broke. Commerce is better, in every way. Nobody gets killed, all parties become better off, and anybody can play, or not, as they like. Since most do, what happens is that both the entrepreneurial state (the one that used to be doing the conquering) and the native society (the one they used to conquer) become wealthier as time goes by. How could anyone think this a less desirable situation than war?

And so it is that peace between States should be, and now generally is, accepted as the international norm. Unfortunately, it is accepted as such by grudging governments, who now turn their attention to other means of bedeviling ordinary people as well as to clandestine support of political violence. In organizations such as the European Union, the lessons of peace and mutual benefit are accompanied by thousands of pages of restrictions on all kinds of commercial activity, created and enforced by legions of bureaucrats, while States not members of the organization are subjected to highly discriminatory, effectively jingoistic protectionist measures as of old. But even so, it's better than having these people shooting at each other.

In too many cases, such as much of Africa and the contemporary Middle East, peace is a cloak for arming militants. The point made above, that just cause of armed efforts to avoid tyranny cannot rationally be confined to relations between nations as such, is reinforced by such observations.

PACIFISM

Pacifism is the thesis that we ought not to fight even if our backs are up against the wall. That is to say, the pacifist wants to avoid war even when the other guy starts shooting. As a generic doctrine, pacifism calls for nonviolence no matter what. However, we need to make a distinction between what we might call the "personal" version and the "political" version. The former calls for nonresistance to violence of all kinds, by individuals as well as institutions; the latter says only that we, as nations, should never resort to war. This is an immense difference, since personal nonviolence stretches credibility to the breaking point. Are we really going to use no violence to protect wives and children from being butchered, if it comes to that? Having doubts about interstate war is more plausible.

Some who call themselves pacifist will say that their doctrines and practices are such that, if we play our cards right, the other side will stop being "other" and won't reach for its guns in the first place. This interesting idea has several problems. One is that it's very "iffy": What does it take to play those cards right, and how many must one play? In addition, it's hard to find much in the way of empirical support for the proposition. The pacifist attitude probably would not have stopped the trains to Auschwitz or the Islamic functionaries from decapitating their chosen enemies.

There is, in truth, much backpedaling among pacifists. Here's the problem. Everyone—well, everyone who counts anyway (you and I, especially!)—is in favor of peace. That is, we're in favor of the situation in which nobody is shooting or is intending to shoot at anybody. But the pacifist view says much more than that: It says that we should not make very much of the question, "who's the aggressor?" Most of us think this question is very important. As the Just War tradition says, we want to go to the negotiating table first; we want to explore peaceful means of settling disputes first. The question is only whether there is going to be a "second"; that is, if the other fellow rejects all compromise and orders the troops to march, what do we do about it? Proposing that we should just let them walk in and take over has the merit of novelty, at any rate, but not much else. Proposing instead that we should only tell our troops to march if theirs do first is not novel but is the normal view, the view of common sense.

Why would anybody take the pacifist view? Usually it's because they suppose that violence is evil. Unfortunately, the term "evil" here applies at two different points. Looked at abstractly, injuries and deaths are, of course, evils. They are things we don't want to happen to us, things we want to avoid. But that doesn't settle the question what to do about people determined to inflict precisely such evils on us. The claim that anyone who inflicts such evils on others is necessarily also committing a moral wrong does not follow from the first claim. Morality is a set of principles or rules for the assessment of interpersonal conduct among people in general. The fundamental principle here, I have argued, is the nonharm principle, which says, "Do not injure the innocent!" It does not say, "Do not injure anyone under any circumstances!" It imposes a condition: Only the guilty, that is, the aggressors, are eligible targets. All others have a very strong right to nonviolence.

But if we don't impose that condition, then what signal have we sent to the aggressors who disregard it? It looks as though that signal is "So, go right ahead!" That is not the message I want to send to those who would attack what I hold dear. Surely it is not the message that any rational person would so send. Pacifism seems to have fallen afoul of a fairly simple fallacy. The fallacy could easily be fatal.[5]

INTERNATIONAL TRADE

If war is the first subject that comes to mind when we contemplate the phenomenon of a world with many States claiming to be sovereign, the second is the State as a controller of commerce (among other relations) between its own citizens and those of other countries. All countries from time immemorial have claimed the right to impose restrictions on such commerce, and most have used it extensively.

Should they have that right? Whenever any nation imposes a tariff or a quota or any prohibition on the exchange of goods, they do the same sort of thing to their own citizens as when they imposes taxes and regulations of other kinds. If the State is legitimate, then it must somehow finance its operations, and taxes seem inevitable. But taxes apply whatever the source of income of the citizen, and so the question is whether transactions between citizens and noncitizens should be any more eligible for restriction and intervention than transactions between one citizen and another.

Prima facie, the answer to this question is in the negative. Our general principle declares that everyone has the right to engage in any nonharmful action with anyone, anywhere. Nationality, or anything else, has nothing to do with it. Each individual wants the most out of life, and so, she wants the most out of the people she deals with, whoever they may be. Our only proposed restriction on such relations is simply that they be voluntary on both sides and harmless to third parties. This condition is very often met, and conationality appears to have nothing to do with it.

Why, then, do States impose trade restrictions on the basis of membership in the State? In one sense, of course, the question is rhetorical, for the answer is easy: They do it because they can get away with it. But that only raises the further question, why they want to do it. And here, the answer is similar to one pointed to in the discussion of democracy. The costs of imposing import or export restrictions are diffused among millions, while the benefits are concentrated upon a relative few and also redound to the benefit of the legislators and civil servants who certify and administer such programs. If those relative few are otherwise important or rich or numerous or friends of the powers that be, then it's not surprising that the State is inclined to favor them. The only thing that's surprising is why serious thinkers about these matters have ever been taken in by the arguments of those favoring the restrictions.

So it may be well to remind the reader of the general economics of this matter—perhaps the nearest thing there is to an item of general agreement among economists. A restriction on otherwise innocent commerce always benefits some people at the expense of others. The costs to those who pay add up to much more than the benefits to those who benefit. A comparative handful of, say, workers or owners in State A benefit (for awhile): Their wages or profits are protected (for awhile). And everybody in State A who buys what they make pays more for it, while everybody in State B who stood ready to make it at a lower price lose out on potential earnings. It is often true that State B's people are poor, while those in State A are comparatively affluent. Those poor people who are denied the opportunity to go to work for a dollar a day—probably ninety cents more than they earned before—have been denied the chance to effect a major improvement in their lives.

Of course, it is likely that current workers, or perhaps whole businesses, may lose jobs or business if foreign competition is permitted. The same, however, is true when they lose jobs to local competitors. If the fact that some people will have to move to different kinds of work as a result of competition from more efficient producers were enough to justify using the law, and henceforce, to protect the inefficient, then we may as well abandon any thought of the State being justified by its promotion of the common good. Enhancing some at the expense of others is not promoting the common good.

On the other hand, as these same economists point out, the money that the great number of consumers who purchase the products in question now have and which they would not have had if they had had to buy at higher prices is now available for the purchase of further goods and services, thus creating a market that some other entrepreneurs are sure to cater to, if they are allowed to.

Prudence might impel any worker to save or enroll in an insurance scheme designed to tide him over in the event of job loss, just as of any other calamity in life. Some will have more reason to do this than others. Perfectly healthy persons need little in the way of health insurance, while desperately unhealthy ones would not be able to get it from normal suppliers if the latter have their choice. These latter will have to throw themselves on the mercy of their fellows, which is normally more than equal to the task. The others will make do one way or another. But meanwhile, the amount of income now made available for the purchase of other services or goods increases potential demand for those "other" things and so offers occasion for the entrepreneur to come up with goods and services to profit from this extra demand.

This leaves no case for the mercantilist, so far as pure economics is concerned. This is not to deny that a State might be in more or less genuine need of military equipment, say, that it might want to keep out of the hands of the enemy. That takes us beyond the boundaries of civilian economics and absorbs the question into the more general ones about war. But insofar as this is a question of high-level policy regarding, simply, citizens and their well-being, the case is really closed. (Despite this professionally uncontroversial finding, we may note, restrictionist measures preoccupy democratic legislatures everywhere. The lesson is not easily learned, it seems.[6])

ECONOMIC GLOBALIZATION

"Globalization" refers to the tendency for people around the world to relate to others less as members of particular States, or for that matter other kinds of particular groups that are more or less geographically local, and more simply as people, irrespective of those local attachments. In recent times, there has been much talk about globalization, and much of that talk has been expressive of concern.

Why the concern? That is our question here. The potential benefits of globalization in the narrowly economic sphere are apparent to any observer. We have but to walk down any modern street in any sizable town in North America or Europe to see automobiles from many nations, restaurants with all sorts of cuisines—many of them exotic—clothing, and all sorts of consumer goods (notably computers and cell phones) made in a variety of countries. A quick look at the relevant consumer features and prices of these goods and services explains why consumers spend their money on these things of multiple origins rather than buying local. Only those who do not approve of people making their own choices and living their own preferred lives can seriously object to globalization insofar as these things are its manifestation. Those who would advance such things as reasons relevant to politics are not liberals.

MULTINATIONAL CORPORATIONS AND OTHER ASSOCIATIONS

The modern world has no end of associations that casually overlap and ignore national boundaries: The Roman Catholic Church, the National Hockey League, the Toyota Motor Corporation, and countless others, large and small. The interests of these innumerable associations simply have no particular relation to considerations of nationality, and any attention paid to that variable is due, by and large, to the insistence of various States on getting a piece of the action somehow or other.

The importance of these institutions is that they are not political ones. They arise from the fact that a lot of people have interests that they can pursue best by acting in cooperation with a lot of others, many of whom are far away. In the case of commercial associations like GM, Microsoft, and so many more, people enter in different ways: by becoming an employee, investor, or customer. Whatever specific role an individual plays, he or she plays it voluntarily, for whatever benefit can be derived from it.

It is fascinating that a great many people these days profess to find multinationals vaguely sinister and evil, since on the face of it they are benign and indeed, hugely beneficial. Hundreds of millions of people in contemporary China, for example, owe their much-improved quality of life mainly to the operation of these giant associations, while corresponding hundreds of millions in various Western countries owe appreciably increased quality of life to the same sources. They are accused, for example, of human rights abuse when they pay much lower wages than prevail in the wealthy countries. This very same "abuse" of course is precisely what enables the people in those countries at last to enjoy steady incomes instead of the unreliable and often nonexistent incomes that were their lot prior to the onset of business by the local branch of the multinational corporations in question. Or we read, for example, of "Burmese citizens who alleged that government police forces carried out a program of violence, torture, rape, forced relocation and forced labor against the Burmese farmers living on the route of a pipeline being built as part of a Unocal-Total project . . . could sue the U.S. companies in U.S. court, and successfully did so."[7] Note that it was agents of the government of Burma that evidently committed these atrocities. Why are American companies taken to court in response?

It is surely true that among the many misuses of State power is the tendency to compel citizens into accepting the costs of business activity instead of having the relevant companies settle things by the proper and normal methods of business, namely negotiation and purchase. But the point here is that those are misuses of State power. No company, of whatever size, is permitted to operate a repressive police force, and any police forces that do operate improperly on their behalf are operated by a government—usually, but by no means always, a dictatorship. To be sure, the companies in question may have encouraged that participation, just as companies, individuals, and associations are forever attempting, too often successfully, to get the power of government behind their particular interests. The point is that those governments have no legitimate reason for doing that.

HIGH CULTURE

Europeans and defenders of things European defend the practice of immense State subsidy of the arts. As one who has devoted much of his life to the mounting of concerts of classical music, I should be much attracted by this. But I'm not. I am acutely aware that a great many people (estimate, 98 percent) do not share my interest in, say, Haydn quartets, and I am hard put to understand why we of highbrow taste should be allowed to exact support from hoi polloi for this admittedly noble and exalted purpose. The point is not that anybody's taste is as good as anybody else's. Indeed, it's not. I acknowledge some few as having still better taste than I, and I regard most people's tastes in these matters as not to be taken seriously. Still, the question for political philosophy is, Who's Boss? The correct answer is No one is—including me and my fellow designated highbrows.

Meanwhile, cultural globalization, as we might call it, takes two different forms. On the one hand, there is exposure to other cultures of the world, which is increasingly evident in today's world, especially by the Internet. On the other hand, there is the mixing of cultures, the fear being that somehow we will all come to a kind of insipid mélange of nothing in particular and everything in general.

Is this last a genuine fear? No. New cultures are forming all the time, as almost anyone with teenage children can attest. Cultural variety is limitless in principle. And as to ancient cultures, most are now dead and studied by anthropologists. We should not mourn the loss of the ancient Mayan culture, with its high incidence of sacrifice of humans to the gods, or those involving cults with self-destructive rites. But people interested in "high" culture should enthuse that there are symphony orchestras playing Beethoven and Tchaikovsky in cities all over the world. This is hardly something to fear or lament, from the point of view of us music lovers. Nor, I would think, from anyone's, so long as the people who enjoy and value this kind of activity bear its costs as well. That restriction, of course, is often violated in today's world. But there is no necessary connection between the globalization of great art and its subvention by governments. Freedom of cultural achievement scarcely needs a special name. It is obviously part of the basic freedom we should all be concerned about, and if it is in place, artistic activity will flourish.[8]

IMMIGRATION: WHO SHOULD BE A CITIZEN?

Among the pressing issues facing modern States is whom to allow in. Putting the question this way implies that the borders of States identify important realities of some sort—that the question of whom to "let in" is a serious one. Since those borders don't constitute such important realities, so far as I can see, the issue must be wrongly put. Why should the "we" who comprise a given State be the relevant decision-makers in relation to someone from a remote part of the world?

It isn't that nobody is relevant. Potential employers, landlords, and neighbors should have quite a lot to say about it. The question is only: Would the opinions of a set of government bureaucrats be better? Would they be better if the government in question was, as is nowadays the norm, elected by the citizenry?

There is a looming paradox in the current view. Governments everywhere screen applicants for citizenship. And, it is said, this is something they should be able to do. Well . . . screen with a view to what? On a liberal view, surely, the answer is mostly, or perhaps entirely, with a view to seeing whether the new applicant could make it as a citizen in the recipient country. Would he or she be able to find employment at a level compatible with paying the rent? There is also the question of criminal potential. Would this person be likely to try to make his living by imposing losses on others? But the two together are sides of the same coin, which is whether the individual in question is likely to be a net positive, or at least nonnegative, addition to the community.

What promises paradox in the view that only government can do this is that what they propose to screen for is precisely what a free market does screen for. You "make it" on a market only if your returns at least equal your costs. Someone proposing to move to Manhattan with no prospect of an income and faced with nonsubsidized housing and other costs will not make ends meet. Normal people move from A to B only because they suppose they will do better in B. They certainly don't need a government to make that decision for them. What they need instead is employment skills that are more highly valued by someone in B than they are in their current circumstances in A. For this we need information that is not usually provided or known by government agencies and in any case is in the interest of potential employers to provide.

What about acceptance by neighbors? Will the newcomer make a good neighbor? Perhaps this above all is what is to be provided by governments— or is it? One important question, of course, is what kind of criteria the potential new neighbors will employ. In densely populated urban cores, where the new neighbor moves into the apartment down the hall in a thirty-story high-rise, the answer may well be that virtually no criteria are employed. Typically, no one in this neighborhood even meets this new individual. The same, of course, is decidedly not so in the suburbs, where newcomers are scrutinized in many ways. But government departments using those criteria would be accused of discrimination, since in all likelihood criteria such as race, ethnicity, accent, taste in automobiles, and any number of others of similar kind will be employed. And too, most neighborhoods usually do not claim a right to decide whether some newcomer is to be allowed in. Either the newcomer, N, buys the property or signs the rental contract, in which case N is in, or not, in which case N is not in. In condominia, there are rules that all signers must accept, and sometimes these include a measure of democratic control of the common property, such as sidewalks and yards, around the buildings. Those cases illustrate further the kinds of considerations that are widely relevant.

Why would a government agency be allowed to overrule all this? The newest answer is that the newcomer might be a terrorist. Many countries, notably large ones such as the United States, are making extreme efforts to turn their immigration policies into effective filters on this one dimension.

As 9/11, the mafia, various Nazis, and assorted imported criminal gangs illustrate, governments' previous efforts were often crucially ineffective, and whether new ones will do better is hard to say. What isn't hard to say is that the level of imposition on all that these new efforts entails will be high; very much higher than ever before. Too high? Trying to protect several hundred million people against the threat of terrorism is not an easy business at best. Whether immigration restrictions will do the job is hard to say, but if there is one relevant reason for refusing admission to someone, it's the fact that he's intent on murdering as many of his new neighbors as possible. Yet finding this out in an interview is not all that easy, and we may be sure that for every potential terrorist excluded, several thousand potentially desirable citizens will be so as well.

Many writers argue that there is a need to restrict immigration because otherwise public services such as welfare and health will be overwhelmed by free-riders from the outside world. Those services are often enough overwhelmed by persons of similar description from inside State boundaries, of course. One might laconically note that the argument points up the lack of foundation in the way of a genuine human right for the services in question. But there is a simple solution to this: Don't have welfare state services in the first place. Immigrants, like anyone else, should be in a sink-or-swim situation. In the heyday of American immigration, in the late ninteenth century, that was their situation, and virtually all of them did "swim," creating the backbone of the affluent society that country is famed for being today.

NATIONALISM AND COMMUNITARIANISM

In recent times, a fairly popular version of political theory proposes that the right model for the State is the community, and that considerations of community and its needs are what justify the State and the various involvements of the State that so many have come to put their faith in. We saw in chapter 1 that community is the wrong model for the State. It is wrong in three ways, actually. In the first place, an entity the size and complexity of the modern State simply is not and cannot be a community. In the second place, communities have shared values and high levels of mutual attachment, suitable for generating considerable claims of obligation among the members. But such bases of obligation are wholly lacking in the State, and people who claim that they are not are rightly suspected of being up to no good. (Remember the Nazi celebration of "Gemeinschaft.") And thirdly, what is true about communities is that there are a great many of them, at many levels, with innumerably different commitments and obligations. There is no way to make the State out to be just one among these innumerable groupings. Good communities are essentially voluntary associations, in the sense not that people join them on purpose—though they often do—but rather that they may leave, at costs that are not artificially imposed as they are by States, but rather, as determined by market considerations. That's why there are so many communities and what contributes to the unsuitability of community as a model for the political State.

The communitarian model must be rejected. But it is true, and very interesting, that many States have sometimes been in the grip of popular nationalism—a belief that this particular State is animated by a special soul of its own, entitling it to glory and a "place in the sun." And it must be admitted that a great many people, down through history, have been animated by nationalism. Is this a con job on the part of the State? Of course the rulers of the State want its citizens to hold the State in high esteem and be ready to sacrifice for it, including their lives if need be. Our question is whether they should get what they want in this respect. Our answer, on the whole, should be negative.

Of course, there are lots of States out there, and the stage gets rather crowded with these sun-worshippers in fairly short order—and then what? Historically we again hear the clash of swords over at stage right. And if that isn't what is wanted, then what is? To propose that we want a world in which people deal with each other simply as people, peaceably, but otherwise in infinite diversity, is the liberal's answer. It seems to me that it's the right answer.

NOTES

1. Woodrow Wilson, speech to the Joint Session of the American Congress, January 8, 1918.

2. Russell Hardin, *Liberalism, Constitutionalism, and Democracy* (New York: Oxford University Press, 1999).

3. http://en.wikipedia.org/wiki/Genghis_Khan. See also www.greenkiwi.co.nz/footprints/mongolia/ghengis_history.htm.

4. For a compact but full account of Just War theory, see Brian Orend, *The Morality of War* (Peterborough, Ontario: Broadview Press, 2006).

5. See Jan Narveson, "Pacifism: A Philosophical Analysis," *Ethics*, vol. 75, no. 4 (July 1965): 259–271. For my much more recent thoughts on the matter, see "Is Pacifism Self-Refuting?" in Barbara Bleisch and Jean-Daniel Strub (eds.), *Pazifismus. Ideengeschichte, Theorie und Praxis* (Bern/Stuttgart/Wien: Haupt, 2006), 127–144.

6. A recent study, Bryan Caplan's *The Myth of the Rational Voter: Why Democracies Choose Bad Policies* (Princeton, NJ: Princeton University Press, 2007), provides much insight into this particular bit of economic ignorance, among much else. See pages 69 and 71 for discussion about them, especially.

7. http://www.geocities.com/~virtualtruth/multi.htm.

8. Tyler Cowen makes the case for the effectiveness of freedom in the arts in *In Praise of Commercial Culture* (Cambridge, MA: Harvard University Press, 1998).

8

Taking Anarchism Seriously

Anarchy is the condition of a society with no government. Anarch*ism* is the theory that society should do without government. It is usually stated in terms of the State's being immoral or illegitimate; that is, the most popular version. But that needn't be the reason for proposing anarchy. It could be held to be better simply because it would work better. For whatever reason, almost all writers on political philosophy today dismiss anarchism with scant or no discussion. In the past, and still often today, there is an idea that anarchy would be chaotic, a condition of social turmoil, of the Hobbesian jungle, or the like.

An essential distinction here is between philosophical anarchism and what we might call practical anarchism. Philosophical anarchism is the view that the State is not in principle justified, that there is no fundamental authority such as is claimed by States. But that is compatible with a recognition that the State is inevitable, say, and certainly that some States are better than others—for that matter, possibly much, much better. Practical anarchism is the view that anarchy really could work in practice and that we should work toward it. There could be anarchist parties or movements whose purpose is to promote the onset of anarchy.

Philosophical anarchism would be irresponsible, even frivolous, if it did not include defense of the thesis that anarchism is possible in the sense of being coherently conceivable and not based on any general assumptions that are clearly false or clearly ruled out by what we know about human nature. A lot of the discussion of anarchism is certainly going to be devoted to refutations of claims of impossibility or disaster. If such claims can be refuted, then the next question is whether it has anything going for it philosophically that the State perhaps does not. There the anarchist comes on much stronger, for as has been argued at many points in the preceding chapters, the State has basic moral problems. If those cannot be solved, then advocacy of the State should leave us uncomfortable. That is also a view I will support here.

BACKGROUND ISSUE: THE STATUS OF MORALS

Anarchists feel free to make many value judgments about States. What sort of anarchism we have, however, will be a function in part of what the underlying morality is. What does the anarchist need to assume along this line?

The strongest answer is that anarchism presumes a "natural" morality, one that he is pretty sure essentially everyone does hold to or would hold to and would recognize as the proper basis for settling disagreements among people. In the preceding chapters, it has been argued—and then more or less presumed—that this natural morality is the libertarian principle, or the nonharm or nonaggression principle, as we may indifferently refer to it.

To see how this interacts with the major question about the feasibility of anarchism, consider the kind of view associated with that name in the late nineteenth century by many proponents. Those anarchists held strongly not only to the nonharm principle but also to a principle of equality. A famous book by Pierre-Joseph Proudhon bore the title *Property Is Theft!* It is easy to see that any such view is going to entail major problems of self-enforcement. Property is an extremely prominent and familiar feature of the human scene. Some people with a lot of it have indeed been persuaded, in quasi-religious fashion, to give up all that they have and give it to the poor, etc. But not very many—not surprisingly. If the anarchist proposes to respond to them by simply taking their property by force, then the problem is that the two parts of the anarchist's program are in conflict with each other. The nonharm principle gives way to the equality principle, thus losing all the advantages that the nonharm principle itself has, in the way of universal appeal. That version, "socialist anarchism" as we may call it, appears to be hopeless and will not further be considered in this chapter. By contrast, however, the capitalist version, as we might with some reservations call it, has all those advantages. What makes it possible for anarchism to be taken seriously is precisely the coherence and self-reinforcing nature of that version.

DO WE NEED GOVERNMENT?:
ANARCHIST REPLIES TO LOCKE

Back in chapter 2, we looked at the Hobbesian and then the Lockean arguments for government. Locke argues, plausibly, that in order to cope with problems that we could surely expect to arise in a "state of nature"—that is, an anarchic condition—we need three functions that, he supposed, can only be supplied by government:

- a policing function
- a judicial function
- a legislating function

Is Locke right? Things now get complicated. For we may agree that we need functions of some such general type but deny Locke's argument for the State nonetheless. That is because we might argue that all of these functions can be done without going all the way to government.[1] Let's look at each in some detail.

Police

Take policing. It is simply not true that the only way to have effective administration of the moral law against violence, theft, and fraud is by having a single, centralized police force. Quite small groups of people—even, for that matter, two-person groups exchanging goods with each other—can arrange for protection. Traders setting forth to do business can take armed guards along with them, guards whose job it is to protect these particular merchants and not just anyone and everyone. Many people would, and do, hire such agents. Many more might, and again, do actually, form volunteer protective associations. In sizable groups, we may expect that some will advertise their services, claiming to offer good service at low cost; competitors may arise who claim to offer better service or lower costs or more specialized kinds of protection, and so on. In fact, as students of modern textbooks in political philosophy seem rarely to realize, we do this now. In today's societies, there are actually many more "private" police than "public" ones. Moreover, the efficiency and serviceability of the public police can be and often is called into question. People do still get murdered and robbed, despite the police. Others remain safe by means of nonpublic methods: They install burglar alarms, they register with companies that monitor their homes while they are away, they become experts at firearms, and so on. Is it really true that we can't be safe without government-sponsored police? Indeed, will we really be safe if we do trust in government police instead of taking things much more extensively into our own hands? We need to think about this. The anarchist's response on this point is powerful and profound and points to a major hole in the classical arguments for the State: insofar as those arguments do point to something we need, it is by no means obvious that the solution is government,[2] and it is not even obvious that the government solution is a very good one.

Judicial Functions

What about judging? First, we need to ask precisely what this function is. We may divide the judge's functions into two, though they are closely related. One thing judges do is to apply the law in the sense that they attempt to infer from the general propositions in the code of law under which they operate to particular cases. Did this person "murder" that one? Or only kill him negligently? Or perhaps, given the evidence, not at all? (Juries also participate in such deliberations, of course. But they are doing the same thing.)

Another thing judges do is try to decide, as between two people who have a problem of interaction, which of them should give way and how much. For this purpose, we do not have a body of legislated law, primarily. Instead, we have something like the common law, which is an accumulation of cases and decisions going back very far and only very partially codified. The principles of common law have a status very much like that of the basic non-harm principle of moral theory: They are thought to arise, intrinsically, from the nature of the matters in dispute and be applicable for that very reason.

An important, or even, arguably, essential feature of a judicial system is that arguments come to an end. Eventually, there is an authoritative, definitive decision—the one the parties to the dispute will simply have to live with, and that's that.

Or is there? Well, of course, as things stand court decisions are often appealed to higher courts, and the whole process of going from lowest to highest may take years as well as a great deal of money. In the case of decisions from the Supreme Court of the country in question, there will be learned dispute for years afterward whether Their Honors came to the right conclusion.

The main single thing that anarchists don't like about government is what we may call its arrogance. At some point, decisions are simply forced on us; we have no choice, and yet we do not think justice was done. With government, there is no need to explain, and rarely is explanation forthcoming. Anarchism hopes to avoid this last problem by insisting that all cases be tried by judges agreeable to both parties. No one is to be dragged unwillingly into court and then dragged out of it with a sense that he has been "had" by the State. Can this work? Let us see.

Civil Law

We normally distinguish two kinds of legal judgments that need making: civil and criminal. Here again, the anarchist's response is of great interest. Let's address the two separately, beginning with civil. In such cases, there is just the sort of dispute Locke has in mind: What really belongs to whom?

In many cases, the parties are subject to some rules of various associations to which they belong, and then the question is, who is qualified for what under those rules? In others, there may be a general claim of damage by one, denied by the other. Interestingly enough, a very large proportion of such cases are even now settled outside of public courts. In arbitrations, the two parties both agree on an arbitrator, who then goes over the evidence with them and makes a decision, which both usually accept. Why do they? If they've chosen a good arbitrator and one who is experienced in these matters, it is likely that he or she will present a really good argument whose merits can be seen by both. Moreover, the more the case is pursued, the more expense is incurred—judges, and perhaps lawyers, need to be paid for their services, and the loser at the first round has a good chance of losing again. This provides motivation to settle. And so cases are settled by a process leading to agreement of the contending parties, without ever going to government. Locke's hastily put argument fails to distinguish the one kind of settlement from the other. Would we ever "need" to go to a government court? It is not obvious why we would.

Notice that, as we observed above, civil action does not usually depend upon specifically legislated law for the kind of case at hand. Much more typically, judges are dealing in "natural" law, in which the rival claims are weighed on merits that arise out of the nature of the case as well as of the rules previously accepted by the two parties and especially by the agreements they have made. So the claim that we need government judiciaries because we need governments to make the laws that settle cases is false in the area of civil law.

The specter of interminable decision-making processes cannot be theoretically eliminated, to be sure. But there is a very major catch. In the foregoing, we noted that the parties have a motive to settle in that not settling costs them. We didn't say just what kind of "costs" might be entailed, but a short excursion into fundamental moral theory can help to bring it out. The contractarian theorist posits that, as it were, in the beginning there is no law at all, and anything goes. Everyone is fair game to everyone else; nobody has any protection, and nothing that anyone does to anyone can be "wrong." We adopt morality precisely because of that; precisely because life without principles to regulate social interaction is likely to be awful, and very short.

Now consider the position of the man who absolutely will not settle in court. He won't take any decision, however well reasoned, for an answer. When he steps outside the courtroom, though, he has a problem. For in disavowing all law, he also disavails himself of appeal to law. If his opponent wears out his patience and shoots him, what can the latter's complaint be, if he refuses to accept any law? Apparently none.

In the societies we live in, this is unlikely. It is far from impossible: The people sentenced to life imprisonment or the gallows for horrendous crimes often have no moral sense whatever, rather than claiming that they didn't do it. The rest of us need have no sympathy for such people. You go around killing us, and if we can get you, we will. And obviously you will have no complaint. Thus a legal system, even with many imperfections, is far preferable, and at the same time, provides the basis for real solutions that is just what we seek here.

Criminal Matters

What about crime? The most interesting question here is whether the familiar distinction between criminal and civil really holds up. The general object of civil law is to restore to the aggrieved party what was his, if possible, or as close as possible if it is not. But criminal damage is not incidental or accidental, but intended and deliberate. When that is so, we are rightly concerned. People who do not acknowledge others as having any rights are dangerous. What to do about them?

The anarchist's answer is nevertheless, that we are really doing the same thing that we do in civil cases. Criminals are so because they have taken something from someone else, something that is that person's and is not the criminal's, but taken it without consent and very much to the detriment of the victim. The task of justice, says the anarchist, is to restore, as nearly as possible, the just situation ex ante. The criminal is to be required to restore whatever he has taken. If it's a robbery, we can put a value on this. But the criminal's "bill" doesn't stop there, for since it's his fault, we also get to charge him for the costs he imposes on us is in the way of tracking him down and bringing him to justice.

In the case where the victim has been murdered, of course, we have a different problem. Now the only people who can be compensated are those who suffer from the victim's loss. One of the forms of compensation they might opt for is to have the malefactor killed as well. In that respect, restitution could approximate to the familiar theory known as retribution. But retribution is not the public point: Restitution is. Many thinkers have explored this idea in depth and are worth consulting about this kind of theory, which departs radically from contemporary practice.[3]

What about the model of consensuality? Some few criminals may claim they were justified in their depredations, and their case can be heard. Most will not. Few robbers are against property laws; indeed, they expect protection of their own property if one of their fellow robbers decides to break in on them.

Here again, the point made by Hobbes needs to be born in mind. People who insist on remaining in the "state of nature" are people who acknowledge no law. And if they acknowledge no law, then from their point of view, what's to stop us from doing anything we like to them? "The fact that you were breaking this man's arm/killing him/robbing him of his life's work meant nothing to you. Why should the fact that what we propose to do to you will do the same be anything you can object to? Or if you do, why should we pay any attention?" Bang! Case closed.

This last scenario sounds draconian to the modern citizen of a State. We are accustomed to thinking that all, even murderers, have rights. It is plausible to say that we have the right to a fair trial, say, one in which the truth about what we did will be discerned. True, but once it is discerned, it may turn out that our criminal is a vicious person to whom other people's rights mean absolutely nothing. Do we still owe him a whole lot of nice treatment? Must we put him in jail, at enormous expense and some danger to ourselves, when we could just treat him the way he treats others? Governments in the past have treated criminals far more severely than we do now. Why think that we are right and they are wrong? That important question will have to be left for later consideration. What matters now is that there is a basis for settling even the most serious disagreements, in ways that no one can reasonably complain of, and without resort to government. The government alternative looks arbitrary and clumsy by comparison.

Legislation

Finally, what about legislation? Here too the anarchist has serious criticisms of the "statist" view. First, Hobbes and Locke, and others, identify first principles that are extremely plausible, yet not in need of or even susceptible of, what we usually think of as "legislation." No legislature can make murder wrong when it wasn't before; no legislature can bring it about that it is wrongful to break a carefully made contract. Locke, according to the anarchist, was right to think that the legislature's function is essentially derivative, not fundamental. What legislatures do can be done well or badly. It is of enormous importance that an institution for making law be reasonably likely to make life better for people, not worse. In fact, much legislation is seriously defective. Whether it is so defective that we would do better not to have an institution such as Locke envisages the legislature to be—is the question before us. Most writers, and perhaps most ordinary people, never think to question this. They should.

Second, it is crucial here to distinguish between the rules of voluntary associations and the sort of thing we usually term law, where the latter refers to legislative statutes, backable by force. If we think about this, an important fact confronts us: Hardly any of the rules that really matter in our lives are made by legislatures. On the contrary, the rules that matter to us, mostly, are the rules of associations to which we belong, large or small, including two-person "associations" in which one person makes a conditional promise to another. For example, you sign a contract. This contract spells out the duties of both parties to it. If one fails to perform as called for, that one is subject to penalties that are also, or can be, spelled out in the contract, or in some background rules of the institution making the contract. And so on. There are rules all over the place, having the status of law in that deviations from them are subject to penalties—but it's all a matter of agreement between individuals or associations. Such "laws" do not apply to everybody, but rather, to all the signatories.

Almost all significant rules for our lives are like that. But some are not. Some do indeed come from legislatures. Are these further, extra rules really necessary? Or could we get along without them altogether, relying entirely on structures of rule to which all relevant parties have agreed? This would be in marked contrast to legislatures, where the "agreement" of the citizen is not voluntary. If we are claimed to "agree" to legislation in the usual sense, it is because our participation is coerced.

If legislation can be justified at all, it must be by showing that we benefit from legislation despite, or better, because of, its involuntary nature. Why are writers on these matters so convinced that government is in the right when it makes law? Perhaps they should not be. At any rate, argument is required, and argument of a level that goes very far beyond the kind provided by Locke.[4] Locke isn't wrong in thinking there could be a need for something of the kind of things he argues for. But does it need to be the case that "The Community comes to be Umpire, by settled standing Rules, indifferent, and the same to all Parties; and by Men having Authority from the Community, for the execution of those Rules, decides all the differences that may happen between any Members of that Society, concerning any matter of right . . ."? He is wrong in thinking that what he describes is clearly needed in such a way as to provide a solid argument for government. Whether we can get there from here is a good question; the point is that we are not there yet.

Again we have to emphasize that the fundamental principle of morals, the nonharm principle, is assumed by the anarchist, as it was by Locke under the title the "Law of Nature," to be "in place"—valid always and everywhere. Are there some who do not recognize it? In practice, of course, there are outlaws: thieves, rapists, con artists, and so on. But the existence of such people certainly doesn't cast any doubt on the validity of the nonharm principle. Their status as people who deserve to have their liberties cut short and to be required to pay compensation to their victims is clear to all.

Law under anarchy is often said to be "polycentric." Various different sets of laws would apply to the members of various different groups, but not to others. Since members of these groups interact, there might be problems, if person A supposes he can treat person B in accordance with certain rules that he, A, recognizes but B does not. Now, of course, the general reaction to this is that A is in the wrong to assume that; he should check it out first.

The A group and the B group might have to send representatives to a meeting to try to make some adjustments. But there is nothing logically difficult about this; again, it is done all the time. International ice hockey is played on a somewhat different-sized rink and under some slightly different rules from North American professional hockey. There is not much difficulty adjusting, so far as rules are concerned.

WHY PRIVATE PROPERTY SOLVES SO MUCH

The leading social organizing device of anarchy is property. Essentially everything belongs to someone, or some association of voluntarily acting people. And so there is no one who has the current public's relation to its various functions; namely, irresponsible (according to the anarchist) authority and the power to ignore some people and simply trample over the wishes of others. When something is privately owned, we know who's responsible: the owner is. That person gets not only whatever profits or rents or whatever that he or she might be able to earn with the asset but also he or she is responsible for any negative effects that might issue. Pollution, for example: When there is pollution, someone is discomfited or outrightly damaged in some way, and the polluter can be required to compensate or desist, by agreement with the pollutees, as we might call them.

How much pollution will there be? It depends, of course. In prosperous modern times, we can afford to be fairly picky about our air, water, and land: It's worth a fair bit to have it clean. But much longer ago, cleaning up the environment was definitely not worth it. Better to be warm, well-fed and well-clothed, and somewhat polluted than to have a clean-as-a-whistle atmosphere and scarcely anything to wear, eat, or for that matter, do.

How about roads and sidewalks and such? Many public areas, as they now are, should remain so because they are public by custom. Lots of people walk on various paths that have been there since anyone can remember, and the convenience of keeping it that way is overwhelming. Those who live nearby will likely become shareholders in a sort of public-land company, which would do a bit of supervision and maintenance. Frequent users would be asked to contribute or could even be charged by the people who have shares in the company to help with those costs.

What about the public's health? The anarchist will claim—with a lot of evidence—that government agencies nowadays are mostly making a mess of this, driving small pharmaceutical firms out of business because of the enormous cost of meeting regulatory requirements and depriving people who would be willing to take risks in the process of trying to cure fatal diseases, many of whom are dead because the government agency refuses to allow the drug that would cure them to be marketed as yet. And so on.

The anarchist looks with fondness on the American organization called Underwriters' Laboratories, that sells a sort of imprimatur of safety to products that pass its rigorous tests. Wise customers look for the UL approved sticker. Governments are not needed here. The idea is applicable very widely, and there's every reason to think it would work very well.

Critics sometimes complain that an anarchic society of this general sort would be a bunch of tightfisted people fretting about lawsuits by fastidious neighbors. Lawsuits in the United States today are often frivolous and driven by the principle that the party with more money should be made to pay, never mind what he's guilty of. This is unlikely to happen where the court has to be selected by both parties and if someone is shown to be acting frivolously or in bad faith, then that one is going to be footing the major share, or likely all, of the bill, perhaps with an extra charge for wasting the defendant's and the court's time.

These and numerous other issues make for fascinating exercises in thought. Anarchism looks pretty good on the score of feasibility in principle. But would it ever happen? Or are people so cross-grained that somebody will always seize power and turn society back into a State? Of course, few of us suppose that we will get to anarchy in the first place, from the contemporary State with all of its vested interests and fiefdoms. This melancholy thought perhaps suggests the next topic.

GOVERNMENT AND WAR

Many thoughtful people have conceded that the anarchist has a strong case, after all. But these same people often raise an objection of a rather different kind to the above: What about war? More precisely, what about national defense? Suppose that the anarchist is right and that some large part of the globe might be occupied by peaceable, busy people leading useful, orderly lives without relying on the State. But suppose, as is uncomfortably likely, that some other area of the globe is, as at present, under the control of some government, and that this State takes it into its head to attack the anarchic area. Wouldn't it be a pushover? After all, modern warfare, especially, requires levels of organization and expense that nongovernmental institutions are scarcely capable of. When you have a government, you are equipped to "invade and despoil" in ways that promise success, unlike such efforts at the level of one-on-one or few-on-few.

This raises three interesting issues.

The first is whether it's really true that even the threat of international-type warfare can't be met adequately without a State.

The second is whether this provides a strong argument for the State even when all the usual ones fail.

And the third—perhaps the most important of all—is what this tells us about the nature of the State and what we can learn from that.

Discussing the first issue adequately would surely require a book in itself. Modern warfare is indeed very expensive. But it is also true that modern corporations manage to assemble vast capitals. Many of today's major businesses have budgets far larger than most of the States in today's world. The Microsoft Corporation, for example, has an assessed valuation much greater than the entirety of most third-world countries' GNP today. Even so, to be sure, it is dwarfed by the American government's military budget.

On the other hand, the main enemy that the American army is fighting at the present time has a trivial budget by world standards. The terrorists giving that army such a hard time do it with weapons of modest cost but manage nevertheless to make life miserable for the American and other armies trying to deal with them. Whether they can "win" the "war" they are currently mounting by these means is another matter. Almost certainly they cannot, and it seems reasonable to think that they won't, but the sheer fact that they can do what they have done with the resources at their disposal must make one hesitate to pronounce on the impossibility of contemporary warfare without the State. For after all, the terrorists do not have a State—yet.

How would a legitimate and just anarchy respond to a threat of external attack by a State? Everything depends on how much of a threat it is, of course. But if we suppose it is a sizable but "conventional" threat, we can imagine a response such as the following. A private agency undertakes military training for a small army of volunteers, whose training, equipment, and salaries are provided by a citizen organization concerned about such possibilities. If the external threat is considerable, we suppose that they will first call for financial support from everyone. They can present good evidence that their ways of life are seriously at risk if the invaders succeed. If the argument is strong, there is ample evidence that people's response will be very substantial. During World War II, the American government raised a great deal of money by selling "war bonds" that were bought voluntarily by individuals. Of course, the bonds were genuine bonds and carried a small amount of interest. But people didn't mainly buy them as sources of future income; rather, they bought them out of patriotism, plus a sense of the extreme importance of winning the war against these peculiarly vicious enemies. In the case of a nongovernmental initiative, we can suppose that if the good guys win, they would be in a position to exact compensation from the invaders, with which income it could perhaps pay off the bonds. Mainly, of course, the Defense Corporation would point out that the "citizens" survived with their lives and property intact and thus got what they were paying for. Finally, and of special interest, the corporation might also be in a position to distinguish between those who supported the war effort and those who did not and be able to point to disadvantages that the non-supporters would endure. Its armies might protect people in certain areas but not in others.

The example of warfare certainly displays in good measure many of the reasons why people think that States might be necessary. The danger of war is such that defense becomes a public good: It is difficult to defend some and not others when the attack is political, aimed at subjugating an entire nation. (As with most public goods, it is not literally impossible, but it is certainly difficult.) No doubt being able to commandeer people's financial support without having to ask them whether they mind is a big advantage in collecting money—it has the "advantages of theft over honest toil," after all. Is that advantage sufficient to outweigh the point that it is theft and therefore prima facie unjust from the start? Napoleon, by utilizing the enormous resources made available by his occupying the dictatorship of France, was able to conquer a large part of Europe. But should people be doing things like that? Obviously not. The habit of regarding the Alexanders, the Genghis Khans, and the Napoleons as world-historical heroes is arguably a piece of romantic nonsense that we have rightly deposited in the "trash basket of history."

This raises our second issue: Would there be any danger of international war if every nation were persuaded of the principle that only defensive war is justifiable? Of course if they were fully persuaded, there would be no such invasions or threats of same, and so the need for an army would be nonexistent anyway. This points to the possibility that this special argument lacks the fundamental nature that is had by the other arguments considered, and rejected, above. If it could be shown that there were domestic functions of clear importance to all that could not be performed without the State, that would be decisive in its favor. The point that such States could not deal with a type of threat that would then be nonexistent anyway is not obviously of the same order of philosophical weight, one may suggest.

The third and most interesting of these issues is rather vague: What is to be learned about the State from the fact that it is so widely involved in wars and war efforts? To be less vague and allusive, the possibility now seriously suggests itself that the State is the sort of thing that will happen whatever we think because it is indeed fundamentally an imposition. The State, it may be suggested, really is a gang of thieves, and there's nothing we can do about that. Therefore, the only room we have for serious consideration is just what kind of State we are going to have, and what sort of modest improvement can be made in its functioning even though we can't show that this functioning justifies the State in the first place. States, on this view, are not justified, they are merely inevitable. (Such is the argument of a recent article by Randall Holcombe.[5])

DOES THE STATE MAKE SENSE?

In the foregoing chapters, one point emerges: This peculiar institution known as "the State" is, despite its fervent and often eloquent press releases, overrated, overpriced, and hugely misused.

It is overrated in that its necessity, which has been trumpeted by almost all writers on the subject and most especially by the State itself, succumbs to analysis with very little remaining. It is fairly clear that in fact the State is not necessary, really, and the question is only whether it is helpful enough to be worth its evident disadvantages.

It is seen to be overpriced when we take a closer look at those disadvantages, which are manifest and enormous. In all modern States, citizens are taxed heavily for things they needn't get from the State and usually don't want, very much. Since the State supplies them at all, it typically does so at twice or more the cost that seems on sober analysis to be likely if they were acquired in the usual way, by negotiation and mutually cooperative activity. And always, they are supplied to people who don't want them as well as to those who do, though the fact that they don't does nothing to mitigate the State's tendency to exact the costs from them anyway.

The State is misused in that it continually arrogates to itself the right to rule over our very lives as well as our fortunes and our liberties and has all too often (indeed, nearly always, in historical retrospect) ruled to the extent of murdering, torturing, and incarcerating or exiling, as well as robbing. It generally deprives people of any number of options in life that they would gladly take if they were available and which the State has no good reason to object to other than it happens to dislike people doing those things.[6]

UP FROM ANARCHY? OR UP TO ANARCHY?

The mists of time are probably too impenetrable to say whether the State should be thought to have arisen from a previous condition of society called "anarchy," and it doesn't really matter.[7] What matters is whether the State is better than a condition of society alternative to it and that is properly termed "anarchy." The image of anarchy over the centuries is one of chaos, disorder, violence. That is not what philosophically serious anarchists hope or expect from the situation resulting from the abdication by the monopolistic, self-righteous, and arrogant institution known as government from the administration of all the many things it does so badly. Are there things left that it does well, and so well that we can't do without government? That is very hard to say, indeed. Critics point out that we have no proper experimental comparisons, since all known societies have governments As well as that governments aren't about to permit experimentation in this area.

Anarchy as depicted here is indeed largely an idea on paper. Moreover, the drums of governments everywhere beat loudly on behalf of the need for government—the more, the better. There will be no experiments if governments have their way. If some small region in, say, Saskatchewan were to declare itself separate from the rest of Canada and were internally lacking in government, we may be sure that some official (and officious) body would quickly rule it out of order, and bureaucrats and gun-waving police would soon descend to restore "order." Under the circumstances, it is not clear quite what the terms of reference are for advocacy of anarchy.

A REAL-WORLD EXAMPLE

The claim that there are no real-world anarchies turns out to be false, though not far from the truth. From reports, most of the area known to the public as Somalia has in fact had no central government since 1991, and it shows little sign of moving over to the politically correct mode, despite the expenditure of billions of dollars and much diplomatic pressure by the UN to get a government established. It seems that the relatively short period just mentioned is misleading, for its basic social structure has existed for hundreds of years, despite conquest and external interventions of various kinds.

The Somali method of dispute settlement is much as described in the foregoing, and its basic law is the property-based, nonharm law so often alluded to here. Apparently that has been the basis of a workable society, which definitely qualifies as an "anarchy." There is now a solidly based account of how it works.[8] Somalia is a quite poor area, though it has been prospering considerably since the misguided American military intervention of the early 1990s. But poverty does not disqualify a people as a workable political society. Somalians can look with disdain at most African states that do have governments, of the kleptokratic variety. It appears that there is, then, some empirical support for the claims advanced by what have been thought to be starry-eyed anarchist dreamers.

TYPES OF ANARCHY

The visions in the heads of persons claiming to be anarchists at the turn of the twentieth century, and still extolled by advocates on the Web, in which private property is abolished and everybody is devoted to everybody in true sibling fashion, are reasonably accounted fantasies.[9] Governments, or nongovernmental polities, must be for people as they are, not as they conceivably might have been had some deity been in charge. For people as they are, there is no substitute for property and individual liberty, with the resulting polity of cooperation enforced, here and there, by persons armed and ready to put down the uncooperative. This reflects the only underlying moral idea that makes any sense: The idea of independent persons making their way in life, that being a life that is generally fairly closely in contact with some few loved ones and multitudinous strangers toward whom we hope for and usually have good will. For that case—which is the standard case of mankind, after all—the "social contract" calls for everyone's recognizing everyone else's general right to pursue their lives as they please, with duties to others a reflection of this recognition. And that, as explained in various parts of this exploration, means private property, rights going to first possessors, and freedom of exchange with willing others, not mandatory sharing and immense compulsory self-sacrifice.

Those principles do not obviously require government. Extensive commercial relations require that there be money, but money does not entail government either. It entails, rather, banks with solid credentials and a reliable record of maintaining the face value of currencies employed. Extensive relations of any kind require that there should be persons available at the direction of aggrieved parties who will wield force when necessary on a basis of clear principle, acceptable to all. But again, as we saw before, these persons need not be employees of a government, as indeed most of them are not, even now.

The only idea of anarchy that makes sense, then, is the "capitalist" version, in which people have control over themselves and such resources as they might get by creating them, finding them, or receiving them from someone else who also got them in those ways, on terms mutually acceptable. This is called by the somewhat ungainly name capitalist anarchism, sometimes shortened to "ancap"—misleadingly, since people often associate the notion of capitalism with something other than the bare principles that enable people to have and exchange private property. (There could not be a chartered corporation in an anarchy, just like that. But as usual, there could easily be a kind of superassociation of companies interested in approximating the status now held by official corporations.) People can, of course, use their freedom and their resources to band together with willing others in whatever ways they can manage, thus creating worker-owned cooperatives, or whatever. But what is only to be expected is what has in fact actually happened for the most part wherever it is allowed—that people will use their freedom to try to make money; that is, to acquire the means of peaceably expanding their repertoires of enjoyed goods and services and to do so by hiring people for agreed sums, in the hope of marketing whatever they produce in greater measure than the costs of so doing. How anyone can object to this is an interesting question. But how they can think that forbidding this way of making one's way in the world is a way of doing without government is more than a conundrum; it is, simply, impossible. So-called socialist anarchism is a neologism.

HOW DIFFERENT WOULD IT BE?

Defenders of the modern State on liberal premises could think that in an anarchic society, things would not be so very different, in many respects. Would there be public schools? No, but the schools we would have would likely range from little ones to ones that approximated contemporary ones, especially at the high school level. Those who compare state universities and private ones note more similarities than differences, allowing for different ages of institution. While there won't be one official police force, there's a fair chance that one sizable force would get most of the business, if we suppose that there are economies of scale therein. And so on. What would be conspicuously missing are things like the drug laws, agricultural subsidies, state-provided welfare agencies with their extensive bureaucracies, and so on. The anarchist may well claim that society would look pretty similar in all the good respects and quite different in the bad ones.

SHOULD WE LOVE AND SERVE OUR NATION?

The short answer to this question may seem to be a resolute negative. But that is only the short of it, for there is also a long and inevitably a more complex one. People often love their nations, or at least profess to. The profession is often sincere—people make considerable sacrifices to serve their country, including putting their lives at risk, and no small number have paid with those lives. We can't deny that these things happen. What we can doubt, however, is that government deserves it. We can certainly doubt that it is entitled to demand it.

People have joined armies, or not resisted conscription in ways they perhaps could, in order to advance the most horrendous of causes; think of the Hitler Youth and no end of conquerors throughout history. Should we take this as evidence that those causes are all right after all? Surely not. We need to return, seriously, to the question just which if any sacrifices individuals ought to be ready to make for "their country."[10] Making sacrifices for worthy causes is pretty normal behavior, though sacrifice of life itself is going very far. The worthiness of those causes will be judged by each individual, no doubt. But sacrificing for the State is a rather special matter. The propensity to do this and to find the State a center of affection and fellow-feeling is unfortunately by no means restricted to supporting decent States. People have died for countries that one is hard put to understand how they could be thought worth the sacrifice.

In a recent article, Daniel Klein takes up the question of why people love the State. His general answer is found in what he calls "The People's Romance." It is essentially a desire for coordination, of an emotionally-driven kind, with not just your fellow members of voluntary associations, but with everybody, or at least everybody that your particular government manages to bring under its control. The romance is pretty independent of subject matter: those who feel it can unite behind perfectly horrible actions of the State. But it is also forwarded in democratic society by the idea that somehow we all approve of all this, indeed, that it's "our doing," "our" State. "The democratic notion of popular sovereignty tells the ordinary person that he gives license to the government, as he does to a voluntary association or club. This superstition makes the whole undertaking tolerable."[11] But of course, as Klein says, it is a superstition, and there is ample reason to think that it is "tolerable" only in the sense that things could be a lot worse. When people are dragged off to jail at the arbitrary whim of the rulers, when half their incomes are wasted on counterproductive schemes for the supposed benefit of the poor or the sick or the rest of the world, or when its policies drag down people in most other States in the world, and in short, when the main benefit of government is rah-rah, may we not raise the question of the emperor's new clothes?

In any case, national feeling can be harnessed in more useful ways. The Olympic Games, the World Cup, and many other competitions for national-level sports teams certainly focus the citizenry in ways much less counterproductive than when they support wars. Anyone who thinks that society without the State lacks the resources for rewarding association with one's fellows must be living in great ignorance of our social world.

The reader may have associated the negative aspects of national feeling with governments you dislike. The trouble is that all governments, governments in general, do these things in greater or lesser degree, and if they are indeed evils—as they surely are—then it may be time to survey the mirror.

LOVE IT OR LEAVE IT?

One brave way with the State is to claim that it is a voluntary association after all, on the grounds that one can always leave if one doesn't like it. Can this be taken seriously? For one thing, of course, leaving the State can easily be impossible, since it may forbid you to go, and of course someone else must take you on and they might well not. More to the point is that the State can and does deprive you of the option of staying on the sort of terms that anyone else might make available. That is to say: The "leaving" in question won't in fact be voluntary, and the argument is thus shown not to be serious. It is nothing like your decision not to shop at Smith's, or even to quit your job and go elsewhere. When you leave somebody else's property, you are indeed exercising a free choice. But when you leave your own property, you do so out of compulsion. The question is: Why should I be compelled to leave because the State imposes things on me that I don't want? A familiar trick of tyrants is to evacuate whole populations and compel them to move a few hundred miles elsewhere, most of them starving on the way. Should we say, "Well, it was voluntary: They could have stayed home and been shot!"?

The defender of the State has a way of trying to make out that it's actually a voluntary association, even though it doesn't look much like it. The anarchist's challenge is, in effect, put up or shut up. If you think the State is a voluntary organization, let's try making it actually voluntary, rather than warping the notion of voluntariness to fit the State. Instead of saying, "OK, if you don't pay your taxes, you go to jail. But remember, you asked for the system in which this will happen!," let's try eliminating the taxes and substituting a series of offers of services with bills attached, so that the citizen can either accept the service at that price and pay it or decline the service and not pay it. As soon as a State is willing to do that, we should be impressed. Given the nature of the State, we may be sure of a very long wait before that happens.

If the proof of the State lies in their existence and frequent effectiveness as police states, then there is no lack of proof. If it lies in its superiority over voluntary associations, then the case is very far from closed.[12]

NOTES

1. See the pioneering paper by David B. Suits, "On Locke's Argument for Government," originally published in the *Journal of Libertarian Studies*, vol. 1, no. 1 (1977): 195–203. The paper is accessible in my teaching anthology, "Classics of Political and Social Philosophy," at http://www.arts.uwaterloo.ca/~jnarveso/TeachingMaterials/Social-PoliticalPhilosophy/.

2. The economist Bruce Benson has done major work on this subject, in two books: *The Enterprise of Law: Justice without the State* (San Francisco, CA: Pacific Research Institute, 1990), and *To Serve and Protect: Privatization and Community in Criminal Justice* (New York: Independent Institute/New York University Press, 1998).

3. For a full and interestingly worked out presentation of the restitution approach to justice, see Randy Barnett, *The Structure of Liberty: Justice and the Rule of Law* (Oxford, UK: Clarendon Press, 1998). See also Joseph Ellin, "Restitution Defended," in Jan Narveson and Susan Dimock, eds., *Liberalism: New Essays on Liberal Themes* (Dordrecht, the Netherlands: Kluwer Academic, 2000), 151–169.

4. One of the better, and certainly more readable, efforts is found in Joseph Heath, *The Efficient Society: Why Canada Is as Close to Utopia as It Gets* (Toronto: Penguin, 2001).

5. For a strong statement of this view, see Randy Holcombe, "Government: Unnecessary but Inevitable," *The Independent Review*, vol. 8, no. 3 (Winter 2004): 325–342.

6. Robert Higgs assembles much empirical arguments on these theses in *Against Leviathan: Government, Power, and a Free Society* (Oakland, California: Independent Institute, 2004).

7. Robert Nozick, *Anarchy, State, and Utopia* (New York: Basic Books, 1974), produces an intricate argument for the conclusion that the minimal state would be morally justifiable as issuing from an anarchic state of nature. The book has become a classic, though not because of this argument! See also the challenging set of essays in Roderick T. Long and Tibor R. Machan, eds., *Anarchism/Minarchism* (Aldershot, UK, Ashgate Publishing, 2008).

8. See Michael van Notten and Spencer Heath MacCallum (ed.), *The Law of the Somalis* (Trenton, NJ, and Asmara, Eritrea: Red Sea Press, Inc., 2007), especially sections 4 and 6.

9. The literature is enormous. Among the best of these advocates was no doubt Peter Kropotkin, whose *The Conquest of Bread, or Mutual Aid: A Factor of Evolution* (London: Freedom Press, 1998), sound noble but illustrate the hopelessness of their ideal.

10. J. D. Mabbott, *The State and the Citizen* (London: Arrow, 1958), makes the case for this very nicely.

11. Daniel Klein, "The People's Romance: Why People Love Government (as Much as They Do)," *The Independent Review*, vol. X, no. 1 (Summer 2005): 17.

12. An immensely useful (and immense) text for pursuing anarchist theory has just come out: Edward P. Stringham, ed., *Anarchy and the Law: The Political Economy of Choice* (Somerset, NJ: Transaction Publishers, 2007).

Bibliography

Adams, Robert. *Foundations of Political Analysis*. New York: Columbia University Press, 1990.

Aquinas, St. Thomas. *Summa Theologica*. In William P. Baumgarth and Richard J. Regan, eds., *Saint Thomas Aquinas on Law, Morality, and Politics*. Indianapolis, IN: Hackett, 1988.

Aristotle, *Politics*, numerous editions.

Arnold, N. Scott. *The Philosophy and Economics of Market Socialism*. London: Oxford University Press, 1994.

Barnett, Randy. *The Structure of Liberty: Justice and the Rule of Law*. Oxford, UK: Clarendon Press, 1998.

Bartholomew, James. *The Welfare State We're In*. London: Methuen, 2004.

Baumgarth, William P., and Richard J. Regan, eds. *Saint Thomas Acquinas on Law, Morality, and Politics*. Indianapolis, IN: Hackett, 1988.

Benson, Bruce. *The Enterprise of Law: Justice without the State*. San Francisco, CA: Pacific Research Institute, 1990.

———. *To Serve and Protect: Privatization and Community in Criminal Justice*. New York: Independent Institute/New York University Press, 1998.

Bernstein, Leonard. *Candide*.

Bleisch, Barbara, and Jean-Daniel Strub, eds. *Pazifismus. Ideengeschichte, Theorie und Praxis*. Bern: Haupt, 2006.

Buchanan, Allen. *Ethics, Efficiency, and the Market*. Totowa, NJ: Rowman and Allanheld, 1985.

Caplan, Bryan. *The Myth of the Rational Voter: Why Democracies Choose Bad Policies*. Princeton, NJ: Princeton University Press, 2007.

Christman, John. *The Myth of Property*. New York: Oxford University Press, 1994.

Cohen, G. A. *If You're an Egalitarian, How Come You're So Rich?* Cambridge, MA: Harvard Univeristy Press, 2000.

Conway, David. *Classical Liberalism—The Unvanquished Ideal.* London: Macmillan, 1995.

Courtois, Stéphane, et al. *The Black Book of Communism: Crimes, Terror, Repression.* English translation. Cambridge, MA: Harvard University Press, 1999.

Cowen, Tyler. *In Praise of Commercial Culture.* Cambridge, MA: Harvard University Press, 1998.

Dahl, Robert A. *On Democracy.* New Haven, CT: Yale University Press, 1998.

de Bruxelles, Simon. "'Dragon' sausages burnt by trade laws." *The Times* (of London), November 18, 2006.

de Jasay, Anthony. "Market Socialism: 'This Square Circle.'" *Justice and Its Surroundings.* Indianapolis, IN: Liberty Press, 2002.

de Secondat, Charles-Louis, Baron de La Brède et de Montesquieu. *De l'Esprit des Loix (The Spirit of Laws),* 1748.

Diamond, Jared. *Guns, Germs, and Steel: The Fates of Human Societies.* New York: Norton, 1996.

Doherty, Brian. *Radicals for Capitalism: A Freewheeling History of the Modern American Libertarian Movement.* New York: Public Affairs, 2007.

Doyle, Michael. "Kant, Liberal Legacies and Foreign Affairs." *Philosophy and Public Affairs* (1984).

Dworkin, Ronald. *Taking Rights Seriously.* Cambridge, MA: Harvard University Press, 1977.

———. "The Place of Liberty" in *Sovereign Virtue.* Cambridge, MA: Harvard University Press, 2000.

Edwards, James Rolf. "The Costs of Public Income Redistribution and Private Charity." *Journal of Libertarian Studies,* vol. 21, no. 2 (2007): 8.

Ellin, Joseph. "Restitution Defended." Jan Narveson and Susan Dimock, eds., *Liberalism: New Essays on Liberal Themes.* Dordrecht, The Netherlands: Kluwer Academic, 2000.

Engels, Friedrich. *Socialism, Utopian and Scientific* (Engels, 1880; authorized English version, 1890).

Farrelly, Colin. An Introduction to Contemporary Political Theory. London: Sage, 2004.

Feldman, Noah. "Islam, Terror and the Second Nuclear Age" in *The New York Times Magazine,* October 29, 2006. www.nytimes.com/2006/10/29/magazine/29islam.html?_r=1&oref=slogin.

Flyvbjerg, Bent, Nils Bruzelius, and Werner Rothengatter. *Megaprojects and Risk: An Anatomy of Ambition.* Cambridge: Cambridge University Press, 2003.

Gauthier, David. *Morals by Agreement.* New York: Oxford University Press, 1986.

Gratzer, David. *The Cure: How Capitalism Can Save American Health Care.* New York: Encounter Books, 2006.

Green, Leslie. *The Authority of the State.* Oxford, UK: Clarendon Press, 1988.

Gwartney, James W., and Richard Stroup. *What Everyone Should Know about Wealth and Prosperity.* Vancouver: Fraser Institute, 1993.

Hardin, Russell. *Liberalism, Constitutionalism, and Democracy.* New York: Oxford University Press, 1999.

———. "Street-Level Epistemology and Democratic Participation," *Journal of Political Philosophy,* vol. 10, no. 2 (2002): 211–229.

Hayek, F. A. *Law, Legislation, and Liberty, vol. 2: The Mirage of Social Justice.* Chicago, IL: University of Chicago Press, 1976.

Heath, Joseph. *The Efficient Society: Why Canada Is as Close to Utopia as It Gets.* Toronto: Penguin, 2001.

Higgs, Robert. *Crisis and Leviathan: Critical Episodes in the Growth of American Government.* New York: Oxford University Press, 1987.

———. *Against Leviathan: Government, Power, and a Free Society.* Oakland, CA: Independent Institute, 2004a.

———. "The U.S. Food and Drug Administration: A Billy Club Is Not a Substitute for Eyeglasses." *Against Leviathan: Government, Power, and a Free Society.* Oakland, CA: Independent Institute, 2004b.

Higgs, Robert, and Carl P. Close, eds. *Re-thinking Green: Alternatives to Environmental Bureaucracy.* Oakland, CA: Independent Institute, 2005.

Hobbes, Thomas. *Leviathan.* 1660.

Holcombe, Randy. "Government: Unnecessary but Inevitable." *The Independent Review*, vol. 8, no. 3 (Winter 2004): 325–342.

Hummel, Jeffrey Rogers. *Emancipating Slaves, Enslaving Free Men: A History of the American Civil War.* Chicago, IL: Open Court, 1996.

Johnston, Ian. Lecture given at Malaspina University-College, Nanaimo, British Columbia, Canada. www.mala.bc.ca/~Johnstoi/introser/machiavelli.htm.

Kant, Immanuel. *Perpetual Peace*, numerous editions.

Kekes, John. *A Case for Conservatism.* Ithaca, NY: Cornell University Press, 1998.

Kirk, Russell. *The Portable Conservative Reader.* New York: Penguin, 1982.

Klein, Daniel. "The People's Romance: Why People Love Government (as Much as They Do)." *The Independent Review*, vol. X, no. 1 (Summer 2005): 17.

Kropotkin, Peter. *The Conquest of Bread, or Mutual Aid: A Factor of Evolution.* London: Freedom Press, 1998.

Kymlicka, Will. *Liberalism, Community and Culture.* New York: Oxford University Press, 1989.

———. *Contemporary Political Philosophy, 2nd ed.* New York: Oxford University Press, 2001.

Lester, Jan. *Escape from Leviathan: Liberty, Welfare, and Anarchy Reconciled.* New York: St. Martin's Press, 2000.

Locke, John. *Second Treatise of Civil Government,* 1690.

Long, Roderick, and Tibor Machan. *Anarchism/Minarchism.* Aldershot, UK: Ashgate Publishing, 2008.

Mabbott, J. D. *The State and the Citizen.* London: Arrow, 1958.

Machan, Tibor. (See Roderick Long.)

———. *The Passion for Liberty.* Lanham, MD: Rowman & Littlefield, 2003.

Machiavelli, Niccolo. *The Prince,* numerous editions.

Martin, Michael. *Atheism: A Philosophical Justification.* Philadelphia, PA: Temple University Press, 1990.

Marx, Karl. *Capital: A Critique of Political Economy,* numerous editions.

Marx, Karl, and Friedrich Engels. *The Communist Manifesto,* numerous editions.

Mill, John Stuart. *Considerations on Representative Government,* numerous editions.

Murray, Charles. *Losing Ground: American Social Policy, 1950–1980.* New York: Basic Books, 1984.

Narveson, Jan. "Pacifism: A Philosophical Analysis," *Ethics*, vol. 75, no. 4 (July 1965): 259–71.

——. *Morality and Utility*. Baltimore, MD: The Johns Hopkins University Press, 1967.

——. *Respecting Persons in Theory and Practice*. Lanham, MD: Rowman & Littlefield, 2002.

——. "The Invisible Hand." *Journal of Business Ethics*, vol. 46, no. 3 (2003): 201–212.

——. "Is Pacifism Self-Refuting?," in Bleisch, Barbara, and Strub, Jean-Daniel, eds., *Pazifismus. Ideengeschichte, Theorie und Praxis*. Bern, Haupt: 2006, 127–144.

Nozick, Robert. *Anarchy, State, and Utopia*. New York: Basic Books, 1974.

Orend, Brian. *The Morality of War*. Peterborough, Ontario: Broadview Press, 2006.

O'Rourke, P. J. *Parliament of Whores: A Lone Humorist Attempts to Explain the Entire U.S. Government*. New York: Atlantic Monthly Press, 1991.

Payne, James L. *Overcoming Welfare*. New York: Basic Books, 1998.

Plato. *Euthyphro*, numerous editions.

——. *Republic*, numerous editions.

Rand, Ayn. "Government Financing in a Free Society." *The Virtue of Selfishness*. New York: Signet Books, 1961.

Rawls, John. *A Theory of Justice*. Cambridge, MA: Harvard University Press, 1971.

——. *Political Liberalism*. New York: Columbia University Press, 1993.

Sarlo, Chris. *Poverty in Canada*, 3rd ed. Vancouver, British Columbia: Fraser Institute, 2006.

Schmidtz, David. *The Limits of Government: An Essay on the Public Goods Argument*. Boulder, CO: Westview, 1991.

Schweickart, David. *Capitalism or Worker Control?* New York: Praeger, 1980.

Scruton, Roger. "How I Became a Conservative." *Gentle Regrets: Thoughts from a Life*. London: Continuum, 2005.

Sedjo, Roger A. "The World's Forests: Conflicting Signals." Ronald Bailey, ed., *The True State of the Planet*. New York: Free Press, 1995.

Simmons, John. *Introduction to Political Philosophy*. Oxford, UK: Oxford University Press, 2008.

Simmons, A. John. *Moral Principles and Political Obligations*. Princeton, NJ: Princeton University Press, 1979.

Smiley, Gene. *Rethinking the Great Depression*. Chicago, IL: Ivan R. Dee, 2002.

Smith, David B. *Living with Leviathan: Public Spending, Taxes, and Economic Performance*. London: Institute of Economic Affairs, 2006.

Steele, David Ramsay. *From Marx to Mises: Post-Capitalist Society and the Challenge of Economic Calculation*. New York: Open Court Publishing Company, 1992.

——. "The Mystery of Fascism." www.freerepublic.com/focus/f-news/916286/posts.

——. *Atheism Explained*. Chicago, IL: Open Court Publishing Company, 2008.

Stringham, Edward P., ed. *Anarchy and the Law: The Political Economy of Choice*. Somerset, NJ: Transaction Publishers, 2007.

Suits, Bernard. *The Grasshopper—Games, Life, and Utopia*. Peterborough, Ont.: Broadview Press, 2005.